Creative, Efficient, and Effective Project Management

Ralph L. Kliem, PMP

CRC Press
Taylor & Francis Group
Boca Raton London New York

CRC Press is an imprint of the
Taylor & Francis Group, an **informa** business

AN AUERBACH BOOK

CRC Press
Taylor & Francis Group
6000 Broken Sound Parkway NW, Suite 300
Boca Raton, FL 33487-2742

First issued in paperback 2019

© 2014 by Taylor & Francis Group, LLC
CRC Press is an imprint of Taylor & Francis Group, an Informa business

No claim to original U.S. Government works

ISBN-13: 978-1-4665-7692-6 (hbk)
ISBN-13: 978-0-367-37933-9 (pbk)

Library of Congress Cataloging-in-Publication Data

Kliem, Ralph L.
  Creative, efficient, and effective project management / Ralph L. Kliem.
      pages cm
  Includes bibliographical references and index.
  ISBN 978-1-4665-7692-6 (hardcover : alk. paper)
  1. Project management. 2. Creative thinking. I. Title.

HD69.P75K577 2014
658.4'04--dc23   2013030836

Visit the Taylor & Francis Web site at
http://www.taylorandfrancis.com

and the CRC Press Web site at
http://www.crcpress.com

To my wonderful family:

Priscilla, Tonia, Mom, Mulder, and Ludwig von Canine

Contents

List of Figures

List of Tables

Preface

Creativity is a word that means so many things to so many different people. Yet, like most abstract concepts, everyone has an intuitive sense of what it is but has difficulty explaining it in concrete terms. Many people and organizations seek to grasp it, knowing all too well that, once in possession, it can turn mediocre performance to levels of greatness not foreseen by any individual or organization.

While this book also covers creativity for individuals, the primary purpose is to enable and harness the creativity of project teams to achieve even greater than expected levels of performance.

In my thirty-plus years in the corporate environment, I have had the pleasure of witnessing and managing teams that had creativity lie dormant and, when the circumstances became right, let the creative juices flow. These juices, if not managed and led satisfactorily, can either destroy or enhance a person's and an organization's performance.

Project managers need to identify ways to capitalize on the creative talents of their people and manage them in a way that not only achieves the vision of a project but does so in a way that exceeds expectations. By exceeding expectations, I am not advocating gold plating, which is giving customers more than what they want. Rather, I mean enticing stakeholders, especially the project team, to perform in a manner that far exceeds the expectations of everyone by creating and improving processes and products, as well as services, which result in innovation.

If you think creativity does not matter, just look at the differences between those companies that place little value on it and those that do. Companies that fail to embrace the importance of creativity often discover themselves lacking the ability to adapt and thrive in a dynamic, changing economy. While their products or services may have reigned supreme for a moment in time, their success is often eclipsed by their overconfidence and arrogance. They get complacent and their output of products or services becomes routine and protective. They are too reluctant to change their processes or products. Firms can arise out of nowhere, taking down a behemoth in an industry through the application of creativity, and become the new market leaders.

I remember watching a television interview with Bill Gates, the founder of Microsoft. He said something to the effect that one of his biggest fears is that someone in a garage could develop software that could essentially jeopardize his company. That's just how powerful creativity is.

Contrary to popular belief, creativity is not reserved for madmen or people of dysfunctional behavior. Everyone on a project team has it, and every team uses it to some degree or another. Unfortunately, creativity is like energy. It resides in everyone, but for the most part remains untapped. In this book, I want to provide project managers with thoughts, tools, and techniques that will enable them to tap creative energy and direct it to achieving the goals and objectives of projects.

I also want to thank Ameeta Chainani for taking time to review the manuscript and providing insights for improving it.

Ralph Kliem
President, LeanPM, LLC
http://www.theleanpm.com
Ralph@theleanpm.com

About the Author

Ralph L. Kliem, PMP, has more than twenty-five years of experience with Fortune 500 firms in the financial and aerospace industries. His vast and varied experience in project and program management includes managing compliance, business continuity, and information technology projects and programs.

In addition to being the author of more than 15 books, which have been translated into several languages, he has published more than 200 articles in leading business and information systems publications.

Kliem is an adjunct faculty member of City University in Seattle and a former member of the Seattle Pacific University faculty, an instructor with Bellevue College and Cascadia Community College, and a frequent presenter to the Puget Sound chapter of the Project Management Institute and other professional organizations. He also teaches Project Management Professional (PMP) certification and other project management seminars and workshops in the United States and abroad.

1

Creativity and Project Management

INTRODUCTION

Perhaps the best phrase that describes the need for creativity on projects is the one offered by Daniel Goleman, notable author on emotional intelligence, when he presented the maxim "I have to do it myself, and I can't do it alone."[1] A project requires the contribution of individuals, which includes their knowledge and creativity. A project, however, also requires that the individuals on the team work together to achieve common goals and objectives.

Creativity on a project requires both operating independently while simultaneously having everyone working together. If a project was simply an amalgamation of independent creative geniuses, the likelihood of achieving success is less than working together synergistically. In other words, they exercise creative collaboration, which involves individuals applying their creativity both separately and also as a team member to achieve the vision of a project.

BENEFITS OF CREATIVITY

There are many obvious, and not so obvious, benefits of harnessing creativity on projects. These benefits include:

- Building emotional involvement
- Generating new ideas
- Increasing teaming
- Leading to competitive advantage
- Leveraging and increasing knowledge

- Opening minds
- Stretching the performance of people

Building Emotional Involvement

Creativity encourages emotional involvement because of the challenge it offers to people. Challenging the status quo is not for the faint hearted because the areas they enter were once deemed taboo. Mental adrenalin begins to flow as the prospect of making a significant change—whether in theory or reality—causes one to stay emotionally engaged even in the midst of potential overwhelming failure. It is, in essence, the thrill of the hunt that keeps people engaged when exercising creativity. Their engagement becomes so emotionally involved that they lose any sense of time, awareness, or physical debilitation.

Generating New Ideas

Creativity, by its very nature, challenges the status quo. It questions the existing order of doing business, whether in regard to a process or product or service. It requires asking questions like "Why?" and "How?". Essentially, it requires being destructive before generating something new, whether a product, process, service, or system. Roger von Oech concurs, noting: "Creative thinking is not only constructive, it is also destructive."[2]

History is replete, of course, with examples where creativity was the instrument for generating new ideas. Everything from political theory to technological advancement creativity has a played a key role, whether coming from an individual or a group. It is quite obvious that without creativity, advancements in so many fields would not occur.

Increasing Teaming

Creativity, when involving more than one person (e.g., a team), frequently results in people working together in trying to acquire that "Aha!" feeling that happens when something creative arises, for example, having insight to a solution in a problematical impasse. A team, especially after operating as just a collection of individuals, finds its members jamming or jelling around the idea. All attention focuses on furthering the development of the idea, and just as importantly, encouraging everyone to use their creativity to make it a reality. A breakthrough idea often builds commitment, which energizes everyone with a feeling that they are part of something greater than themselves.

Leading to Competitive Advantage

Even though James Higgins's list of primary challenges was formulated in the 1990s, the circumstances that affect a firm's ability to adapt ring as true today as they did back then. Higgins, in *Innovate or Evaporate,* identifies ten challenges that firms face that require creative, adaptive responses:

1. Accelerating rates of change
2. Globalization of business competition
3. Increasing complexity of the environment
4. Increasing demands of constituents
5. Increasing levels of competition
6. More diverse workforce
7. Rapid technological change
8. Resource shortage
9. Transition from industrial to knowledge-based society
10. Unstable market and economic conditions[3]

If companies harvest and harness the creativity of individuals and groups alike, they can compete more effectively and efficiently in such environments. Unfortunately, the pressure to maintain the existing order of a firm, which is essential, can constrain the creativity of individuals and teams simply to satisfy a firm's need for obedience. Extreme compliance can result in people, to use an overwrought phrase, thinking outside the box. Individuals and teams alike then constrain their creativity because what often gets rewarded in an organization is compliance, not creativity, even if it leads to innovation. The result is an organization that fails to adapt and respond to a dynamic environment. Creative actions provide the means for a project and organization to adapt to such an environment.

Leveraging and Increasing Knowledge

Accumulation of knowledge for knowledge's sake is fine, but its real advantage comes when it is mixed with creativity. Creativity serves as the catalyst that puts knowledge into action to change reality. When both are combined, either on an individual or team level, the results can become synergistic. While limited knowledge can sometimes lead to more creative outcomes, the chances increase with more knowledge about a domain or subject, because there is greater opportunity for innovative thought. Little knowledge often leads to subscribing to beliefs and assumptions that are treated as facts, thereby constraining one's ability to think creatively. Further combination of teams and cumulative knowledge and creativity can have an explosive effect. Business and science are replete with examples of greater knowledge being coupled with creativity. Knowledge and creativity share a common characteristic: they are both cumulative. Knowledge begets more knowledge; creativity begets greater creativity.

Opening Minds

Creativity requires and causes minds to open up to possibilities and realities that have never before existed. Due to its destructiveness, creativity increases knowledge and awareness because it breaks down the mental paradigms, or models, that many people hold dear for confronting reality. Sometimes creativity opens minds dramatically by attacking fundamental premises held sacrosanct by so many; at other times, it advances existing paradigms by reinforcing the basic tenets. Sometimes, however, it simply results in incremental improvements that gradually lead to change, but cumulatively over time, leads to dramatic change. Individuals and teams often find their awareness so strong that what they viewed as "sacred" seems no longer relevant and gives them no other choice but to accept change.

Stretching the Performance of People

Contrary to popular opinion, creativity often involves hard work. It requires effort to understand the status quo and then challenge it—not an easy task. Issues of unlearning and relearning, changing and challenging assumptions, taking a new perspective, rearranging what others perceive as reality, just to list a few shifts, require considerable mental and even physical work. Creativity causes not just the status quo to become stressed and potentially broken, but can also do the same for the person doing the creating. Legendary stories abound of individuals and teams working late into the night or for innumerable days, to the point of exhaustion and emotional breakdown.

MISPERCEPTIONS ABOUT CREATIVITY

Despite the immense advantages of creativity, some common misperceptions exist about the subject. Some of the more common ones are:

- Creativity involves some degree of mental illness
- Not everyone is creative
- Only individuals, not groups, are creative
- Creativity is restricted to certain fields
- Only certain segments of the population are creative

Creativity Involves Some Degree of Mental Illness

Perhaps, since the publication of *Society and Its Discontents* by Sigmund Freud, the perception exists within society that creativity only resides in those who are affectionately referred to as eccentric fruitcakes. Such misperceptions serve only to prevent people from realizing their creative potential. So extreme is the perception, that people believe that to be creative requires dressing and acting in an asocial fashion. Sadly, this misperception inhibits creativity among many people as organizations reward conformity rather than creativity. Yet, business in general, and projects in particular, would be better served if they discarded such perceptions of anomalous behavior. The people on a project team who dress or act differently are not more creative than any other person. To tap the creative potential of all team members, project managers need to avoid falling into the stereotype.

Not Everyone Is Creative

While not everyone can be on the level of a Leonardo da Vinci or a Pablo Picasso, we all have some capacity to be creative. According to Gerard Nierenberg in *The Art of Creative Thinking,* people can use creativity to produce ideas and objects, and then relationships, either by accident or intention.[4] Without some level of creative spirit, human beings would simply be robots or organisms predicated on stimulus–response.

Unfortunately, socialization can squash creativity, almost to the point of making it nonexistent. From the moment parents start disciplining their children, to the time that individuals become full-fledged instruments of production during their careers, creativity either remains dormant, crushed by the levers of familial corporate power, or gradually dissipates due to disuse. James Higgins, in *Innovate or Evaporate,* observes that although people and organizations have some degree of creativity, it essentially lies dormant.[5]

Sadly, in the world of project management, most people on teams simply become willing instruments of production, working at best as applied rather than critical thinkers. Project managers can find it difficult to arouse and encourage creativity due to socialization in work environments. Yet, as just mentioned, creativity resides within all of us. The challenge is for project managers to get team members to recognize their own creativity and also to lay the groundwork for it to surface on their projects.

Only Individuals, Not Groups, Are Creative

A common perception is that only individuals are creative, often citing the lonely discontent isolated by society doing his own thing. In some cases, that is true. In today's environment of technological complexity and with the cost of innovation, such a perception makes this scenario the exception rather than the rule. Increasingly, projects consist of teams that harvest and harness the creativity of the individuals. If managed appropriately, teams can be as creative, if not more so, than any individual. It is difficult to visualize an individual being solely responsible for the creation, for example, of a game-changing plane or even an iPhone®. The complexity behind all technologies, initiatives, and so on necessitates a team approach. Project managers need to orchestrate creativity in a way that builds truly innovative results. Co-author Daniel Goleman observes that creative problem solving is as much a team effort as it is an individual one, especially in today's environment requiring both collaboration and competition.[6]

Creativity Is Restricted to Certain Fields

Perhaps because computing technology has dramatically changed modern society and the relationship among individuals, a frequent misperception is that creativity lies solely in the domain of information technology. Other fields, from literature to medicine, however, are also making major contributions. Yet the prevailing perception seems to override the visibility of other creative advancements in the other domains.

The truth is that creativity exists in all domains, not just that of information technology. Technology in general, and information technology in particular, is an enabler, no different than a pencil or pen; owning a laptop, for example, just having it or using it does not mean a person is creative. Technology is, more often, a tool to help an individual or group create.

Creativity, in reality, is often enhanced when one crosses domains. Creative people often transfer their knowledge and skills from one field and apply them to another. They have the advantage of seeing the new domain from different perspectives and of making significant changes. It behooves project managers, therefore, to have teams of a diverse mixture, consisting of diverse backgrounds, experiences, and skills to enable their teams to contribute creative insights.

Only Certain Segments of the Population Are Creative

For many people, the perception exists that only certain segments of the population are creative. For example, some people believe that only the young are creative. Some evidence exists that supports this notion if one is subscribing to the belief that artists, writers, and physicists, for example, are the only creative people. Yet there are many examples to the contrary. Creativity actually spans across all categories of ages, races, gender, and nationality. In fact, creativity blossoms among these categories at different times and places, just as it does with others. Unfortunately, stereotypes cause some people to be pigeon-holed into not being creative, and, like the Pygmalion Effect, turn out not to be so.

DOWNSIDES OF CREATIVITY

With benefits come the downsides that exist with just about everything. Engendering and allowing creativity on a project team pose some challenges:

- Cause of anxiety and fear
- Challenge authority
- People may leave
- Upset team

- Upsetting the status quo
- Waste of resources

Cause of Anxiety and Fear

Because it challenges the status quo and disrupts the familiar, creativity can cause anxiety and fear among some stakeholders. People desiring stability through order and discipline often do not care for the unknown that creativity frequently causes, especially in medium and large organizations. Such institutions depend on order and discipline to ensure delivery of services and goods to internal and external customers. Creativity potentially disrupts that delivery system for at least a short while, causing instability in an organization. Project managers must make an effort to at least acknowledge the challenge and then take measures to allay any anxiety and fear arising from a team being creative. Failure to do so can cause division among the team, lower productivity, and may hurt *esprit de corps*. Yet a project manager should not eliminate division totally because it can spark creativity in others and can lead to action.[7]

Challenge Authority

Creativity, as mentioned so much already, requires asking questions that bother people, especially of people who do not want to be second-guessed. Creative individuals—and not to imply all of them—ask questions that may appear to challenge people in positions of authority, such as the project manager and executive sponsors for a project. People in authority, especially people who rest behind their positions within a hierarchy, may not like being questioned regarding an idea, strategy, or approach that they have chosen; they may view questioning as being insubordinate. Whatever the perception, a team of creative people can sometimes be viewed as unruly and appear as not focusing on accomplishing the goals and objectives of a project.

As a common saying goes, project managers will likely be walking a tight rope. On the one hand, they want team members to be creative and provide ideas furthering the project along. On the other hand, they want team members to work together in support of accomplishing not only the goals and objectives of the project, but also the ones established by senior and executive management of the parent organization. This can cause a layered cake-like situation to arise, whereby the project and the parent organization are not supporting each other, thereby potentially putting the project manager at odds with both stakeholders.

People May Leave

Because creativity causes disruptions to people and process alike, some team members, and other stakeholders, may elect to leave a project. Very creative types, who are unlike people who are used to routine and are highly applied thinkers, often subscribe to the notion of "this is how it is done" or "this is the way it is done." The disorder that often accompanies a creative environment will entice such people to leave a more stable, predictable environment. Gerard Nierenberg, in his classic text *The Art of Creative Thinking*, observes that the human mind creates a system of logic based upon knowledge and experience, which, coupled with our ego, affects the way we see the world around us and determines how we perceive and respond to it.[8]

Upset Team

Related to the last point, creativity can cause dissension among team members. This dissension is primarily because of the exploratory nature of being creative. People ask critical questions about ideas, challenging their validity and identifying flaws. Sometimes people get their egos wrapped up in their ideas, which can result in severe differences surfacing between, and among, team members.

Project managers must make every effort to ensure that the questioning that accompanies creativity does not lead to clashes over personality rather than ideas. Otherwise, creativity will quickly deteriorate into counterproductive differences. Teaming is as essential as creativity in completing a project successfully; it behooves the project manager to ensure that team members work hand in hand, sometimes not an easy feat.

Upsetting the Status Quo

By its very nature, creativity challenges the existing way of doing business, whether incrementally or on a grand level. It often requires destruction before putting anything new in place. Creativity will challenge and destroy long-established processes, procedures, and routines that often follow out of obedience, and because people are used to them and are rewarded in some way for compliance. Upsetting the status quo on a project, for example, could force management to make uncomfortable decisions about whether to sponsor a creative idea or discard it due to the ramifications, for example, greater project costs or going to a change board to receive approval. It may also be construed by others that the original vision for the project was flawed after so many egos were invested in the outcome. Edward de Bono agrees, noting in *Serious Creativity*, that creativity brings forth something unprecedented that can have messy consequences. For that unprecedented something, it must add value if it is to be adopted.[9] James Adams agrees with de Bono. He says that people need a reason to create and innovate, such as addressing a problem and then employing rigorous questioning to create a meaningful solution.[10]

Waste of Resources

Sometimes, maybe often, creativity and efficiency, at least in the short term, do not go together. Creativity frequently requires an environment of stop and go, unlike a material good or service that can be produced repetitively or routinely. Creativity is not like a machine that can be turned on or off like a lawn mower or automobile; repetition and routine are frequently anathema to it.

In a creative environment, waste is the norm rather than the exception, at least in the short term. In the long term, a creative breakthrough can result in a payback that can yield value way beyond following a repetitive, routine process. However, when creativity fails, it can do so big time, resulting in considerable loss in time, effort, and money.

The best of creative projects generate waste because rework occurs. When a project team is creative in addressing problems, waste in time, effort, and money can occur as team members struggle to find a solution.

WHAT EXACTLY *IS* CREATIVITY?

Creativity can be defined many ways, and is a reflection of its perceptions and misperceptions.

Daniel Goleman says that creativity is something that is novel and appropriate,[11] while Mihal Csikszentmihalyi refers to it as a process in which a domain is changed.[12] Howard Gardner appears to agree with Csikszentmihalyi, noting, "the creating individual is one who regularly solves problems or fashions products in a domain, and whose work is considered both novel and acceptable by knowledgeable members of a field."[13] Arthur Koestler states that creativity involves taking seemingly unrelated components or elements to form something more than the sum of its parts.[14]

To others, creativity is more than producing something different or unique. It also has to produce something that is meaningful, that is, of value to others. Goleman further notes that it must "work," being "correct, useful, valuable, meaningful."[15] James Higgins agrees, stating, "creativity is the process of generating something new that has value,"[16] while John Kao in *Jamming* describes it as "the entire process by which ideas are generated, developed, and transformed into value. ... it connotes both the art of giving birth to new ideas and the discipline of shaping and developing those ideas to the next stage of realized value."[17]

This notion that creativity is developing something novel and that has value is really, from a business perspective, called *innovation*. Innovation is creative output that produces something of value to a person or organization.[18] Of course, creativity should not stop at innovation, which is producing something simply of value. It must also be implemented in the so-called real world to ensure that people realize its benefit. Quite often, creativity stops at the point of innovation. The final act is to implement it into the environment, which is not easy.

That gratification, however, does not come easily. Projects, by their very nature, involve creating something that is novel and unique that should result in a product or service adding value to the customer; otherwise, a customer would not bother paying for the project in the first place. It also requires implementing that product or service so the customer realizes the value of their investment. Hence, from the author's perspective, creativity can be defined as developing a new or improved product or service that adds value to the customer upon its implementation. This definition encompasses a complete project life cycle perspective. Hence, if the creativity could be compressed into a simple formula, it would be "novelty + value + implementation." Novelty, in the sense that the product or service is incrementally or completely unique; value, in that the product or service offering satisfies a need; and its implementation becomes part of the customer's reality.

WHAT IS THE RELATIONSHIP BETWEEN CREATIVITY AND PROJECTS?

As mentioned earlier, projects are collaborative efforts; rarely is a project the result of a single individual effort, although that occurs from time to time. In today's modern environment, however, experts agree that projects are largely done in a team environment due to a myriad of factors, for example, magnitude, complexity. Warren Bennis agrees, observing that a project's success requires the help of a number of creative individuals. Rarely is it the work of one creative person. The complexities and interconnections among the stakeholders and technological elements require collaboration.[19] Accepting the fact that projects are collective endeavors, it requires what Bennis calls *creative collaboration*, whereby the individual and group work in concert to achieve a common goal. Individual and group are not considered a mutually exclusive relationship. Bennis observes that the key is to have the right balance between individual autonomy and the team that results in achieving a common goal.[20] It is therefore clear that projects do not consist of an assembly of individuals who operate independently of each other. They require all members to contribute, including creative ones. All team members have the capacity to be creative, and the team, with the leadership of the project manager, should work to ensure that everyone has that opportunity.

The contributions of individuals and groups often center on four elements. These four elements are people, process, product (or service), and performance.

People are important because they have the creative capacity that will be applied on a project. Unless this capacity is released, creativity cannot affect the other three areas: process, product (or service), and performance. A hard dependency exists among people and the other three elements.

Process is important because it relates to managing the work or building interim deliverables and the final product (or service).

An incremental or dramatic improvement in a process can lead to significant gains in the quality of the product (or service) delivered to the customer.

Product (or service) is important because it is what the customer expects to receive as an outcome of a project. Creative contributions to the product (or service) can have a variety of impacts on a project, including accelerating the delivery schedule, reducing costs, and improving output.

Performance is important because it builds customer confidence in the product or service being delivered. In large part, creative contributions by people to process and product (or service) result in better performance. However, performance in this context means making creative contributions to identify and meet the expectations of the customer. These creative contributions might entail making creative contributions on reporting about schedule, cost, and quality.

People, process, product (or service), and performance are all elements of a project that are in need of creative contributions of individuals and the team as a whole. Like the fingers of a hand, they need to collaborate to develop creative ideas to further the vision of a project.

Before discussing the relationship between project management and creativity, a discussion is warranted about what project management is and some of its major features. This understanding will make it easier to see the relationship between project management and creativity.

A project is temporary endeavor to achieve a specific result, such as developing a product or delivering a service for the first time. It has specific start and stop dates, consumes a finite quantity of resources, and does not include phases like operations and maintenance. Once complete, a project is over.

A project has several resource elements that require management. These are people, processes, systems, data, time, equipment, and supplies. The quantity and quality of each one can have an impact on the performance of a project.

People are perhaps the most important element because of their contribution to the outcome of a project. If motivated and employed in a value-added fashion, they can apply all the other elements efficiently and effectively. Naturally, one of the greatest contributions of the people element is the creativity and innovation generated and applied to a project.

The other elements are really employed based upon the knowledge, experience, expertise, and creativity of the individuals making up the team. Creativity is the enabler, not just for applying these elements more effectively and efficiently, but also doing so in a way that exceeds expectations that result in creative and innovative outputs.

Several project management methodologies exist. Some of these project management life cycles treat project management as if it occurs sequentially, such as ones using a waterfall life cycle, while others treat the subject iteratively, such as Agile. Fundamentally all projects, regardless of life-cycle approach, share some common characteristics.

First, all project processes involve stakeholders who are people or organizations that have an interest in the outcome of a project. The interest of these stakeholders can vary in depth and degree, and can oscillate throughout the life cycle of a project. Some stakeholders may be more powerful than others in terms of influencing the outcome of a project. However, the project manager is the only stakeholder who regularly interacts with all the stakeholders.

Second, all project processes have deliverables. These deliverables include technical and project management ones. The technical deliverables relate to building the product, such as requirements documents and detail designs. The project management deliverables, the focus of this book, are related to managing the work, such as developing a work breakdown structure or building a schedule.

Third, all project processes consume resources. These resources consist of labor and nonlabor, such as supplies, equipment, and time. Naturally, all these resources translate into money. Some processes consume more money than others, usually for planning and executing. Naturally, the project manager and the team need to consume resources efficiently and effectively. Four, all processes have some type of checkpoint or gate. The purpose of the checkpoint is to ensure that all the project management and technical deliverables have been developed and that they comply with criteria. Checkpoint reviews require a go/no-go decision before progressing to the next process.

Finally, all processes require inputs and outputs that feed one or more processes. Just to name a few, the inputs include information, templates, completed deliverables, reviews, approvals, and decisions. The outputs also consist of new or revised information, deliverables, reviews, approvals, decisions, and so on. The symbiotic relationships among the processes depend on the quantity, but perhaps most importantly, the quality of the inputs and outputs.

The product life cycle represents phases to manage the technical output of a project, as opposed to a project life cycle, which is oriented toward managing the work. The product life cycle consists of several phases that can fundamentally be segmented into five primary phases: defining, designing, developing, and deploying. *Defining* is identifying the requirements, *designing* is creating the architecture, *developing* is building the product or service, and *deploying* is implementing it. The final phase is sometimes added to represent the postimplementation of a product or service, often called *operations and maintenance*, and includes, for example, fixes, upgrades, and warranty coverage. This last phase is not considered part of a project.

Within each of these five phases is the application of six project management processes. These six processes also vary from one project management methodology to another, but can be fundamentally defined in these categories: defining, planning, organizing, execution, monitoring and control, and closing.

The defining process requires determining, at a high level, the goals, scope, deliverables, major tasks, responsibility assignments, schedule milestones, risks, and other pertinent issues and concerns. Major project management deliverables are the charter and the statement of work. The planning process requires determining the roadmap for achieving the high-level information identified in the defining process. Its deliverables include building a work breakdown structure, detailed and summary schedules, responsibility assignment matrices, cost and schedule estimates, risk assessment, and much more. The organizing process involves identifying and putting in place the infrastructure for effectively and efficiently managing a project. Its deliverables include setting up a repository, selecting project management tools, setting up mechanisms to enable good communications, and other ones that provide good support for the people supporting the project. The execution process is the actual application of the plan to achieve the goals and objectives of the project. Its major deliverables include managing stakeholder expectations, the labor and nonlabor resources, and ensuring compliance with standards. Monitoring and controlling processes involve collecting and assessing information about the performance of a project and taking the necessary corrective actions to improve that performance. Its major deliverables include performance information, change management, and actions to improve performance. Closing involves bringing a project to a conclusion efficiently and effectively. Its major deliverables include administrative and financial documentation, as well as completing all remaining tasks.

The summary chart in Figure 1.1 shows the relationship of project management processes and some of the more common deliverables produced for each one.

With an understanding of project management processes, the next step is to show the relationship of those processes to the phases within the creative cycle. The creative cycle adopted for this book is the traditional approach described earlier. It has the following phases: preparation, concentration, incubation, illumination, and verification and production.

Like the processes of project management, the phases of creativity share some common characteristics but also have their differences.

First, they arc nonlinear in most cases. The processes and phases are often iterative, meaning that the entirety of both can be repeated, leading to results that are of greater breadth (e.g., expansion of knowledge) and depth, (e.g., greater detail).

Second, they create a result. The only real difference is that the phases of the creativity cycle often have a less tangible quality to them. In the end, however, the results of the phases of creativity facilitate the development of deliverables produced by the project management phases.

Third, they consume resources. The key difference between project management processes and creativity phases is that the resources of the former tend to be physical in nature (e.g., labor and supplies) while the latter tend more toward the intangible (e.g., brain power). In many cases, project managers can take a more mechanical, step-by-step approach and "dump" more resources to produce deliverables of lesser quality. Of course, a threshold exists for how much resource can be dumped to create project management deliverables before the value of their contribution decreases (e.g., loss of efficiency and effectiveness). In many respects, the effort to increase creativity can prove counterproductive because unlike project management processes, creativity seeks to enhance the performance of existing resources.

Despite the similarities and especially the differences, the project management processes and the phases of creativity can work well together. This integration takes the form of the creativity phases occurring within each of the project management processes that occur in the project management life cycle, as shown in Figure 1.2.

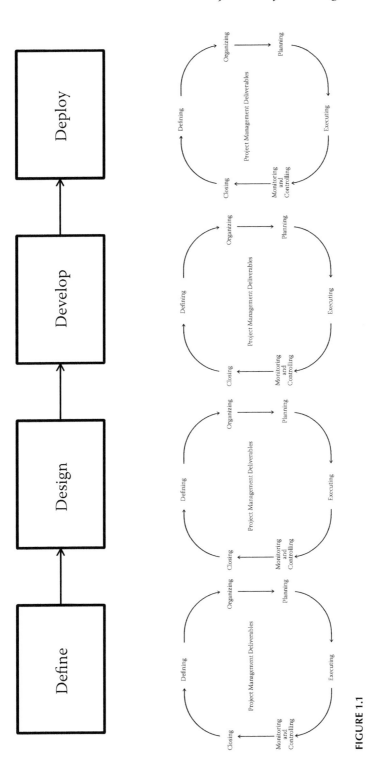

FIGURE 1.1
Product/project management life-cycles relationship.

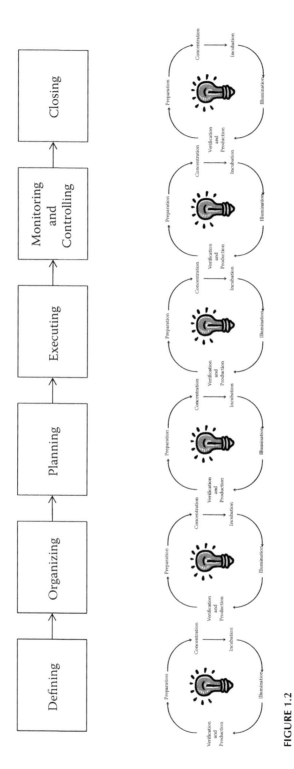

FIGURE 1.2
Project management processes/creativity phases relationship.

CONCLUSION

Creativity is a key ingredient in the success of almost all projects simply because projects rarely go as smoothly as planned. Obstacles, issues, risks, and showstoppers are just some of the debris that falls in the path of completing a project. This debris requires that people be creative in dealing with it so that the product or service being built and delivered meets the needs of the customer. This creativity can happen both on individual and group levels; ideally, the levels should be integrated in a way that melds the creativity of the individual with that of the group to increase the likelihood of the successful completion of a project.

Getting Started Checklist

Question	Yes	No
1. What is your definition of creativity?		
2. Which of the following benefits will creativity offer your project?		
Building emotional involvement		
Generating new ideas		
Increasing teaming		
Leading to competitive advantage		
Leveraging and increasing knowledge		
Opening minds		
Stretching the performance of people		
Other(s):		
3. What are some of the misperceptions about creativity that exist in your project's environment?		
Creativity involves some degree of mental illness.		
Not everyone is creative.		
Only individuals, not groups, are creative.		
Creativity is restricted to certain fields.		
Only certain segments of the population are creative.		
Other(s):		
4. What are some of the downsides of creativity that could impact your project?		
Cause of anxiety and fear		
Challenge authority		
People may leave		
Upset team		
Upsetting the status quo		
Waste of resources		
Other(s):		

ENDNOTES

1. Daniel Goleman, Paul Kaufman, and Michael Ray, *The Creative Spirit* (New York: Dutton: 1992), p. 122.
2. Roger von Oech, *A Whack on the Side of the Head* (New York: Warner Books, Inc., 1990), p. 57.
3. James M. Higgins, *Innovate or Evaporate* (Winter Park, FL: New Management Publishing Company, 1995), p. 8.
4. Gerard I. Nirenberg, *The Art of Creative Thinking* (New York: Cornerstone Library, 1982), p. 17.
5. Higgins, *Innovate or Evaporate*, p. 41.
6. Goleman, Kaufman, and Ray, *The Creative Spirit*, p. 94.
7. Goleman, Kaufman, and Ray, *The Creative Spirit*, p. 145.
8. Nierenberg, *The Art of Creative Thinking*, p. 90.
9. Edward de Bono, *Serious Creativity* (New York: HarperBusiness, 1992), p. 3.
10. James L. Adams, *Conceptual Blockbusting*, 2nd ed. (New York: W. W. Norton & Company, 1979).
11. Goleman, Kaufman, and Ray, *The Creative Spirit*, p. 24.
12. Mihaly Csikszentmihalyi, *Creativity* (New York: HarperCollins, 1996), p. 8.
13. Howard Gardner, *Frames of Mind* (New York: Basic Books, 1983), p. xvii.
14. Adams, *Conceptual Blockbusting*, p. 76.
15. Goleman, Kaufman, and Ray, *The Creative Spirit*, p. 24.
16. James M. Higgins, *101 Creative Problem-Solving Techniques* (New York: The New Management, 1994), p. 3.
17. John Kao, *Jamming* (New York: HarperCollins, 1997), p. xvii.
18. Higgins, *101 Creative Problem-Solving Techniques*, pp. 3–4.
19. Warren Bennis and Patricia Biederman, *Organizing Genius* (Reading, MA: Addison-Wesley Publishing Co., Inc., 1997), p. 2.
20. Bennis and Biederman, *Organizing Genius*, p. 20.

2

Creative Thinking Abilities

INTRODUCTION

Creativity is not some spontaneous act, as often construed by people who think it is something only certain people have. The premise of this book is that everyone has the ability to be creative. Naturally, some people have certain abilities that are more pronounced and innate than others, but everyone has creative abilities. Through conscious effort, people can tap these abilities and augment them over time with experience.

A WORD ABOUT BRAIN HEMISPHERES

Both hemispheres are needed to create, of course. Using one side of the brain only restricts deploying the output of the right brain into the real world, the one for turning creativity into innovation. It is not an either/or proposition between the two. It is more like a Venn diagram where the two sides overlap to produce something creative and innovative.

Unfortunately, it often appears that a dichotomous choice is made, resulting in an unbalanced view of creativity. Think about it. An environment completely dominated by a left-brain perspective is one that is devoid of ambiguity, humor, and challenge; these characteristics hardly engender creativity. An environment completely dominated by a right-brain perspective is devoid of focus, practicality, and logic; these characteristics hardly engender innovation. A blend of both sides of the brain enables an atmosphere of creativity and innovation, resulting in turning an idea into a reality. In other words, the environment combines the art and science behind creativity and innovation, as discussed in the succeeding paragraphs.

David Pink, in his excellent book *A Whole New Mind*, describes the importance of using both sides of the brain. His view is that for a considerable time, the left-brain dominants have, for lack of a better word, dominated the business environment. Today, for many reasons, the right-brain dominants are coming into their own. Advancements in technology are a major contributor to this shift from left to right brain emphasis. Pink adds that other factors, too, add to this mental shift, to include material abundance and globalization.[1] He refers to the ability to detect patterns and combine unrelated ideas as *high concept*, and emotional intelligence and human interaction as *high touch*.[2] Western thought and our educational system have indeed emphasized left-brain thinking to the exclusion of the right side. Project management tends to continue this emphasis, resulting in skewing thinking on how to approach a project. Fortunately, this dominance is starting to crack with greater attention toward subjects like the human side of project management, for example, creativity and emotional intelligence and different approaches to projects, such as Agile.

CREATIVE THINKING ABILITIES

Creative thinking requires having certain abilities. These include the following abilities:

- Cross-domain thinking
- Having fun
- Listening to your intuition
- Shifting perspectives
- Being an iconoclast, even nihilistic
- Unlearning and relearning
- Looking from the outside, in
- Reverse thinking
- Conceptualizing
- Embracing ambiguity
- Seeing multiple answers
- Defining the problem
- Being observant
- Tinkering
- Determining the essence of something

- Being self-aware
- Competing and collaborating
- Persevering
- Shifting thinking
- Shifting perspectives
- Suspending judgment
- Tinker
- Communicating

Cross-Domain Thinking

This means being able to shift to, or transcend from, one field of study to another, and applying the tools, concepts, and techniques to derive something creative in the new field. Essentially, the creative person becomes interdisciplinary. This ability becomes invaluable when trying to provide a different insight and when overcoming a roadblock in another domain. Many creations of the past involved people coming from one domain and pollinating another with new thoughts and ideas. Unfortunately, too many people, especially in highly specialized fields or in stovepipe organizations, take the attitude of "not my area," which hinders their capacity to adopt a different perspective and to generate creative ideas and options.

Their experience enables them to see phenomena and obtain perspectives that ordinary people do not see. They often pollinate two or more fields based on using their knowledge and experiences obtained in other areas. Their diverse background helps them identify opportunities that may be blind to others. However, this does not mean that they are ignorant about the field in which they are working; it does mean that they often do not get drowned in details and emotionally involved. They can learn about and play around with different topics. With a greater breadth of views, they can also respond to their environment.[3]

Having Fun

The more fun one has when creating, the greater the likelihood something original will result. If being creative is laborious and burdensome, then the likelihood of diminishing creativity will occur. It must be enjoyable; otherwise, too much effort is expended to create, which, ironically, only inhibits it even more. Having fun often has an element of craziness that appears as something less than normal.[4]

Naturally, the joy of creating provides the opportunity to self-actualize in a way that seems to stop any sense of time or other constraint (other than the laws of physics) when engaged in the creative act. They become totally consumed in what they do while simultaneously finding themselves rooted in reality. Creating becomes a release from the trials and tribulations of the moment. Time seems to fly when they are literally having fun. This experience is referred to as *flow*, whereby people experience a match between their consciousness and the act of creation. Less energy is expended as time and self-consciousness seem to dissolve.[5] They are involved in the moment.

Listening to Your Intuition

Being logical requires operating on a presumed set of valid assumptions. Logic and reasoning require agreement, or at least consensus, over assumptions, if for no other reason than to have a dispassionate discussion over an issue or problem. Using the basic assumptions (items presumed factual until proven otherwise) as premises, logic becomes structured.

The downside of simply relying on logic may lead to a paradigm or mental model that intellectually makes sense but does not fit reality. The model is out of sync with what exists in the real world. It presumes that assumptions are valid, absent of facts and data, which can result in intolerance of anything that does not support a paradigm; that is, ambiguity, unpredictability, and invalidation of a logical construct, for example, a model. Ambiguity often plays a significant role by causing uncertainty, which challenges the very premises behind logical reasoning.

Being intuitive is one of the most recognized capabilities of the right side of the brain. It is commonly referred to as *instinct*, *gut feel*, or *inner voice*. It is what some people refer to as the emotional capability of the brain. The emphasis is less on facts and algorithms and more on a subconscious belief on how something should or does work. Naturally, it is quick and requires less effort than using logic and calculations.

It is that gut feeling or sense, frequently unconsciously derived, that tells you that perhaps you should try or do something different.[6] Intuition is often cited by inventors, artists, writers, and so on, as an important ability to tap during their creative pursuits. Too much emphasis on logic often stifles one's sense of intuition. Hence, many creative people are often not even cognizant of their mental processes when creating, and rely on the subconscious and intuition.[7] Daniel Goleman agrees, noting the importance of the unconscious in creating in the early stages of the creative process.[8] Logic often overrides the unconscious and intuition, however, restricting creativity and, hence, options and perspectives. Logic dispels inconsistency and contradiction, two catalysts to creativity. To some extent, it is a conflict between the inner and outer voice, the former being akin to the identity, and the latter to the ego or superego—if one is taking a Freudian perspective.

Yet, a great degree of creative thinking is spontaneous.[9] Spontaneity allows creative people to shift gears, moving from one perspective to another, simply because they have an independence of mind. Their observation skills facilitate abandoning assumptions and biases using facts and data. Closely tied to spontaneity are flexibility, adaptability, and effectiveness when circumstances dictate them.[10] Also tied to spontaneity is the ability to free the unconscious to allow the former to arise. If unable to free their unconscious, they will struggle to allow spontaneity in their thinking simply because the mental gates in their minds are shut.

Creativity therefore requires that people pay attention to both gut feelings and logical thinking. They can discern when a creative opportunity may exist and determine whether it is worth pursuing. Being intuitive does not mean, of course, foregoing logical thinking and simply relying on emotions. Rather, it means listening to intuition, and at the same time applying logic to creative thinking. Intuition, though, has the upper hand and often does not involve logic.[11] Inventors know this, as Jacob Rabinow notes: "Inventing is not a logical process. It's only a logical process after the fact."[12]

Shifting Perspectives

When you shift perspectives it enables the ability to see a problem from multiple vantage points. By doing so, creative people can step beyond their own paradigm, which is often a restrictive viewpoint, and open their minds to new possibilities. In other words, they can broaden how they see a problem so that they generate and evaluate their ideas more effectively. Different perspectives also increase their knowledge and awareness about a specific topic.

Different perspectives can come from a defilade, point of view, angle, or macroscopic level to a microscopic one.[13] The mind is often the biggest constraint when viewing the world as it pertains to creativity. As noted earlier, Gerard Nierenberg says that our ego affects how we perceive and respond to the world around us, some of the phenomena radically affecting our perceptions.[14] With creativity, of course, systems, logic, and common sense are often challenged, causing reorganization of patterns.

By shifting perspectives, they have the ability and capacity to see beyond the constraints in which others take refuge when thinking. They can pull themselves above their milieu, including the accepted facts and assumptions of their time. This ability to think outside the box enables them to become more independent, which in turn allows them to become excellent observers of any topic or domain under study by distancing themselves from the subject. Such a perspective allows them to see a subject from unique, multiple perspectives, often by seeking multiple points of view.

Being an Iconoclast, Even Nihilistic

While creativity can involve incremental innovation, often the biggest gain is when it entails what some people refer to as "big bang" creativity, resulting in significant change. Creativity is one side of a coin; destruction is the other. One cannot exist without the other. Having investment in the status quo, whether an idea or object, does not encourage radical thinking if it means total destruction to create something new; it simply puts too much at risk. Nothing, when it comes to true creativity, should be sacrosanct if the intent is to create something radical, such as the way of doing business that often involves pressure to follow the policies, procedures, rules, and so on. This attitude, of course, is upsetting to people who find themselves invested in the status quo whereby they adhere to a paradigm. Such an investment will be likely to inhibit creative thinking. Tradition and taboos work against individuals who challenge the rules.[15] Other factors confronting the iconoclast are repression, concealment, denial of reality, and self-censorship.[16] Perhaps the biggest resistance to the iconoclast is, however, success, which breeds comfort with, and acceptance of, the status quo.[17] They realize that to create, they must destroy the status quo. Creativity involves building something new, different from what exists now. To build something, like an idea or object, different from the past, requires destroying the present to provide something for the future. They look for that opportunity to destroy, noting that may be a reward in itself. As Richard Nicolosi notes, "Sacred cows make great steaks."[18] Creative people, therefore, step beyond the boundaries by stretching or breaking the rules. They recognize that they will face tangible and intangible constraints in whatever they do. They also do not view them as sacrosanct, meaning inviolable. While they appreciate rules as a necessity, they also recognize how rules can inhibit perspectives and options. They try to circumvent them. This behavior is not something that is usually rewarded. If the first attempt does not work, for example, they take a different approach with a different orientation.[19] They know that they must think and do something different and that requires "breaking set."[20] They break set by challenging relationships, order, and structure; combining and recombining them; and discarding and replacing them.

Unlearning and Relearning

We are all products of our environment, which molds us positively and negatively. This molding includes not only our behavior but our thinking too, both of which are highly interlinked. We find ourselves stuck in a paradigm, for example, on how we view the world, entrapping us in some type of mental prison. Daniel Goleman has come up with an apt term for being so rigid in thinking: *psychosclerosis*.[21] Part of this rigidity is due to the human tendency to impose structure, order, and relation, which constrain as well as enable thinking.[22] An important key to creativity is the ability to break out of this paradigm to generate new ideas. Unlearning requires removing the shackles, so to speak, of the paradigm to ensure false assumptions and beliefs do not inhibit thinking. Relearning requires viewing the world under a different paradigm, adhering to a different set of assumptions and beliefs, breaking out of the prison of familiarity. This may explain in part why certain people come from one domain and enter into another one and operate successfully. In the end, it all boils down to two types of thinkers that can affect creativity. Says Kenneth Boulding, "There are two kinds of people in this world; those who divide everything into groups and those who don't."[23] Creative people don't.

Looking from the Outside In

Instead of viewing something within a paradigm, the creative thinker has the ability to look at the object of study from an independent, objective perspective. While true objectivity can never be attained, creative thinkers strive to disassociate from whatever they are studying, by looking at it from a somewhat unattached perspective. They can see what is positive and negative and change their thoughts, assumptions, beliefs, and so on accordingly. This is not easy because sometimes it requires being brutally honest in self-criticism about what they create.

Reverse Thinking

This one involves taking, when creating, the opposite perspective of whatever may be the prevailing thoughts. For example, if the prevailing thought is black, then creative people think white. The objective is to see the object of study as the opposite of what everyone thinks, and then to identify the differences, and perhaps even more so, leverage them. The ability to take the opposite view often leads to changes that no one else foresees.

Too often, people see the world in black but not necessarily in white, or vice versa. This restrictive thinking locks people into a rigid mental model that restricts seeing the world as multifaceted. It also limits options. Through reverse thinking, creative individuals can turn their views upside down, revealing one or more answers to a problem or issue that an opposite perspective can only disclose.

Conceptualizing

Conceptualization involves developing ideas.[24] Creative individuals are *idea people* who develop concepts concerning a problem or issue and synthesize them into a model or paradigm. To some extent, they take a childlike view of their topic, taking components and constructing a model that reflects what they perceive as happening, and just as importantly, not happening. This allows them to take a *big-picture* view of the phenomena, understanding and creating a unique, novel idea through different connections of concepts.[25] Creative people often have the ability to take conceptualization one step further, and develop and combine unrelated ideas to form new models or paradigms. They can even do so by leveraging a small idea to create a model or paradigm of considerable complexity, resulting in breakthrough innovation.[26] Conceptualizing can result in concrete consequences that add value. A danger exists, however, that the more thinking and intuition that go into an idea, the more complex the idea can become and then require greater effort to translate; simplification seems to go to the wayside. Complexity does not necessarily equate to creativity. A threshold seems to occur when the complexity simply obfuscates the idea and all creative thinking becomes difficult. Simplification in conceptualization represents creativity when inventing.[27] Simplification, then, is a critical ingredient of creativity and people often reflect after the fact.[28]

Deployment of a new product, process, or service, however, must be done in the real world, thereby requiring enabling acceptance and refinement. Otherwise, the only person receiving any consolation or gain is the creator. If truly innovative, by definition it must provide value to someone else, usually the customer. Implementation, of course, can be a great challenge, requiring good organizational skills, as Steve Wozniak observed about his friend Steve Jobs: "[Jobs] was able to manage projects, set up schedules, make sure everything was done that needed to get done. He could persuade people to do things that normally couldn't get done."[29]

Embracing Ambiguity

Precision operates on the premise that an exact answer exists for everything; there is a right and wrong answer. The left brain seeks to find the answer by looking for a tangible, concrete result upon inquiry. A major premise is that only one right answer exists which is specific and exact; there are no shades of gray as are associated with fuzzy thinking. Precision is paramount.

The downside is that reliance on left brain thinking assumes reality is predictable, such as through mathematics and measurement. Such thinking can lead to the disregard of other important phenomena simply because it is not measurable. It can also lead to thinking that has very little tolerance for being wrong or imprecise. The desire to suffice is intolerable to someone who prefers precision.

The left brain is structured, concrete, and logical. Ambiguity, intuition, and emotion have very little value to this side of the brain. Algorithms, verbal translation, and other modes of thinking have much more value to those who are left brain–dominant than metaphorical, visual thinking does for the right brained individuals.

Ambiguity goes hand in hand with creativity. The reason is that creativity involves change, which in turn involves causing some degree of unpredictability. With unpredictability come known and unforeseen impacts. Some people are fine, even thrive in such environments. Others find such environments disquieting, even intolerable. Creativity often arises best when some ambiguity exists because it gives people the latitude to create by reducing or disregarding restraints and constraints, such as rules, procedures, guidelines, standards, and so on. Ambiguity furthers the freedom and courage to create what a more regimented environment would not allow.

Creative people will leap into the unknown, going to places that no one dared to, or is willing to go. The novel experience entices them to step into the abyss in the hope of creating something that was thought impractical.

They may have a sense of danger; they are willing to explore despite the arrows that they know will be coming at them, because the reward—not necessarily financial—is greater than the pain. They also like to tinker with ideas, approaches, and so on, to uncover something new and different.[30] They know that creativity means diving into the unknown, the distant waters consisting of monsters and other creatures that could mean failure or quitting. However, their vision of what to create causes them to proceed into that vast ocean, hoping that something better will result, whether incrementally or on a grand scale. It takes considerable guts to challenge a well-accepted process, product, or service, for example, and to not expect an onslaught of criticism, even ostracism. Naiveté may be necessary perhaps. Not without its costs, however. The more creative you get, the greater potential for pain to increase. Perseverance then becomes an important quality.[31] Some are virtual gamblers; others take on more calculated risks. Regardless, they are willing to step into the unknown based upon some notion of potential gain by taking a risk. Again, the idea in their mind is that the gain exceeds the pain. Risk taking is not easy for most people, partly due to personality and to their past. For example, risk taking rarely gets rewarded in schools because it often requires breaking the rules, something schools do not usually encourage.[32] So people seek safety, which usually does not lead to creativity.[33] Creative people also know that risk taking involves probability of failure. Indeed, more often than not, the odds are in favor of failure when taking a risk. They also know that if they experience success, the rewards will likely exceed the costs. Not surprisingly, they tend to make more mistakes but develop more ideas as a result than their colleagues.[34] Albert Einstein agrees, commenting that "A person who never made a mistake, never tried anything new."[35] Creative people are often ahead of their time because, in many cases, timing, as an old saying goes, is everything. They also learn through failure. Failure, therefore, becomes a springboard to move forward when creating.

Seeing Multiple Answers

The left side of the brain tolerates little ambiguity and unpredictability. Linear relationships reflected in serial thinking, reasons, and precisions are its core competencies. The right brain is unstructured, abstract, and emotional. The emphasis is more on the subjective, relational, and intangible qualities of a person. Precision is not what is important. What is important is being "good enough" to understand what is going on and to create something that may only partially address complexity. Generally, what matters most is deriving general rules and patterns of behavior. It requires developing a high level of abstraction for understanding and predicting behavior with some reliability. Tolerance needs to exist for fuzzy logic, ambiguity, and being wrong occasionally. It also requires less time and effort than using the capabilities, for example, precision, of the left brain.

Creative individuals understand the need to acknowledge that many right answers can exist. Creativity necessitates exploring different ways to come up with an answer. In typically unambiguous environments, the perception reigns that only one right answer exists. When creating, however, there are often multiple right answers, and the challenge is choosing among two or more "best" ones. A combination of intuition and logic, or the subjective and objective, respectively, helps of course, but oftentimes it requires relying more on the former because the one-size-fits-all answer does, more often than not fit. In many respects, the educational system emphasizes the importance of having the right answer. The wrong answer ends up in low grades and disfavor among peers. Also, one's own prejudices, values, and so on, can influence the types of questions asked. An example is the leading question used on the witness stand where the answer is predictable.

Defining the Problem

This one enables creativity to be targeted toward building something innovative rather than allowing creative energy to dissipate into activities resulting in a solution failing to address a problem or issue. Quite often, people spend too much time jumping to a solution before defining the problem or issue. Impatience is partly the reason. It is partly because developing a solution is more fun than spending time defining the problem or issue. Finally, according to Daniel Goleman, the rational, analytical mind seeks an answer too.[36] Not surprisingly, solutions are often short-term fixes and become irrelevant as the problem or issue resurfaces or gets worse over time.

Being Observant

Observation is critical to understanding what is happening when creating. Good observation requires being able to divorce yourself from the process and results to ascertain whether your creativity adds value by solving the problem or issue. Good observation also includes determining if time may be necessary to change approaches, techniques, and so on to meet expectations.[37]

Failing to observe can result in a host of difficulties when being creative. These difficulties include misunderstanding the problem or issue, coming up with an inadequate solution, and overlooking important information. Creative individuals, contrary to popular belief, know that the devil is, indeed, in the details, and any detail often requires being observant, such as experimenting after building a prototype.

Tinkering

This ability is a good one to see what works and what does not work. Tinkering requires occasionally straying from a plan to determine how something works or should work, and then using that knowledge to develop something innovative. It also reveals when something does not work, leading down a different path resulting in an unexpected creative insight. Deviating, through tinkering, often brings accidental, unexpected solutions.

Not surprisingly, creative people like to tinker with an object or idea to see its strengths, weaknesses, responses, features, and so on, to learn more and expand their awareness and perspectives and to know how things work. Their curiosity is allied with all the other characteristics because without it, creativity may be impossible. In addition, they are comfortable asking questions that often result in multiple answers rather than the "right" answer. They like to uncover a problem as much as solve it. Even failure can fire up curiosity.[38] If they cannot find an answer, no worries. An infantile curiosity helps, too.[39]

Determining the Essence of Something

Too many times, people add superfluous detail to describe an idea, process, or technique, which only confuses both the originator and receiver. More is not necessarily better because additional, irrelevant facts and data only clutter the mind, and consequently the understanding. As human beings, we will never be able to eradicate complexity, but can, and need to, distill the essence of the subject to reduce complexity. Modeling works best to ascertain the essence of the subject that currently exists and then identify different options to develop an innovative solution. However, like all models, they are a distillation of details that simplify but potentially can eliminate or overlook a key detail.

When sifting through assumptions, data, and facts, creative people discern the essence of something by uncovering patterns, which improves understanding of a problem as well as enables the development of a creative idea that addresses the problem or issue being solved.[40] Often, patterns of behavior exist that enable simplifying phenomena for understandability. These patterns center on the probability of certain behaviors that enable reliable and confident prediction of behavior. These patterns reflect one of the following: part versus whole, verbal versus configuration, serial versus simultaneous, and so on.[41]

Being Self-Aware

Being self-critical means performing a self-analysis regarding your values, beliefs, assumptions, and perspectives when creating. This ability is not easy to exercise as people are all products of a milieu. Being self-critical, however, is needed to determine if prejudices are interfering with, or preventing, creativity. Without the ability to be self-critical, a paradigm trap or mental straightjacket may preclude thinking creatively. This ability enables a level of objectivity often reserved for outsiders not sharing similar beliefs, values, and assumptions. In the end, a balance must exist between being self-critical and creative, even to the point of rejecting one's own ideas.

Creative people can identify where their creativity works; they can also identify where it falls short of expectations. They know what does, and just as importantly, what does not work. They will revise and refine and, if necessary, destroy what they already created and start over. While standards in a domain or organization are important, they consider their own to be higher. They also have the ability to question their own ideas, no matter how close they feel toward it. They also know confidence is critical to engage on a journey of creativity. Albert Bandura refers to this as "self-efficacy," meaning creative people have a sense of being able to handle what confronts them.[42] Creativity is not for the weak of heart because of the potential for failure and the consequences that often accompany it. With self-confidence, they can proceed too, without internal or external criticism. Or, if they are bothered by it, they can direct their angst into their work as they shrug their shoulders and continue with their creative pursuit. In many respects, the very existence of anxiety enhances their desire to create by embracing the angst that often accompanies the act of creation.[43] Finally, they know that creativity requires attention and focus on whatever they do. Consequently, they do not allow others to distract them from their work. They are also self-disciplined in the sense that they apply their tools and techniques, knowledge, and experience, which respects the domain under which they work. Form plays a key role in creativity, meaning it is not just an act of free style or freedom (unless, of course, it is chosen as a deliberate way to create).

Competing and Collaborating

Competition, for the most part, furthers creativity; it does not retard it. Examples of historical relationships fill the history pages of individuals competing with each other. Such competition can only go so far, especially in today's technological age. They realize that they have to collaborate, if for no other reason than to get their ideas accepted and implemented by others. Creativity is no longer an island unto itself. It frequently requires the tacit acceptance of others. As Daniel Goleman notes, it necessitates having a sense of compassion rather than the strict competitive position of a winner-takes-all mentality.[44]

Creative people, therefore, know that they have to collaborate if they hope to get their ideas implemented. This situation is especially true in the case where the environment is highly specialized and the final product or service requires the participation of people working in different disciplines. Without collaboration, competitive success is frequently meaningless.

Persevering

This one is closely allied with embracing ambiguity; the difference here is that the forces against being creative are coupled often with ambiguity. Creativity means stepping into the unknown, the distant waters of monsters and other creatures that could mean failure or quitting. However, their vision of what to create causes them to proceed into that vast ocean, hoping that something better will result, whether incrementally or on a grand scale. It takes considerable guts to challenge a well-accepted process, product, or service, for example, and to not expect an onslaught of criticism, even ostracism. Hence, the more creative you get, the greater the potential for pain to increase. In the face of criticism and other less than desirable reactions, they doggedly pursue their final goal. There will always be the naysayers and mockers of institutional pressures to conform.[45] The creative people persist, nonetheless, because of a belief in themselves and their vision. They have a high adversity quotient, relying on two key values: persistency and perseverance. Inventor Wilson Greatbatch calls it "stick-to-it-iveness."[46] They have the willpower to turn their goals into reality.[47] In some cases, pushback from others can encourage a greater sense of purpose.[48]

Shifting Thinking

Creative individuals can shift their thinking in three ways: from divergent to convergent and vice versa, from linear to nonlinear, and from analysis to synthesis.

Divergent thinking involves taking a more free-form type of thinking whereby one collects as much data and information as possible and generates a wide range of ideas. Principally, a person exercising divergent thinking suspends judgment in the collection of data and generation of ideas. The individual is simply keeping his or her mind open, serving as a mental sponge. It is a learning experience. Convergent thinking, in contrast, focuses upon some scoping or narrow criterion. The emphasis is on solving a specific problem or issue; the excess is eliminated as creativity is directed toward addressing a specific goal or objective.

Next, linear thinking involves viewing the world as sequential, such as left to right, or step 1 then step 2. Nonlinear thinking involves seeing the world at a much higher degree of complexity whereby activities occur simultaneously and proportionally, depending on a given set of relationships with nonlinear thinking; the patterns are more random and the relationships complex, resulting in a higher degree of difficulty in predicting behavior. Nonlinearity is a characteristic of complex systems, whether an idea or object under study. The basic concept here is that relationships among components are difficult to understand and predict. The right side of the brain allows it to handle nonlinearity because it can tolerate and understand a certain degree of complexity in relationships that is hard to predict mathematically through narrative description. Nonlinearity often leads to ambiguity and unpredictability, which the right side of the brain can tolerate up to some threshold.

Both linear and nonlinear thinking are crucial for creativity to allow for greater exploration of alternatives. This type of behavior is often associated with complex systems, meaning that the components and variables have multilinear relationships. Simultaneous behavior makes understandability and control much more difficult due to the level of integration and interdependence of the components and relationships. The right side of the brain enables the capacity of people to deal with complex systems. A simple flow on a control chart, for example, do A, then B, then C, as opposed to a data flow diagram reflecting two processes occurring at the same time, which is an example of simultaneous behavior.

Finally, analysis is breaking the object of study into components. Analysis is key to understanding the current pre-creative state of the object under study and creating something new. Linear thinking helps simplify reality into a set of predictable mathematically precise behaviors. One plus one equals two is the anticipated result. It involves dealing with the world in a logical way because such thinking is predicated on predictability, that is, it presumes relationships are stable and predictable with little tolerance for ambiguity or anomalies. The downside is that linearity tends to break down as the complexity of a system increases, that is, augmenting the number of variables and their relationships. Simple mathematical equations predicated on a handful of assumptions no longer apply.

Synthesis is putting all the components together into some coherent whole. This ability requires exploding a concept or object into components, perhaps in varying levels of details in an effort to tackle the complexity supporting it. The old notion of how do you stirfry an elephant applies here—one piece at a time. Also, by breaking something down, the idea is that you can mix and match the pieces to come up with a new idea. The challenge, though, with exploding something into components is loss of synergy, the notion that an idea or object had before being exploded into components. This loss of connectedness, or relationships, involving integration and interdependence among the components gets lost while trying to understand the pieces of a puzzle. Additionally, the eventual recombination of the components may never be the same, depending on the complexity of what is being exploded into components. In other words, simplicity may result in the actual understanding of an issue or problem. It may also result in a person losing sight of the big picture after drilling down into the details. In synthesis is important to do the same thing, except this time, the pieces are put together to see how all the components fit and to uncover patterns that reveal the essence of how something works. Unlike analysis, which requires breaking down an idea or object into components, synthesis entails putting all the parts together. Emphasis shifts, therefore, from parts to relationships. Instead of decoupling, the right side of the brain couples components to understand the overall idea or object. It also enables seeing the big picture, as opposed to getting buried in the details, to enable seeing how components fit together.

Suspending Judgment

Too often the tendency is to make a judgment first before even really understanding the problem or issue. Creativity initially requires the free flow of ideas, for example, applying divergent thinking, and then down-selecting ideas until one of them is truly innovative. When letting judgment rule in the beginning, people think only within their assumptions. If they find a solution, it may not be creative or lasting. Suspending judgment precludes limiting the number of ideas, and creativity is frequently a numbers game.

Creative individuals essentially hold little if anything sacred. Assumptions, values, and so on are all subject to challenge, especially if they hope to come up with a truly creative idea. As noted earlier, their tolerance for ambiguity, being iconoclastic, and the ability to unlearn as well as relearn helps, but does not eliminate the propensity to make premature judgments.

Communicating

As Confucius says, a picture is worth a thousand words. Visual display of data and information is preferred by right brain-dominant people. A visual image allows them to see the big picture with all the components working together. It is easier, for example, to see how the parts fit together, giving a person a holistic, or gestalt, perspective. A visual image capitalizes on the power of synthesis and requires less effort and time to communicate a large amount of information. It also enables seeing from different perspectives.

The downside of visual display is that it can either confuse people more or oversimplify understanding of how something works. It also does not satisfy people who have other modes for processing information, for example, auditory or kinesthetic. Also, important details may be overlooked, which causes people to acquire an erroneous appreciation of the complexity.

Verbalizing requires using language to process data in a way that involves decomposing and translating. The mechanical side of language requires serial processing in the left brain. Individuals select certain parts of a language, code and decode it, and translate it into literal meaning, that is, detonative. Contrast that with understanding the emotional meaning of the language done in the right side of the brain. Precision and detail, albeit less important than the meaning, that is, connotative, is what typifies this side of the brain.

The downside, however, is that verbal learning is just one mode; other modes include graphical learning. It also can lead to intellectual blindness, which is screening important data or information simply because something cannot be described verbally. It also requires considerable effort and time to be verbal and leads to varying interpretation of elements of the language.

TOOLS FOR PROJECT MANAGERS

There are, of course, psychological tools that project managers can apply to enhance managing the creative side of projects. What follows is a high-level summary of the more prevalent models employed on projects. Some of the following models address human behavior on a general level while others are specifically oriented toward creativity and innovation.

The models described below are by no means exhaustive. They are simply presented to encourage the reader to determine whether they are harnessing the strengths, and compensating for weaknesses, of the different styles people exhibit on projects. By using one or more of the models, creativity has a greater chance of success on projects. Before applying these models on projects to further creativity, however, it is important to state general insights.

First, most people do not fit neatly in a category. The reality is that many people have elements of each characteristic associated with a particular personality.

Second, the typologies do not mean people act the same all the time. Under stressful conditions, they may resort to a different style within a particular typology.

Third, there will likely never be enough information to help you determine the appropriate category for an individual within a model. There are too many intangible aspects about human behavior to allow accurate determination of a person's personality type. Using the models more often than not requires making a best guess and looking for subtle clues about that person.

Finally, too many unknowns and so much variation exists about a person that predictability of a person's behavior under a designated category makes accurate predictability impossible. The best hope is for a decent probability or likelihood of success.

Birkman Model

The Birkman Model, once well-known but seemingly fading in the background, is a model predicated on four psychological profiles represented by colors. This model looks at the relationships of two continuums, direct and indirect, as well as task and people orientation. Each style—Red, Green, Blue, and Yellow—has its own set of strengths and weaknesses. Reds tend to be decisive, energetic, preferring to focus on achieving results. Greens tend to be assertive, competitive, and enthusiastic about change, seeking to influence people. Yellows are cautious, orderly, preferring structure, routine, and so on. Blues are thoughtful, reflective, preferring creative activities and interests. According to Roger Birkman, the key is to reduce as much dissonance between a person's true self and socialized behavior. True style is reflected in a person's tendency to lean toward one of the four colors, or styles.

Birkman notes that each style has a preference when it comes to interests, needs, styles, and stress. Project managers can capitalize on this information when assigning people to develop deliverables for a project. Using the strengths of a Red, Green, Yellow, or Blue, in other words, depends on the needs of the project at the time. Hence, Reds prefer action when implementing an idea. Blues and Greens may be best to generate ideas. Yellows might be good at identifying the downsides of making a change that everyone else embraces.[49]

Hartman Color Code

The Color Code by Taylor Hartman is another psychological model that project managers can tap to unleash the creativity of team members, individually and as a group. Like the Birkman Model, the Color Code identifies four personalities. The Color Code assumes that everyone has a core personality to direct their behavior. Each personality is based upon three variables: motive, needs, and wants. The colors are Red, Blue, White, and Yellow.[50]

Reds seek power, need to be right and respected, and want to be productive and adventurous. Blues seek intimacy, need to be appreciated and accepted, and want autonomy and security. Whites seek peace, need tolerance and respect, and want to be independent and contented. Yellows seek fun, need to be noticed and praised, and want to be playful and free. Again, like other creative typologies, few people completely fit into one category; rather, most people have some of the others to one degree or another. Also, congruence with the personality and the work a person does engenders greater passion; the work he or she does can only lead to greater productivity.

In terms of creativity, Blues tend to be the creative ones, generating ideas. Reds tend to be innovative, preferring creative ideas that add value and produce results. Whites are also creative, and like Blues, are doers but lack the intensity of Reds to make things happen. Yellows seek change and innovation like Reds, but the avoid a confrontational approach. Reds like to challenge and Yellows like the adventure that comes with being creative.

Myers-Briggs

Myers-Briggs is another tool to help engender and employ the creativity of individuals. Predicated on the work of the famed psychologist Carl Jung, Myers-Briggs offers an assessment for identifying sixteen patterns of behavior regarding individuals' personalities.

The assessment identifies four pairs of temperaments that, when combined, create the sixteen personalities. These pairs of temperaments are:

- Extraversion (E) versus Introversion (I): People who are extraverted are externally focused, being social and relationship oriented. Introverts are internally focused and territorial.
- Sensation (S) versus Intuition (N): People who have a sensation orientation emphasize experience and pride themselves on being realistic. Intuitive people emphasize hunches, or gut feel, and pride themselves on being imaginative.
- Thinking (T) versus Feeling (F): People who are thinkers strive for objectivity and value laws and standards over intimacy. Feeling people are subjective and emphasize intimacy and social values.

- Perceiving (P) versus Judging (J): Perceiving people tend to be flexible and open ended, adapting as circumstances warrant. People who are judging are decisive and fixed in their decisions, having a preference to produce.[51]

The result of these four categories of temperament is sixteen personalities:

ISTJ	ESTP	ISFP	ESFP
ISFJ	ESFJ	ISTJ	ESTJ
INTP	ENTP	INTJ	ENTJ
INFJ	ENFJ	INFP	ENFP

All sixteen personalities can, of course, play an important role in the creative process by contributing at specific points during the creative process. SPs prefer action in an impulsive, independent manner. SJs prefer duty, follow-through on obligations, and hard work. NTs seek to understand, explain, and predict through competency. NFs are exploratory in the pursuit of goals, especially personal ones, as a means of self-actualization and providing integrity in their behavior and expressions, becoming somewhat of a true believer until their enthusiasm wanes.

Based upon the description above, NFs can be used to motivate the project team to exercise its creativity. SJs can ensure the creative work gets done on their own and other's dedication. NTs can help ensure that logic and a systematic approach are adhered to. SPs can provide the spontaneous insight to develop different ideas and options, and the others will help turn a creative thought into reality.[52]

The Enneagram

The Enneagram is yet another psychological approach project managers can use during the creative process. Unlike the previous models, being reflected in a quadrant, the Enneagram identifies nine personality types that are grouped into what are called *triads*: Feeling Triad, Doing Triad, and Relation Triad. The Feeling Triad pertains to emotions, the Doing Triad to the ability to act, and the Relation Triad to how one deals with the real world.[53] These triads determine a person's positive or negative orientation.[54] Richard Rohr calls the triads by different names that are associated with parts of the human anatomy; gut, head, and heart. The gut deals with the sexual aspects of the human being, symbolized by the digestive system. The head deals with the objectivity and introspection, symbolized by the brain. The heart heals with relationships with others, symbolized by the heart and circulatory system.[55] Using the triad model, each one consists of three of nine personalities. These personalities have a unique number, that is, 1 through 9, but author Don Riso gave them names that are referred to in this book and help further visualize the nine personalities more meaningfully.

The Feeling Triad consists of the Helper, someone who cares for and encourages others positively, but can be negative by being manipulative. The Status Seeker is confident and ambitious, but from a negative narcissistic perspective. The Artist is the third personality, and is positively creative but negatively can be depressive.

The Doing Triad consists of the Thinker, who is positively perceptive, analytical but eccentric, even simplistic. The Loyalist emphasizes duty but is dependent and passive-aggressive. The Generalist is the third personality in this triad, and is, in a positive sense, successful but seen as excessive at times.

The Relating Triad consists of the Leader, who is positively confident but is negatively aggressive. The Peacemaker is reassuring and easygoing but is complacent. The Reformer is the third personality in this triad, and emphasizes rationality but is very much a perfectionist.[56]

All three triads and the nine personalities are reflected in a circle with nine points placed around its circumference, all interconnected by arrays to show their relationship to one another.

According to Riso, keep the following points in mind about the nine personality types, which to a large degree relate to the other personality tools discussed in this chapter. Each personality is universal, being independent of race, religion, and so on. No personality is better than another. Finally, it is very difficult for a personality to change his or her personality.[57] Each personality has a continuum that spans from positive orientation (referred to as *integration*) to negative (referred to as *disintegration*). Hence, each personality can be reflected on a continuum, ranging from healthy (positive, integration) to unhealthy (negative, disintegration).[58]

Multiple Intelligences

Although not a personality profile, the work of Howard Gardner coined the term *multiple intelligence*. He identified several intelligences, each one being useful when applied during the creative process.

Gardner refers to those intelligences as intellectual proclivities that involve creative insights for a particular domain, such as disciplines or crafts. He notes that many independent "human intellectual competencies" exist, which he refers as "frames of mind."[59] He observes that, in large part, damage to certain parts of the brain affect people's exhibition of these difference intelligences. He also notes, as evidence, the use of symbolic systems to create, for which no theories of explanation exist.[60] He also adds that genetic factors play a role.[61] Just as importantly, which has relevance to project managers, Gardner notes that the right environment can also allow people with one or more proclivities toward specific intelligences to grow.[62] By allowing these proclivities to grow, individual team members can focus on solving problems and addressing difficulties, or reveal other problems.[63]

The following is a description of each of the intelligences identified by Howard Gardner:

- **Musical Intelligence** relates to perceiving and creating rhythms, melodies, and so on. This intelligence is exhibited through playing an instrument, composing, and other activities. It also involves considerable analyzing, listening, and critiquing.
- **Body-Kinesthetic Intelligence** relates to exercise, such as running or walking. This intelligence is exhibited by preparing, cleaning, and so on. It also involves assembling and crafting.
- **Interpersonal Intelligence** relates to communicating and empathizing. Often, this is exhibited through supervising, negotiating, rewarding, and motivating. It also involves confronting and collaborating.
- **Linguistic Intelligence** relates to telling, informing, and instructing. This intelligence is exhibited through teaching, writing, editing, and other language-related activities. It also involves listening and interpreting.
- **Logical-Mathematical Intelligence** relates to numbers and reasoning. Often, this intelligence is exhibited through activities like budgeting and estimating. It also involves systematizing and classifying.
- **Spatial Intelligence** relates to visualizing and illustrating. This intelligence is exhibited through activities like drawing, building maps, and photography.

- **Intrapersonal Intelligence** relates to self-awareness and making decisions. This intelligence is exhibited through activities like setting goals and objectives and planning to achieve them.[64]

MODELS OF CREATIVE INDIVIDUALS

Creative Roles

Roger von Oech, author of several best sellers on creativity, essentially describes the role of four creative types of people, which in many ways reflects the creative process. These roles enable developing, and just as importantly, implementing new ideas. The four roles are the Explorer, the Artist, the Judge, and the Warrior. Loosely parallel to these four roles and the creative process are the discovery of information, conversion of information into an idea, evaluation of the idea, and implementation of it, respectively.

Explorers are people who go on a journey of discovery. This journey can uncover all sorts of data, information, concepts, techniques, and so on, which are useful either to address a problem or issue or to define one. This requires paying attention to what is, and perhaps what is not, which are available by taking macroscopic and microscopic perspectives. The key, however, is to have an open mind that enables uncovering what is needed through an inquisitive mind.[65] Artists are the people who take the information gathered by the Explorers and develop a new idea to address the issue or problem. Artists are like sculptors, taking the clay and molding it into something meaningful. They take a different perspective combined with imagination and connect everything to come up with a new insight. The Artist adds, deletes, connects, and compares the information to come up with a new idea.[66]

Judges are the people who determine the fate of the ideas from the Artists. They are the critics who ask the questions that any realist would feel compelled to ask. These questions often center on the feasibility of the idea, such as: How much will it cost? Will people see value in it? Is there anything overlooked, such as the downsides? What are the rules? Are the assumptions valid? What's the likelihood of success? These, and many other questions, cause one to question the very premises of an idea before the Warrior takes over.[67] Warriors are the people who make it happen. They are the people who take the idea and put it in the real world. They strategize, plan, and "land on the beach," so to speak, with the idea. Character traits like being courageous, persistent, and focused are essential for an idea to become a reality. Many times an idea does well until it reaches the Warriors when most people find reality just hard to face and quit. With the spirit of the Warrior, an idea has a chance to survive and even thrive if they succeed.[68] Again, although von Oech describes the four categories as mindsets, they can be sequenced in a logical order in a way that reflects the creative process that works quite well: discover information (Explorer), convert information into ideas (Artist), evaluate the idea (Judge), and implement it (Warrior).

Five Mental Skills of Creativity

Annette Moser-Wellman provides another approach that follows the different types of creative people, but can also serve as a process for creativity. She identifies five mental skills that are quite useful for being creative in business in general and projects in particular. They are Seer, Observer, Alchemist, Fool, and Sage. These mental skills fall short of implementing a creative idea, but still prove valuable in understanding what the process of creativity entails.

Seers are the people who imagine. That is, they visualize the idea or generate multiple ones. This visualization involves not some vague idea initially, but the ability to do so in detail, to give it the breadth and depth necessary to eventually turn the idea into reality. Through imagining, they have the ability to manipulate the details to derive a variety of alternative ideas. Some of these ideas may be construed by some people as unconventional. Seers, however, can often imagine without fear of criticism from others or being restricted by certain assumptions deemed as truths. The focus is on what could be and not be. In addition, Seers take the details from the image and manipulate the relations among the details to come up with alternatives.[69]

Observers take a somewhat different approach when generating ideas. Observers compile data and information and generate ideas from the bottom up, so to speak. The smallest piece of data may rise, from the Observer's perspective, to a major idea. To the "normal" person, a datum might seem of little value; to an Observer it may be something akin to gold because it generates a valuable idea. The emphasis on detail is fueled by an Observer's acute curiosity about how the universe operates, to

understand its meaning and the lessons that may arise from that understanding. Data is the fuel that helps generate information, which in turn
creates ideas.[70]

Alchemists, as the name implies, are people who generate ideas from
a myriad of sources. Their ability is mixing and matching material to
come up with new ideas. Alchemists' fuel is connections because it is
through the manipulation of different components and the relationships among them that new ideas come forth. Alchemists capitalize to
a large extent on what was done in the past; sometimes, this may not
seem original. Yet, history is replete with examples of people coming
from one field to another and combining existing ideas, techniques, and
so on and inventing a wholly new way of doing business. They have the
ability, therefore, to reinvent the present by creating new relationships.
To be an Alchemist requires having a broad background to avoid being
myopic.[71]

Fools have the ability to see things that people often do not think
about. They have little or no desire to just sit by and accept something as
the truth. Instead, they have no problem looking at something considered inviolable and turning it upside down to generate a new idea. They
capitalize on imperfections and see discrepancies as catalysts to generate
new ideas. Fools are rarely popular, despite the value of their creative ideas
because absurdity, even mockery, is their tool. They capitalize on finding
a weakness and then push it until a new idea arises. Inversion is the fuel
that moves Fools forward. They look at the opposite of what is construed
as truth to come up with a creative idea. Naturally, when Fools take on the
status quo or anything sacrosanct, resistance by others is strong and the
attacks unrelenting. Thanks to courage that accompanies perseverance,
Fools persist until they come up with a good idea.[72]

Sages are the final type of creators. They have the ability to "cut to the
chase," that is, take away the chaff and simplify. Using simplification, they
come up with an idea that after the fact seems so simple that others wonder why they never thought about it. The primary tool for this simplification is the vision that they hold in their head and use to align everything
else to it. If something does not contribute to the vision, then it goes to the
wayside. Their fuel is the ability to discover or uncover the fundamental
issues and take that information and generate an idea. In other words,
simplicity leads to eloquence. History is a useful tool for Sages because
they can ascertain what is or is not relevant based upon that historical
experience.[73]

CONCLUSION

As stated earlier, everyone has the abilities to be creative—if they seek to tap them. These abilities, albeit not clearly divided between the left and right brain, are often seen as unconnected. The reality is that people need both sides of the brain to create and innovate. When managing their projects, project managers need to be aware of and to capitalize by tapping the abilities of both sides of people.

Getting Started Checklist

Question	Yes	No
1. Which of the following abilities are best exhibited by most of the members of your team?		
Cross-domain thinking		
Having fun		
Listening to your own intuition		
Shifting perspectives		
Being an iconoclast, even a nihilist		
Unlearning and relearning		
Looking from the outside in		
Reverse thinking		
Conceptualizing		
Embracing ambiguity		
Seeing multiple answers		
Defining the problem		
Being observant		
Tinkering		
Determining the essence of something		
Being self-aware		
Competing and collaborating		
Persevering		
Shifting thinking		
Suspending judgment		
Communicating		
2. Which of the following abilities need improvement for most of the members of your team?		
Cross-domain thinking		
Having fun		
Listening to your own intuition		
Shifting perspectives		

(*Continued*)

Getting Started Checklist

Question	Yes	No
Being an iconoclast, even a nihilist		
Unlearning and relearning		
Looking from the outside in		
Reverse thinking		
Conceptualizing		
Embracing ambiguity		
Seeing multiple answers		
Defining the problem		
Being observant		
Tinkering		
Determining the essence of something		
Being self-aware		
Competing and collaborating		
Persevering		
Shifting thinking		
Suspending judgment		
Communicating		

3. List the ways in which you can best use the abilities identified in number 1 above?

   Way(s):

4. List the actions you can take to improve the abilities listed in number 2 above?

   Action(s):

5. Determine which models to use for assessing individual creativity:

   Birkman Model

   Hartman Color Code

   Myers-Briggs

   Enneagram

   Multiple Intelligences

   Von Oech's Creative Roles

   Moser-Wellman's Mental Skills

   Other:

ENDNOTES

1. Daniel H. Pink, *A Whole New Mind* (New York: Riverhead Books, 2006), p. 2.
2. Pink, *A Whole New Mind*, pp. 2–3.
3. Gerard Nierenberg, *The Art of Creative Thinking* (New York: Cornerstone Library, 1982), p. 85.

4. James L. Adams, *Conceptual Blockbusting*, 2nd ed. (New York: W. W. Norton & Company, 1979), p. 126.
5. Daniel Goleman, Paul Kaufman, and Michael Ray, *The Creative Spirit* (New York: Dutton: 1992), pp. 47–48.
6. Adams, *Conceptual Blockbusting*, p. 126.
7. Adams, *Conceptual Blockbusting*, p. 42.
8. Goleman, Kaufman, and Ray, *The Creative Spirit*, pp. 19–22.
9. Adams, *Conceptual Blockbusting*, p. 3.
10. Goleman, Kaufman, and Ray, *The Creative Spirit*, pp. 49–50.
11. Goleman, Kaufman, and Ray, *The Creative Spirit*, p. 68.
12. Kenneth A. Brown, *Inventors at Work* (Redmond, WA: Tempus Books, 1988), p. 190.
13. Nierenberg, *The Art of Creative Thinking*, pp. 40, 89.
14. Nierenberg, *The Art of Creative Thinking*, p. 90.
15. Adams, *Conceptual Blockbusting*, pp. 63–64.
16. Goleman, Kaufman, and Ray, *The Creative Spirit*, pp. 104–105.
17. Goleman, Kaufman, and Ray, *The Creative Spirit*, p. 19.
18. Roger von Oech, *A Whack in the Side of the Head* (New York: Warner Books, Inc., 1990), p. 64.
19. von Oech, *A Whack in the Side of the Head*, p. 29.
20. von Oech, *A Whack in the Side of the Head*, p. 92.
21. Goleman, Kaufman, and Ray, *The Creative Spirit*, p. 18.
22. Nierenberg, *The Art of Creative Thinking*, p. 26.
23. von Oech, *A Whack in the Side of the Head*, p. 36.
24. Adams, *Conceptual Blockbusting*, p. 3.
25. von Oech. *A Kick in the Seat of the Pants* (New York: Harper and Row, 1986), p. 70.
26. von Oech, *A Whack in the Side of the Head*, p. 166.
27. Brown, *Inventors at Work*, p. 81.
28. Brown, *Inventors at Work*, p. 104.
29. Brown, *Inventors at Work*, p. 227.
30. von Oech, *A Whack in the Side of the Head*, p. 7.
31. Goleman, Kaufman, and Ray, *The Creative Spirit*, p. 31.
32. Goleman, Kaufman, and Ray, *The Creative Spirit*, p. 68.
33. Dove Allen, Matt Kingdon, and Kris Murrin *What If?* (Oxford: Capstone Publishing Limited, 1999), p. 218.
34. Goleman, Kaufman, and Ray, *The Creative Spirit*, p. 43.
35. Goleman, Kaufman, and Ray, *The Creative Spirit*, p. 35.
36. Goleman, Kaufman, and Ray, *The Creative Spirit*, p. 19.
37. Adams, *Conceptual Blockbusting*, p. 126.
38. Brown, *Inventors at Work*, p. 279.
39. Brown, *Inventors at Work*, p. 285.
40. Adams, *Conceptual Blockbusting*, p. 126.
41. Linda V. Williams, *Teaching for the Two-Sided Mind* (New York: Touchstone, 1983), p. 26.
42. Goleman, Kaufman, and Ray, *The Creative Spirit*, p. 65.
43. Goleman, Kaufman, and Ray, *The Creative Spirit*, p. 44.
44. Goleman, Kaufman, and Ray, *The Creative Spirit*, p. 38.
45. Brown, *Inventors at Work*, p. 149.
46. Brown, *Inventors at Work*, p. 31.
47. Goleman, Kaufman, and Ray, *The Creative Spirit*, p. 68.

48. Brown, *Inventors at Work*, p. 360.
49. Roger Birkman, *True Colors* (Ontario: Thomas Nelson, Inc., 1997), pp. 37–49.
50. Taylor Hartman, *The Color Code* (New York: Fireside, 1998), pp. 43–51.
51. David Keirsey and Marilyn Bates, *Please Understand Me* (Del Mar, CA: Prometheus Nemesis Book Company, 1984), pp. 27–66.
52. David Keirsey, *Please Understand Me II* (Del Mar, CA: Prometheus Nemesis Book Company, 1998), pp. 18–20.
53. Don R. Riso, *Personality Types* (Boston: Houghton Mifflin, 1990), p. 7.
54. Riso, *Personality Types*, p. 10.
55. Richard Rohr and Andreas Ebert, *Discovering the Enneagram* (New York: Crossroad Publishing Company, 1997), pp. 25–28.
56. Riso, *Personality Types*, pp. 7–8.
57. Riso, *Personality Types*, pp. 28–29.
58. Riso, *Personality Types*, p. 42.
59. Howard Gardner, *Frames of Mind* (New York: Basic Books, 1983), p. 8–9.
60. Gardner, *Frames of Mind*, pp. 24–25.
61. Gardner, *Frames of Mind*, p. 33.
62. Gardner, *Frames of Mind*, p. 33.
63. Gardner, *Frames of Mind*, pp. 60–61.
64. Thomas Armstrong, *7 Kinds of Smarts* (New York: Plume, 1993), pp. 192–194.
65. von Oech, *A Kick in the Seat of the Pants*, pp. 23–54.
66. von Oech, *A Kick in the Seat of the Pants*, pp. 55–87.
67. von Oech, *A Kick in the Seat of the Pants*, pp. 89–111.
68. von Oech, *A Kick in the Seat of the Pants*, pp. 113–135.
69. Annette Moser-Wellman, *The Five Faces of Genius* (New York: penguin, 2002), pp. 21–45.
70. Moser-Wellman, *The Five Faces of Genius*, pp. 46–69.
71. Moser-Wellman, *The Five Faces of Genius*, pp. 70–89.
72. Moser-Wellman, *The Five Faces of Genius*, pp. 90–114.
73. Moser-Wellman, *The Five Faces of Genius*, pp. 115–137.

3

Groups and Creativity

INTRODUCTION

Contrary to popular belief, it is not just individuals who are creative. Groups can be equally creative, and in some cases, exceed the creativity of any individual. Like creative individuals, creative groups have characteristics that distinguish them from other groups that are less, or not even as, creative. Few, but some, models exist that help them identify and harness the creative capacity of teams.

CHARACTERISTICS OF CREATIVE GROUPS

What distinguishes creative, from noncreative, teams? Creative teams

- Are synergistic
- Have a diverse membership
- Do not care about the physical environment
- Avoid "noncontributory" activities
- Are emotional and logical
- Are collegial and nonhierarchical
- Have facilitative and supportive leadership
- Have fun
- Allow the individual and group to coexist
- Are unafraid to push boundaries
- Are small in size
- Seek balance among creating, planning, and implementing
- View failure as a learning experience

- Know the priorities
- Share tangible and intangible assets
- Are curious
- Are true believers
- Have high esprit de corps
- Adapt

Synergistic

The output is greater than the sum of the people on teams. The dynamics behind the integration among all the team members, assuming they work together harmoniously, can produce creative output that far exceeds that of a team member working independently. Like the five fingers of a hand, they work best in concert with others, focusing on a common vision. The relationship is likened to one of being symbiotic, whereby relationships depend on individuals collaborating in an interdependent, integrative manner. In *Group Genius*, Keith Sawyer notes that Robert Sternberg, Yale psychologist, refers to *Group ID*, which reflects a team functioning greater than the sum of its members.[1] Keith Sawyer likens it to a sports team, whereby the team doesn't just rely on one exceptional person but rather the entire group to generate the desired results.[2] Sawyer refers to this phenomenon as "group flow," whereby a team performs at the top of its ability, similar to the flow experience of individuals as described by Mihalyi Csiksentmihalyi.[3] According to Sawyer, group flow occurs when an equilibrium exists among a series of oppositional tensions, such as between being analytical and a visionary. This tension serves as a means for propelling a team toward greater creativity. Conflict, however, is another issue.[4] Sternberg also notes that Group IQ is greatest when teams work together with minimal or no conflict.[5] Backstabbing, petty jealousies, and positioning are minimal or nonexistent.[1] What allows for this synergistic effect? It is a shared goal that everyone understands.[6]

Have a Diverse Membership

Regardless of the typology employed, for example, Myers Briggs, Herrmann Brain Dominance, people with different personalities, backgrounds, experiences, and so on, enable more insights and tolerate different perspectives that enhance the opportunity for greater creativity simply because not everyone sees problems, challenges, and issues in the same way. Diversity in thought leads toward helping overcome dysfunctions like groupthink, which is essentially peer pressure affecting individual judgment. Creative teams often have a membership of people with backgrounds transcending multiple disciplines. This background helps to overcome discipline myopia, forming a collaborative team consisting of creative thinkers.[7] One advantage of having a diverse team is that it avoids the extreme conformism that sometimes surfaces in groups. Groupthink can hinder diversity of thought so essential for creativity to arise. It enables bringing together people with diverse skills, experiences, and perspectives, providing the necessary tension resulting from varying opinions.[8] Generally, therefore, homogeneity of team members causes a team to be less creative.[9]

Care Less about the Physical Environment

Their attention is on the work, not the working conditions. Creative teams enjoy the mental challenge. Again, they are willing to work in hell for a noble cause. They will endure conditions that most people would feel are unacceptable to do great, creative work.[10] Warren Bennis and Patricia Biederman note that actually the inverse may exist where the better the degree of comfort in the work environment, the less creativity.[11]

Avoid "Noncontributory" Activities

Attending countless meetings and addressing what some consider bureaucratic red tape, such as generating reports and filling out forms, frustrate them.[12] Creative teams want to focus on the vision, not bureaucratic scatology. Most creative teams have minimal amounts of noncontributory activities, or waste, so they can focus on the goals and objectives and have more time for doing so.[13] They also prefer casual attire, indicated by an informal atmosphere conducive to greater creativity.[14]

Emotional and Logical

Excitement and enthusiasm consumes the team. They have a high energy level that radiates in and among team members. It is as if the team consists of warriors, not soldiers, who thrive on each other. Esprit de corps is high. Everyone and the entire team are on high octane because they share a meaningful goal. They also find the challenges psychologically pleasurable.[15]

Collegial and Nonhierarchical

The typical top-down organizational structure depicted in organization charts often does not sit well with creative teams. Extreme specialization, vertical top-down communications, and hoarding of information reflect traditional hierarchies and do not engender creativity as more entrepreneurial-type organizations.[16] This circumstance does not mean that no leader exists; it does mean that the command-and-control type of style often runs contrary to engendering a creative environment. Hierarchy is minimal within a creative team, allowing for greater sharing of communications and information as well as placing greater emphasis on role rather than position.[17] Therefore, if division of labor prevails on a team, the probability of creative ideas declines.[18] This minimal division of labor does not mean, of course, that a creative team is nothing more than a blob of people; some semblance of structure and order must exist. As Keith Sawyer also observes, such collaboration does not equate to anarchy; it still has some semblance of structure and order.[19] He refers to this type of organization as a "semistructure," a blend of structure and order that allows innovation but prevents an organization, such as a project team, from falling into chaos.[20] The emphasis is on flexibility and connectivity.[21]

Relationships are key, not hierarchy. Creativity is often construed as an independent act. Yet evidence to the contrary suggests that quite often it occurs among two or more people. Relationships, sometimes competitive but frequently collaborative, allow for the questioning and exchange of ideas, approaches, sharing of information, and so on, to determine if creative output is valuable and practical. Relationships become even more important today than ever before, due to the complexity of technology, from medical to aerospace. Sustaining and enhancing such relationships becomes even more important. Even when similarities exist, such as terminology, differences can exist in meaning and nuance, which can challenge relationships among people from different disciplines. The relationships become quite interdependent, entailing greater communication, which results in people working together and helping each other.[22] The relationships are not formal or hierarchical, but rather more collegial and collaborative.[23]

Have Facilitative and Supportive Leadership

The leader of the team and those above him or her do what they can to help the team succeed while keeping the team focused on the vision.[24]

They do what must be done to protect it from interference by groups and individuals not furthering its cause.[25] They exhibit a sincere intention to provide what is necessary to encourage creativity.[26] Some of the more common values that exhibit leadership support for a creative environment include demonstrating endorsement for creativity, encouraging openness, and embracing change.[27] Additional actions include ensuring the sharing of information, reducing stress, and removing obstacles so that talent thrives rather than dies.[28] They also select people to compensate for their own shortcomings and people who fit in the right role within the group.[29] Leaders of creative groups, therefore, concentrate on being more facilitators than controllers, which is not the same as being weak. These leaders work on helping people focus and remove obstacles inhibiting success. Essentially, they are stewards, guiding the team in a way that focuses on the vision.[30] They also give team members challenges worthy of their attention and energies.[31] The style of these leaders can be summed up in two words: encourage and enable.[32] They appear almost as equals with team members.[33]

Have Fun

That's right. The challenge before each team member and the entire team is viewed as an opportunity to enjoy themselves when pursuing an overall goal. The joy of learning, problem solving, and experimentation that accompanies the creative process keeps individuals and teams alike engaged. Playfulness is not a dirty word on creative projects; it enables learning and achievement. Team members even get to the point of acting like adolescents.[34]

Allow the Individual and Group to Coexist

There is no dichotomous choice between an individual and a group. A person can self-actualize in his or her own way while simultaneously contributing to the goals and objectives of a project. Team members do not have to march like soldiers; co-worker pressure to conform is minimal. Individuals and groups can coexist.[35] Everyone can have a sense of autonomy while concentrating simultaneously on a collective goal. In other words, there is room for everyone to have their own space because talent needs to actualize.[36] Yet, everyone recognizes the importance of working together and supporting each other in achieving common goals and objectives.[37] Warren Bennis and Patricia Biederman also agree, noting that autonomy is a crucial ingredient that is necessary without sacrificing on a group goal.[38] Hence, individuals have a shared destiny when each one feels they have a stake in the outcome. If the team fails to achieve its mission, each feels he or she has failed. They are emotionally as well as logically committed to individual and group success. This attitude enables team members to experiment and do whatever it takes to succeed. Following the rules and going through the motions is not enough. Every team member must feel he or she has ownership in the outcome.[39]

As a result, members are comfortable with themselves to such a degree that they allow frank and open dialog without fear of punishment, such as ostracism and ridicule; otherwise, discussions and free thinking become inhibited and no sharing of ideas and information, so vital to creativity, can occur. "Mind guards" and "mental police" have a minimal role or are nonexistent The last thing a creative group wants is to have groupthink infect the beliefs and values to the point that free discussion becomes squashed. In fact, a positive rivalry or competition among viewpoints that allows dissent to arise can further creativity.[40] Each team member should be exposed to the ideas of others to reveal shortcomings in their own and those of colleagues.[41] They should also feel free to pursue the advice of others.[42] Through conversation, therefore, better collaboration can arise.[43]

Unafraid to Push Boundaries

They will take it to the limit to ensure a greater probability of success. They are comfortable breaking the rules.[44] They are more interested in finding out what works and does not work. This is not a license for doing something unethical or illegal; it simply means creative teams are willing to do whatever is legitimately possible within the constraints confronting them. A boundary does not inhibit them; in fact, it may encourage them to bust it. Nothing is sacred when taking a creative approach. As they bust boundaries and shatter rules, they see connections that others cannot see.[45] Hence, they have what Warren Bennis and Patricia Biederman refer to as "creative chutzpah."[46]

Pushing the boundaries means stepping into the unknown, something such teams embrace. Just the experience of facing the void can bring a diverse group of creative individuals together. To a large extent, creativity is tightly interlinked with pursuing the unknown because it involves challenging the status quo and doing something different. The team must have a sense of adventure when tackling the unknown, willing to face danger and risk as a result of feeling adventuresome.[47]

They Are Small in Size

They are not of the magnitude of conventional armies but instead more like guerrilla bands. Small is, indeed, beautiful when it comes to creativity. Large teams often require more rules and regimentation, which can smother creativity to promote efficiency. Large teams also require a more complex flow of communications that can distort messages and require more time for clarifications; small teams allow for more informal, less hierarchical communications.[48] Leadership, therefore, involves creating organizations into small, independent entities when it comes to creativity.[49]

Seek Balance among Creating, Planning, and Implementing

They recognize that creativity often occurs in what some people refer to as the ozone, whereby thoughts, concepts, and alternative viewpoints reign. This does not mean that they are not rooted in reality; quite the contrary! They just realize that they must first develop ideas, concepts, and so on and then, considering reality, make adjustments accordingly; they consider all significant constraints to come up with something realistic. With a diverse team, the opportunity to develop a creative idea or concept increases because someone will likely raise an issue, concern, or shortcoming that the team must consider. The team must then come up with a plan based upon some improvisation that helps them turn an idea into a reality. All the key elements of a good project plan, addressing the who, what, when, where, why, and how exist; however, it may not be at a depth that people associate with implementing an idea. The planning grants enough freedom to improvise along the way to allow for exploration, experimentation, and independence. This latitude is essential to allow creativity and innovation to flourish. A balance is critical for creativity and innovation to arise, observes Keith Sawyer.[50] He advocates developing a general plan that enables sufficient freedom to respond to unexpected situations, thereby reducing the need for in-depth planning. He refers to this type of planning as "opportunistic planning."[51] Still, these groups deliver. As Warren Bennis and Patricia Biederman observe, "Great groups ship."[52]

View Failure as a Learning Experience

It is not an opportunity to blame someone or to treat a member of the team as a scapegoat. All team members share responsibility for results and leverage the experience to further the goals and objectives of their projects. In some cases, failure serves as a catalyst for enhancing collaboration and communication during the next opportunity to be creative as a team. When failure occurs, the culture of the team is supportive. Warren Bennis and Patricia Biederman observe that creative groups do not take a harsh view of failure but use it as a learning opportunity because they realize that risk involves failure sometimes.[53] If they stumble, according to Keith Sawyer, they learn from failure as a way to avoid repeating the same mistake and experience the same mishap in the future. He refers to this concept as "deliberate practice."[54] Creative teams also err on the side of optimism, not pessimism; they are filled with an almost unrealistic sense of confidence.[55]

Know the Priorities

Members focus their creativity on what contributes to critical common goals and objectives.[56] In other words, creativity is not something to dissipates. They know creativity is not easy because, over time, it becomes harder to sustain focus on the vision and maintain a strategy.[57] Additionally, common goals and objectives enable them to see how their individual performance, along with others, contributes to the overall success of the project, provides a measurement for ascertaining how well the project is progressing, and serves as mechanism for resolving disputes that would ordinarily result in an impasse. If one or more team members want to experiment with an idea, they can demonstrate its overall value toward achieving overall project goals and objectives.

Share Tangible and Intangible Assets

If morale is high, sharing becomes easier because competitiveness is focused on achieving the goals and objectives of the project, and not the members. Hoarding is atypical of creative groups because it is only through sharing that a team can succeed. Sharing of ideas, information, tools, and so on contributes to that sense of interdependence and integration. Sharing also builds relationships. Weekly meetings serve as an excellent way to share ideas and information because they offer a venue to allow disagreements to surface.[58] Ongoing spontaneous communication is also useful.[59]

Are Curious

They do not subscribe easily to the party line. They challenge it, and the best vehicle for doing so is to further individual and group inquiry. Facts and assumptions granted from higher-ups are not enough to satisfy their need to know. They feel compelled to challenge those facts and assumptions to satisfy their own sense of validity and reliability. They are driven to determine the reasons behind something, that is, what makes it "tick."

What fuels this zeal? According to Warren Bennis and Patricia Biederman, curiosity is what energizes a group, not problem solving. It is the exploratory nature of creativity that satisfies them, especially for team members with highly inquisitive minds.[60]

Are True Believers

They have such extreme faith in the vision of their projects that they will endure hardships, ranging from long periods of overtime to working in squalid environments, to achieve something significant. They will, using a trite phrase, "be willing to march into hell for a heavenly cause." Creative groups of this nature view themselves as David taking on Goliath, tackling seemingly insurmountable odds.[61] What also fuels the zeal is their perspective of fighting an enemy that must be defeated.[62] This sometimes leads to being unrealistic over its purpose.[63] This is referred to as collective denial and delusional confidence. If members volunteer, their zeal may be greater because they committed themselves, and not by the hands of someone else.[64]

Have High Esprit de Corps

Creative teams have considerable unity and solid morale, thanks largely to a shared vision. These teams have substantial energy and endurance, which enables synergistic performance, feeling like members of a cadre, and being able to ensure hardship and failure. Cohesion can be so intense that the team can develop its own culture and feel isolated from its parent organization.[65]

Adapt

This adaptability can take many forms, from changing a strategy to achieve a project's vision to using a different tool or technique. They are also willing to change roles and relationships if it achieves successful results for a project.[66]

This adaptability is essential for a creative team to accomplish a shared vision. Collaboration is the enabler for adaptability because people can share ideas, experience, knowledge, and so on, on what works, and just as importantly, what does not work. Keith Sawyer suggests that, for instance, inventions reflect an accumulation of "creative sparks" that come together through collaboration to provide breakthrough results.[67]

TEAM TOOLS

From a group creativity perspective, not many models exist relative to those for individuals; however, some useful ones do exist. For the most part, models like Myers-Briggs and the Birkman Model are used to mix and match personalities to create a winning combination. Some models enable project managers to capitalize on the overall synergy of a team. Two common ones are Organizational Engineering and People Styles Typology.

Organizational Engineering

Organizational Engineering is one model. It emphasizes the relationships of four behavior styles predicated on how they process and respond to information, reflecting what is referred to as the *strategic style* of the individual.[68] This strategic style consists of a method and mode; the method refers to how an individual gathers and assimilates information, and the mode refers to how a person responds via decision making. Reactive Stimulator (RS), Relational Innovator (RI), Logical Processor (LP), and Hypothetical Analyzer (HA) are the four strategic styles.

Reactive Stimulators are characterized best by speed in method and mode. They take information only to the extent that is needed to get the job done after generating options and selecting one. They are task oriented and seek results quickly.[69]

Relational Innovators focus on the big picture. They like to investigate problems and possibilities, and prefer autonomy to explore many alternatives. Special emphasis is on defining the problem and weaving information and ideas in a way to create something innovative.[70] Logical Processors focus on specifics that are rooted in reality. Everything must produce tangible results that require taking a step-by-step approach. Being methodical necessitates having clear, unambiguous directions.[71]

Hypothetical Analyzers focus on solving problems by being analytical, using a methodology or framework. As conceptual thinkers, they look at the big picture and are open to new ideas and opportunities after careful analysis. They will then pursue a structured, organized approach to complete work.[72]

Organizational Engineering can prove a useful tool for encouraging creativity on projects. Relational Innovators do not like structure and detail, but like to absorb information from different sources and are prescriptive in orientation. They prefer brainstorming and role playing. Hypothetical Analyzers approach a problem through analysis, using detail to populate a framework and prefer working with texts and numbers. They prefer a structural approach. Logical Processors go after detail. They seek, however, to have detail of the highest quality and use that information in a narrow manner to achieve tangible results. They prefer statistics, observation, and simulation. Reactive Stimulators are descriptive, focusing on what is concrete and the shortest distance between two points. They prefer trial and error, involving active experimentation and trips.[73]

People Styles Typology

Another model is the People Styles Typology best described by Robert Bolton. He looks at how people's behavioral patterns and habits affect their relationship with others in a typology. What makes this approach relevant is that it looks at how one's style influences the behavior of others, which can affect the creative output of a team.

A person's style is exhibited through what he or she does, which in turn reflects his or her traits and how he or she repeatedly acts.[74] Using this information, his style can then be identified in a quadrant created through the intersection of two continuums called *dimensions of behavior*.

The first dimension is *assertiveness*, defined as a person's degree of forcefulness. A person is less or more assertive. This continuum runs horizontal.

The other dimension is *responsiveness*, defined as the degree to which a person is aware of another person's feelings. A person is less or more responsive. This continuum runs vertical.[75]

Together, these two dimensions create four styles that indicate how other people see the way that person behaves. A style reflects a pattern that helps predict how a person likes to interact, such as at work, with others.[76] A style exhibits a pattern through the way they communicate, deal with conflict, handle stress, make decisions, and exhibit body language.

Analytical, Amiable, Expressive, and Driver are the four social styles.

Analyticals tend to focus on the task to get done and less on people. They eschew emotion as their critical thinking and desire for facts and data prevail over most people-oriented concerns. They also tend to be reserved and taciturn in their dealings with people. As you might suspect, they are cautious, not being aggressive risk takers. They prefer structure, order, and precision. They also take an organized, systematic approach in what they do.[77]

Amiables, more so than Analyticals, seek to work with others but in a congenial manner. They are friendly, empathetic, and focus on others over facts and data. Like the Analyticals, they tend toward the cautious side, not being aggressive risk takers. They also tend to be indecisive, not out of having better data but out of fear of causing people to get upset. Hence, they are people, not task, oriented. They are the ultimate team players by getting along with everyone.[78]

Expressives are the people who allow emotions to surface. They are highly active, excitable people who have a restless energy that does not sit well often with people who, like Analyticals and Amiables, are cautious either because the data are imprecise or because they do not want to upset someone. Expressives operate on generalities rather than details and are risk takers, ever mindful of seizing an opportunity. They are highly communicative, albeit not effective listeners. They like and want others to have a good time and as a general rule have a preference to avoid the shackles or order and structure.[79] Drivers are the people who look at the bottom line, or results. They, like the Expressives, are very energetic and active. They tend to be less abstract thinkers and more oriented toward achieving goals and objectives. Purposefulness and resolution are two good words to describe them. Fast paced, they will take a systematic and structured approach and use what they can and discard the rest. Highly task oriented and less responsive to the emotional side of people, they recognize the value of the belief that the shortest route between two points is a straight line.[80]

When using the social styles typology, just about the same guidelines apply as they do with most other typologies. Not everyone fits neatly in a style; everyone usually has an alternate style when under stress, and each style has its positive and negative characteristics. Ultimately, it serves as another tool to help the project manager deploy people on projects to help build a synergistic relationship that engenders, enhances, and sustains creativity. By capitalizing on a style's strengths and compensating for its weaknesses, the performance can be enhanced for individuals and the entire team. As the Boltons observe, no one can be everything to everyone; each person brings a set of skills that supplements and complements each other.[81]

As with all the other tools described on an individual or group basis, project managers can mix and match not only people, but also deploy them at the right point during the project life cycle in general, and more specifically during the creative life cycle. A team can consist of all four personalities. Expressives can be used to identify opportunities; Analyticals, to provide a structure and systematic approach; Amiables, to engender relationship building with the customer and among team members; and Drivers, to keep the project moving forward until the goals and objectives have been accomplished.

Six Thinking Hats

Another creative approach that was quite popular but which, for some reason, has faded in popularity, is Edward de Bono's Six Thinking Hats. This approach involves coming up with a creative idea by wearing different-colored hats for each kind of thinking to develop, evaluate, and implement an idea. Wearing a different-colored hat encourages role playing by assuming that thinking styles are associated with an applicable color. Role playing encourages people to take multiple perspectives and apply different sets of rules and techniques, thereby helping people overcome their prejudices, and therefore become less reactive in their thinking. The creative thinking process goes sequentially from one colored hat to another: white, red, black, yellow, green, and, with possible exception, blue.

The White Hat is concerned with facts and data about a problem or issue. It is, in many respects, these facts and data—their quantity and quality— that provide homework for the roles of the other hats leading to a creative idea to deal with a problem or issue. The general idea is that the White Hat puts the thinker in a more objective frame of mind.[82]

The Red Hat allows the emotional part of people to come forth. This hat enables people's feelings to take over, allowing them to rely on hunches, intuition, and preference. Through emotions, people can look at the facts and data, for example, and select what is relevant due to the context of the situation. It allows for greater understanding of the situation. In the end, the Red Hat enables making choices based upon values and emotions.[83]

The Black Hat takes a negative view of an idea through logic. It requires being skeptical, even pessimistic, by using logic to shoot holes through an idea. It is a cold, calculated approach for determining, through criticism, whether an idea makes sense. Wearing the Black Hat allows people to play the devil's advocate to reveal, for example, errors, faults, incompleteness, inaccuracies, and so on, of an idea. By pointing out the shortcomings, alternatives, or different options, can surface the means to address any shortcomings or risks associated with the idea.[84]

The Yellow Hat is essentially the opposite of the Black Hat. It uses logic to determine the positive aspects of an idea. Its focus is optimistic and on the benefits of the idea. It is a positive assessment. Like the Black Hat, it involves judgment, not emotion, to determine the positive side of an idea. The Yellow Hat also looks at how to make the idea a reality through suggestions and recommendations. However, its primary focus is not being creative; it is simply being positive about an idea by looking at its benefits and its future possibilities.[85]

The Green Hat is where the real creative side of people comes out. It is about coming up with new ways to bring about change by challenging and changing patterns of thought; de Bono's concept of lateral thinking applies here. Using lateral thinking enables looking at an idea differently and using additional ideas to generate even more creative ones. Green Hat thinking then leads toward movement to make an idea a reality by coming up with provocations, such as something "weird." It relies on the illogical or absurd to provoke ways to come up with alternatives to make an idea a reality. It is basically using an earlier idea to generate others, perhaps better than the previous one.[86]

Blue Hat is the sixth and final hat. It is about control and focus to achieve clarity. Control and focus go hand in hand to ensure that the superfluous goes to the wayside and that organization becomes the rule rather than the exception. In other words, it provides discipline by developing and implementing through good managerial practices. The person who wears the Blue Hat ensures that the other hats are worn, making sure people follow some type of order as indicated, for example, through an agenda at a creativity session and clarifying differences when different hats seem to overlap. Basically, the Blue Hat serves like an orchestra leader, bringing in the right hat at the right time and making sure that everything flows in a controlled, focused manner.[87]

CONCLUSION

Creative teams share many of the characteristics of creative individuals. They embrace challenging the status quo and stepping outside the boundaries. They pursue the unknown even in the face of failure. What distinguishes the group from the individual is that the former has a level of diversity and strength in the face of adversity that individuals do not have. Project managers, as they do with individuals, have models to help them harness creativity.

Getting Started Checklist

Question	Yes	No
1. Which creative characteristics are exhibited the most by your team:		
Are synergistic		
Have a diverse membership		
Are careless about the physical environment		
Avoid "noncontributory" activities		
Are emotional and logical		
Are collegial and nonhierarchical		
Have facilitative and supportive leadership		
Have fun		
Allow individual and group to coexist		
Are unafraid to push boundaries		
Are small in size		
Seek balance among creating, planning, and implementing		
View failure as a learning experience		
Know the priorities		
Share tangible and intangible assets		
Are curious		
Are true believers		
Have high esprit de corps		
Adapt		
2. Identify ways you can capitalize on the creative characteristics of your project team:		
Way(s):		

ENDNOTES

1. Warren Bennis and Patricia Biederman, *Organizing Genius* (Reading, MA: Addison-Wesley Publishing Co., Inc. 1997), p. 121.
2. Keith Sawyer, *Group Genius* (New York: Basic Books, 2007), p. 41.
3. Sawyer, *Group Genius*, p. 43.
4. Sawyer, *Group Genius*, p. 56.
5. Daniel Goleman, Paul Kaufman, and Michael Ray, *The Creative Spirit* (New York: Dutton, 1992), p. 121.
6. Sawyer, *Group Genius*, pp. 51–53.
7. Bennis and Biederman, *Organizing Genius*, p. 19.
8. Sawyer, *Group Genius*, p. 71.
9. Sawyer, *Group Genius*, p. 131.
10. Bennis and Biederman, *Organizing Genius*, pp. 10–12.
11. Bennis and Biederman, *Organizing Genius*, p. 127.
12. Bennis and Biederman, *Organizing Genius*, p. 124.
13. Dave Allan et al., *What If?* (Oxford: Capstone Publishing Limited, 1999), pp. 158–166.
14. Bennis and Biederman, *Organizing Genius*, p. 124.
15. Bennis and Biederman, *Organizing Genius*, p. 126.
16. James M. Higgins, *Innovate or Evaporate* (Winter Park, FL: The New Management Publishing Co., 1995), p. 175.
17. Bennis and Biederman, *Organizing Genius*, p. 104.
18. Sawyer, *Group Genius*, p. 68.
19. Sawyer, *Group Genius*, p. 170.
20. Sawyer, *Group Genius*, p. 169.
21. Sawyer, *Group Genius*, p. 175.
22. Sawyer, *Group Genius*, p. 72.
23. Bennis and Biederman, *Organizing Genius*, p. 29.
24. Bennis and Biederman, *Organizing Genius*, p. 104.
25. Bennis and Biederman, *Organizing Genius*, p. 71.
26. Goleman, Kaufman, and Ray, *The Creative Spirit*, pp. 140–142.
27. Higgins, *Innovate or Evaporate*, p. 302.
28. Bennis and Biederman, *Organizing Genius*, pp. 120–125.
29. Bennis and Biederman, *Organizing Genius*, p. 89.
30. Bennis and Biederman, *Organizing Genius*, p. 200.
31. Bennis and Biederman, *Organizing Genius*, pp. 211–212.
32. Bennis and Biederman, *Organizing Genius*, p. 26.
33. Bennis and Biederman, *Organizing Genius*, p. 29.
34. Bennis and Biederman, *Organizing Genius*, p. 161.
35. Bennis and Biederman, *Organizing Genius*, p. 20.
36. Bennis and Biederman, *Organizing Genius*, p. 29.
37. Allan et al., *What If?* p. 149.
38. Bennis and Biederman, *Organizing Genius*, p. 20.
39. Bennis and Biederman, *Organizing Genius*, p. 22.
40. Goleman, Kaufman, and Ray, *The Creative Spirit*, p. 171.
41. Bennis and Biederman, *Organizing Genius*, p. 71.
42. Bennis and Biederman, *Organizing Genius*, p. 191.
43. Sawyer, *Group Genius*, p. 140.
44. Bennis and Biederman, *Organizing Genius*, p. 221.

45. Bennis and Biederman, *Organizing Genius*, p. 12.
46. Bennis and Biederman, *Organizing Genius*, p. 95.
47. Bennis and Biederman, *Organizing Genius*, p. 50.
48. Allan et al. *What If?* pp. 158–166.
49. Goleman, Kaufman, and Ray, *The Creative Spirit*, p. 120.
50. Sawyer, *Group Genius*, p. 29.
51. Sawyer, *Group Genius*, p. 169.
52. Bennis and Biederman, *Organizing Genius*, pp. 214–215.
53. Bennis and Biederman, *Organizing Genius*, p. 21.
54. Sawyer, *Group Genius*, p. 55.
55. Bennis and Biederman, *Organizing Genius*, pp. 209–210.
56. Allan et al. *What If?* p. 149.
57. Sawyer, *Group Genius*, p. 168.
58. Bennis and Biederman, *Organizing Genius*, p. 72.
59. Sawyer, *Group Genius*, p. 53.
60. Bennis and Biederman, *Organizing Genius*, p. 17.
61. Bennis and Biederman, *Organizing Genius*, p. 207.
62. Bennis and Biederman, *Organizing Genius*, pp. 207–208.
63. Bennis and Biederman, *Organizing Genius*, p. 157.
64. Bennis and Biederman, *Organizing Genius*, p. 70.
65. Bennis and Biederman, *Organizing Genius*, pp. 206–207.
66. Bennis and Biederman, *Organizing Genius*, p. 26.
67. Sawyer, *Group Genius*, p. 102.
68. Ralph L. Kliem and Harris B. Anderson, *The Organizational Engineering to Project Management* (Boca Raton, FL: St. Lucie Press, 2003), p. 20.
69. Kliem and Anderson, *The Organizational Engineering to Project Management*, p. 32.
70. Kliem and Anderson, *The Organizational Engineering to Project Management*, p. 32.
71. Kliem and Anderson, *The Organizational Engineering to Project Management*, p. 32.
72. Kliem and Anderson, *The Organizational Engineering to Project Management*, p. 32.
73. Kliem and Anderson, *The Organizational Engineering to Project Management*, pp. 182–184.
74. Robert Bolton and Dorothy G. Bolton, *People Styles at Work* (New York: AMACOM, 1996), p. 11.
75. Bolton and Bolton, *People Styles at Work*, pp. 16–22.
76. Bolton and Bolton, *People Styles at Work*, p. 10.
77. Bolton and Bolton, *People Styles at Work*, pp. 30–33.
78. Bolton and Bolton, *People Styles at Work*, pp. 33–38.
79. Bolton and Bolton, *People Styles at Work*, pp. 38–43.
80. Bolton and Bolton, *People Styles at Work*, pp. 43–46.
81. Bolton and Bolton, *People Styles at Work*, p. 6.
82. Edward de Bono, *Six Thinking Hats* (Boston: Little, Brown, and Company, 1985), pp. 34–55.
83. de Bono, *Six Thinking Hats*, pp. 56–79.
84. de Bono, *Six Thinking Hats*, pp. 80–109.
85. de Bono, *Six Thinking Hats*, pp. 110–134.
86. de Bono, *Six Thinking Hats*, pp. 135–169.
87. de Bono, *Six Thinking Hats*, pp. 170–196.

4

Challenges and Constraints

INTRODUCTION

Enabling creativity in a project environment does not come easily. While it sometimes occurs spontaneously without any help, more often than not, the environment must be conducive for creativity to occur. Identifying some of the challenges and constraints that inhibit creativity goes a long way in helping to foster it in the project environment.

THE LIST

Here are some of the common challenges and constraints inhibiting productivity in the project environment:

- Groupthink
- Mores, beliefs, values
- Fear
- Mismatch
- Lack of tools
- Lack of data and information
- Too much and too little training
- Starting and stopping workflow
- Impatience
- Specialization
- Craving for predictability
- Inability to adapt

- Poor communications
- Poor coordination
- Leaping to judgment
- Faster, better, cheaper philosophy
- Stretching resources too thin
- Silos
- Focusing on the past or future, not the present
- Lack of sharing
- Compliant workforce
- Hierarchy
- Not listening to inner voice
- Taking on only what is known
- Management's lack of responsiveness
- Success
- Too many positive and negative incentives
- Team composition imbalance
- Dominance of brain thinking
- Infighting

Groupthink

William Sonnenschein observes in *The Diversity Toolkit* that people prefer to associate and work with individuals like themselves; working with dissimilar backgrounds widens challenges and our perspectives, augmenting creativity.[1] However, peer pressure is one of the most prevalent pressures inhibiting creativity. The desire to get along with peers is often so strong that it can stifle creativity, both on individual or group levels. Team members may be reluctant to speak up to avoid punishment, ranging from ridicule to ostracism. The pressure can become so immense that denial of reality occurs even in the midst of facts and data to the contrary; *groupthink* is the term to describe this condition. Most people like to get along with others for many reasons, but especially in the work environment. This pressure to conform has intensified. Eugene Raudsepp, in *How Creative Are You?* notes that this conformity has spread like a disease, from the moment we attend school to our work environment, where we become institutionalized.[2] Some of the consequences of this pressure include reliance on others for self-worth and a desire to be accepted by a group.[3] Naturally, few people are willing to create under such circumstances.

From a creativity perspective, here are some ways to counter the affect and effect of groupthink:

- Bring people on board with different backgrounds, knowledge, experience, and personalities.
- Encourage questioning of proposals, ideas, thoughts, and so on.
- Reassign teaming relationships.

Mores, Beliefs, Values

The culture of an organization can have an immense impact on creativity in people. The mores, beliefs, and values may be so strong that any creativity that is contrary to the culture will, either overtly or indirectly, be repressed or suppressed. In some cases, it can lead to punishment to serve as an example of people transgressing what is held dear by an organization or group. Of course, the culture can be interlinked with groupthink, whereby the mores, beliefs, and values become the cement that prevents any creative thought.

What is required is a better understanding of those mores, beliefs, and values that potentially cause what Roger von Oech refers to as mental locks.[4] Understanding of mores, beliefs, and values can help overcome many mental locks. William Sonnenshein agrees, observing that it affects how we perceive and approach the world around us through our behavior and communications.[5] From a creativity perspective, here are some ways to counter the affect and effect of mores, beliefs, and values:

- Assign people whose mores, beliefs, and values are different from the prevalent ones in the group.
- Assign someone the role of being a devil's advocate.
- Investigate other projects' ways of doing business.

Fear

Franklin Roosevelt was right about fear: the only thing we have to fear is fear itself. Fear of reprisal, ostracism, ridicule, and many other forms can stifle individual and group creativity. Fear, such as of a major termination or massive layoffs, can become so intense, that being creative is the last thing anyone wants to do unless it protects them from becoming a victim. Fear can arise from a minor comment, especially from someone in authority or having a substantial influence on us.[6] Fear does not have to result from something negative; it can also originate from something positive. An example would be fear of not receiving a substantial financial award or an opportunity for greater advancement. Positive or negative, fear can inhibit creativity. The ability to overcome fear makes the difference in whether innovation is brought into reality.[7] Naturally, being creative and innovative raises the wall of resistance because it increases the stakes and generates the opportunity for reprisal by some others. Eugene Raudsepp observes that the people having a vested interest in the status quo will defend it and, the more an idea threatens what currently exists, the greater the resistance.[8]

Fear can quickly translate into insecurity. Some people feel vulnerable psychologically, even perhaps physically, if they exercise too much creativity. After all, creativity upsets the status quo, especially for people who hold a vested interest in maintaining it. If some creative people feel they will not be supported or protected, they will cease to create, whether the sense of insecurity is real or imaginary. When people feel insecure, they often side with the one who holds the power, meaning they will support the status quo.

It is rare that a creative person can withstand the onslaught of superiors, peers, and subordinates and continue his or her creative pursuits. To be a creative person requires considerable courage because he or she must confront the protectors of the status quo with an idea that challenges their legitimacy.[9] Additionally, few people can withstand the negative thoughts and actions of others.[10]

From a creativity perspective, here are some ways to counter the affect and effect of fear and insecurity:

- Encourage team members to share their thoughts and experiences with others on the team.
- Encourage team members to stretch the limits of rules, procedures, and so on.
- Keep all key stakeholders engaged in the outcome of creative tasks.
- Perform benchmarking to expose team members to new ideas, processes, and so on.
- Provide frequent one-on-one sessions with the more fearful team members.
- Provide training on relevant tasks to enhance competence and confidence.
- Recognize and reward team members who take risks.

- Use a buddy system; for example, assign two or more people to a difficult task.
- Visit other projects and organizations to learn new ideas, processes, and techniques.

Mismatch

Creativity can be difficult if people are hired into a job or on a team that does not match their talents, knowledge, skills, or personalities. Mismatches can cause people to work hard just to fit in a job that they have been assigned; their focus, though, is on survival, not necessarily being creative. Any attempt at being creative, no matter how significant, could easily make them a target of more experienced peers who could attack them with character assassination or sabotage. History is replete with examples of people who, coming from another field with little experience in the new one, have a creative idea and are then assailed by people established within an organization.

From a creativity perspective, here are some ways to counter the affect and effect of mismatch:

- Allow people to identify or choose tasks on which to work.
- Assign people to tasks after having them take a personality assessment.
- Have periodic one-on-one sessions with individuals to assess task performance.

Lack of Tools

Being creative often requires having the necessary tools, for example, technologies, to develop new ideas. Not having access to these tools can retard activities or add frustration to them when trying to experiment to test their validity. As a result, some people may find it difficult to innovate because they have no sense of probability or likelihood that their creation will work, and if so, whether it will under acceptable, normal conditions.

From a creativity perspective, here are some ways to counter the affect and effect of a lack of tools:

- Have people increase their awareness of technological advancements in their profession.

- Have the latest professional journals available for reference by team members.
- Provide training on technology related to doing work on the project.

Lack of Data and Information

Both are keys to creativity. A lack of data and information makes it difficult to create and receive feedback on the validity of a creation. Otherwise, whether a creation is practical and innovative becomes a matter of conjecture and preference by certain individuals. Data and information help overcome such bias. A symbiotic relationship exists between creativity and the sharing of data and information, if for no other reason than to generate ideas. Creativity, by its very nature, requires and encourages sharing of data, information, and ideas. Unfortunately, the opportunities for sharing often do not exist.[11] From a creativity perspective, here are some ways to counter the affect and effect of a lack of data and information:

- Adopt a policy of sharing data and information.
- Encourage access to other sources of data and information beyond the confines of the project.
- Provide the infrastructure, for example, a common repository.
- Use tools that follow common standards.

Too Much and Too Little Training

Training is important for creating, of course. However, too much training can hinder creativity simply by reinforcing existing ideas and techniques to such an extent that people struggle to see outside the box or to push the boundaries of a paradigm. Too little training can also hinder creativity because people may not be exposed to other ideas and techniques that could open their minds. Instead, they continue to treat assumptions, values, and beliefs as fact. Perhaps the right amount of training is what is important.[12]

From a creativity perspective, here are some ways to counter the affect and effect of too much and too little training:

- Identify relevant training for the project.
- Provide cascade training, for example, people sharing knowledge gained from training elsewhere.
- Tailor training to the specific needs of individuals.

Start and Stop Workflow

In today's changing environment, it is not unusual for people to jump from one responsibility or task to another before completing it. For some reason, management, probably due to immense schedule and cost pressure, thinks people can work at multiple tasks at the same time, which is physically and mentally impossible, especially in highly intellectual disciplines. The constant start and stop at work disrupts creative thought and effort, causing relearning and reapplying of knowledge, tools, and techniques. This start and stop makes it difficult to complete anything in one sitting, let alone think creatively. It is time consuming and wasteful due to time spent getting back up to speed. Dave Allan et al. refer to this circumstance as "bar coding" and describe how it arises and the corresponding consequences. It slices up one's day into discrete pieces that do not provide the time to focus, thereby not only wasting time, but also destroying creativity.[13] From a creativity perspective, here are some ways to counter the affect and effect of starting and stopping workflow:

- Attempt to protect team members from nonproductive requests and activities.
- Avoid continuously changing priorities.
- Keep assignments as consistent as possible.

Impatience

Creativity is not something you can turn on and off like a light switch, although the analogy of idea creation is often in the form of a light bulb. It is, rather, more like a continuous knob light switch, whereby creativity gradually grows and fades. This takes time, but in an environment of faster, better, and cheaper, it does not give creativity the time it needs to percolate to the surface. Whatever creativity does occur is often a quick fix, which at the moment appears creative but is really a band-aid that may introduce greater problems in the future. Sometimes, and perhaps more often than not, getting a solution quickly before all the facts and data are known and verified leads to myopic solutions, sacrificing the big picture for a little one. Eugene Raudsepp refers to this tendency as *premature particularization*.[14] He also says that individuals who do take time often face pressure from peers and self-inflicted guilt because they do not appear to be producing or contributing.[15] From a creativity perspective, here are some ways to counter the affect and effect of impatience:

- Allow time for relaxation.
- Allow time to generate ideas.
- Keep the major goals and objectives in the forefront of team members' minds.

Specialization

In the past few centuries, specialization has become a way of life for most people in the business world. Except for senior leadership, most people are specialists, for example, software engineers, financial accountants, and mechanical engineers. The reason is because the depth of knowledge to succeed in a field now often takes years of education and experience to acquire a good body of knowledge of a specialized subject. Despite the advantages of specialization, it has its drawbacks when it comes to creativity. Specialists see the world through a narrow lens, sometimes filtering key information that would be deemed important in another specialization. It sometimes also makes it difficult to communicate with other people. Creativity suffers because some specialists find it difficult to see the world from a paradigm that is different than the one prevailing in their specialty, thus making it difficult to think outside the box.

From a creativity perspective, here are some ways to counter the affect and effect of specialization:

- Allow for training outside of one's specialization.
- Provide cross-training.
- Provide opportunities for job enrichment.
- Reassign responsibilities whenever possible to broaden knowledge.

Craving for Predictability

In today's dynamic economy, predictability seems like something in the distant past. Yet human nature, as it is, will prefer predictability over chaos because it gives a sense of stability and confidence. Predictability is not often associated with creativity. The latter requires upsetting the status quo by challenging sacred cows. You cannot have one without affecting the other in the opposite way. A high correlation exists; more predictability is associated with less creativity, and less predictability is associated more creativity. In part, this desire for predictability is reflective of an educational system that stresses appropriateness and order.[16] It is also stressed by the prevailing paradigm of our day, says Thomas Kuhn, because of normal science reinforcing the prevailing paradigm through eclectic reinforcement of its premises.[17]

The key is to shake up predictability by doing something creative that is akin to jumping out of a running river, as Dave Allan et al. observes. By jumping, so to speak, it stimulates creative thinking as the river continues to flow.[18]

From a creativity perspective, here are some ways to counter the affect and effect of a craving for predictability:

- Engage stakeholders in developing and managing plans.
- Establish and maintain effective communications.
- Institute good change management discipline.
- Perform risk management.

Inability to Adapt

People may not change, but the context may do so substantially. If people cannot or refuse to change, then their ability to adapt is severely limited, reflecting their inability to be creative. Adaptability requires being creative to survive and grow in a new environment. The inability to create is really, therefore, an inability to adapt and to develop new ideas, processes, products, services, and so on. James Adams identifies some causes of an inability to adapt, including inadequacies related to language skills to articulate ideas, problem-solving definition, and strategizing for dealing with problems.[19] Additionally, inflexibility in thinking sometimes causes one to deny evidence to the contrary. That, in turn, encourages some people to make premature judgments before knowing the facts and data. This premature judgment gets our ego involved, causing people to stick to their judgment despite evidence to the contrary.[20] From a creativity perspective, here are some ways to counter the affect and effect of an inability to adapt:

- Allow for open sharing of data and information.
- Be flexible in applying tools, techniques, and procedures.
- Encourage critical thinking.

- Provide cross-training.
- Provide training.

Poor Communications

A team of creative individuals that do not communicate with each other will likely never be creative as a complete entity. One or two individuals may be creative but not the whole team. To enable a team to be creative, members need to share their ideas and proposals for discussion and evaluation. Without a serious dialog, the group is a committee of people working independently, coming together perhaps only occasionally. For a team to create, its creative members must communicate. Otherwise, likely no one will have any idea what each of the other team members thinks or does.

From a creativity perspective, here are some ways to counter the affect and effect of poor communications:

- Allow for open sharing of data, information, and ideas, for example, team meetings.
- Apply effective listening skills on individual team levels.
- Encourage cross-checking of output as a means to acquire feedback.
- Encourage participating in the planning and management of the project.
- Establish a dispute resolution process.

Poor Coordination

Team members must not only communicate, but also coordinate with each other. The failure to coordinate can result in a wasteful, redundant effort that results not only in duplicate effort but confusion over who is doing what. How does this impact creativity? Simple. It means people are busy spending more time and effort trying to determine who is doing what rather than using it to direct energies into something creative, either individually or as a group.

Even if a creative idea arises, it often requires the participation of others to develop and implement it. Even if we successfully solve a difficult problem or come up with a very worthwhile creative idea, people's receptivity may be low or nonexistent. The cooperation of others will be required even more so if the solution or idea is to become a reality.[21] From a creativity perspective, here are some ways to counter the affect and effect of poor coordination:

- Clearly define roles, responsibilities, and authorities.
- Develop reliable plans involving the participation of key stakeholders.
- Encourage greater integration and interdependence among team members.
- Provide training on team building.

Leaping to Judgment

More often than not, people jump to judgment before listening to someone describe a problem. Instead of defining the problem, even understanding it, some people often develop a solution after very little discussion. From a time perspective, this behavior is advantageous; however, it does little to enable developing a truly creative solution that addresses the root cause of an issue or problem. Creativity is important to develop lasting solutions, but it takes time and a willingness to discuss the positives and negatives of each solution. Few people want to take the time to restrain this tendency because they want a solution quickly, perhaps due to organizational or peer pressure or personal frustration, rather than take the time to generate multiple possible solutions.[22] From a creativity perspective, here are some ways to counter the affect and effect of leaping to judgment:

- Apply brainstorming and other creativity techniques.
- Apply effective listening skills.
- Define problems prior to developing solutions.
- Encourage giving and receiving feedback.
- Practice critical thinking.
- Seek outside perspectives.

Faster, Better, Cheaper Philosophy

Management style coupled with the current economic environment requires just about everything being done faster, better, cheaper. This philosophy more often than not restricts time and effort devoted to creativity. Creativity requires overhead because it cannot be forced or handled like something being built in a manufacturing line. Creativity requires thought, discussion, experimentation, and evaluation, all of which in the short term are not necessarily faster or cheaper, or better. Ironically, creativity is difficult under such circumstances. Allan et al. say this is indicative of an emergency room environment where the stress is on quick analysis, precision in thought, and immediate results. Little time is available to explore ideas and experiment.[23]

From a creativity perspective, here are some ways to counter the affect and effect of a faster, better, cheaper philosophy:

- Emphasize the importance of addressing the cause and not the symptoms of a problem or issue.
- Encourage team members to consult peers on key issues, concerns, and problems.
- Implement change management.
- Take time to define problems prior to developing solutions.

Stretching Resources Too Thin

Today, and for perhaps longer than realized, the emphasis in the work environment is to operate with a minimum amount of resources to accomplish the work. Management wants to keep the overhead low and at the same time increase output. From an efficiency standpoint, this perspective makes sense. However, it can often hinder creativity. People, resources too, struggle to obtain other resources to accomplish their work; they may also get overworked and burned out, thereby affecting their ability to create. Creativity requires sufficient resources, ranging from time to equipment, to allow it to blossom.

On top of all of the above are the constant disruptions at work. These disruptions can range from multiple sources, from telephone calls to ad hoc meetings with peers, allowing little time for creativity.[24] From a creativity perspective, here are some ways to counter the affect and effect of stretching resources too thin:

- Apply resource leveling to have more efficient and effective usage.
- Determine priorities.
- Encourage sharing of knowledge, experience, and expertise.

Silos

Large organizations, despite efforts over the past decade or so of flattening, remain silos that restrict creativity within too-narrow disciplines.

Manufacturing, finance, information systems, personnel, and many other silos within organizations struggle for dominance. This situation impacts creativity because it isolates the experiences of people and compartmentalizes them, making it difficult to become exposed to new ideas. Creative people often have a broad background, and working in a separate environment filled with silos makes that difficult.

Creative ideas can be threatening to organizations and individuals alike, particularly in bureaucratic organizations. According to Eugene Raudsepp, silos affect receptivity toward creative thinking because it may challenge the authority and purview of another person or organization. In other words, creativity and the resulting idea may result in differences, even hostility, on the part of other people or organizations.[25]

From a creativity perspective, here are some ways to counter the affect and effect of silos:

- Address conflict early on and directly.
- Communicate continuously with stakeholders.
- Encourage greater integration and interdependence among key stakeholders.
- Encourage sharing of data and information about project performance and other activities.
- Enlarge the core team to include key stakeholders.

Focusing on the Past or Future, Not the Present

Success in the past and present is excellent for leveraging knowledge and experience to create a new product, process, service, and so on. Sometimes, however, people rest on successes of the past and present, and disregard any need for innovation in the future. They rest, in other words, on their laurels, and by doing so, become complacent, comfortable, and conditioned to not upset the status quo. Naturally, under such circumstances, creativity becomes difficult to exercise. After all, why change anything if the circumstances are quite good right now?

From a creativity perspective, here are some ways to counter the affect and effect of focusing on the past or present, not the future:

- Conduct planning with team members.
- Perform contingency planning with team members.

- Perform risk management with team members.
- Perform visioning with team members.

Lack of Sharing

When people stop sharing ideas or resources, a degree of mistrust exists. People often do not share when they feel it will jeopardize their interests. Sharing usually occurs when the gain is mutual, either for selfish reasons to increase synergy or for encouraging a symbiotic relationship. People not sharing makes creativity difficult because they will not reveal their ideas to others for fear of retribution, theft, or someone else taking credit. Creativity, especially on a team, requires sharing; otherwise, the probability of its occurrence decreases dramatically.

From a creativity perspective, here are some ways to counter the affect and effect of a lack of sharing:

- Build a common data repository.
- Encourage sharing of data, information, knowledge, and experiences.
- Provide a common set of tools.
- Use media, such as file shares and email, to share data, information, knowledge, and experiences.

Compliant Workforce

Ideally, organizations want people who can think creatively while at the same time follow orders and maintain the status quo. Most jobs generally fulfill the former requirements; few do the latter. Creativity, unless sanctioned by management, can threaten sacred cows. In addition, most work does not require creative thinking but rather applied, procedural mental applications that are almost robotic in nature.[26] Eugene Raudepp agrees, observing that management often prefers order over innovation, which means subordinates who are copiers rather than creative innovators. Naturally, this preference can be detrimental to surviving in a highly dynamic competitive environment.[27] To no one's surprise, highly creative people will take flight to somewhere else to exercise their creativity rather than work, as most people do, in a routine environment maintaining existing products, processes, and services. A compliant, as opposed to a creative, workforce will be likely not to take chances that will upset the status quo because it is not in its character or interests to do so. What organizations need to do is to produce what Peter Senge refers to as "creative tension" by clearly articulating the mission and its relationship to the discrepancies that exist in reality.[28] Consequently, management often embraces doing everything "by the book" because of the advantages. It provides predictability. It reduces anxiety because the outcome, if negative, absolves a person from responsibility. It can also provide a roadmap for trekking through the unknown. Rules and regulations for any organization are important for its survival because they offer order in place of chaos.

However, if rules and regulations are taken to the extreme, they will greet ideas with hostility through displays of intolerance and inflexibility.[29] From a creativity standpoint, it can mean horror. A by-the-book attitude makes it difficult to challenge assumptions, principles, concepts, and so on when creating, thereby inhibiting a questioning perspective and relying on intuition—two critical abilities for being creative. Allan et al. recognize that such constraints restrict our ability to come up with creative and innovative ideas.[30] Fortunately, failure from adopting a by-the-book philosophy can, ironically, lead to greater creativity by seeing through the failure to new ideas.[31] In the end, the desire for a compliant workforce and adherence to a by-the-book philosophy results in methodism with overemphasis being placed on compliance with a process, procedure, or technique, at the expense of experimenting with something new. Pressure, in other words, is to conform to the current way of doing business, almost in a manufacturing-like setting. Naturally, any effort to break with the process, procedure, or technique can bring retribution upon the person or organization. Methodism is reflective of what Thomas Kuhn refers to as *normal science*, which is essentially puzzle-solving that does not exactly encourage creativity. Kuhn says that normal science does whatever it can to suppress novel ideas by requiring the use of accepted, known rules and procedures. Under such conditions, creativity and creative output are difficult to achieve due to conditioning of our thinking through knowledge and experience, reinforced through the application of recognized methods and procedures proven by past success.[32] From a creativity perspective, here are some ways to counter the affect and effect of a compliant workforce:

- Allow for flexibility when applying standards, procedures, and techniques.
- Encourage team members to think outside the box.

- Recognize and reward people who initiate taking risks, regardless of outcome.
- Select a diverse team of people, from personality to experience.

Hierarchy

This challenge implies formal power over other people. It also implies that certain people determine direction, values, and priorities. In traditional hierarchies, creativity is difficult at best because parameters and other constraints are heavily imposed. Fortunately, many organizations are working to reduce the layers of hierarchy and the micromanagement that often accompanies it. Less hierarchy enables greater creativity; more hierarchy reduces it. Creativity requires latitude; too much oversight kills it. Eugene Raudsepp sums it up well, noting that an idea often has to travel up the food chain before getting implemented, if it ever gets that opportunity.[33]

From a creativity perspective, here are some ways to counter the affect and effect of hierarchy:

- Allow some team members to assume project management responsibilities.
- Apply job enlargement for team members.
- Have project manager and leads assume some of the responsibilities that other team members have.
- Increase span of control for project manager and leads.
- Provide opportunities for cross-training.

Not Listening to Inner Voice

All too frequently, especially in externally focused cultures, the inner voice that has proven helpful in being creative is squelched. In the corporate environment, the pressure to quiet that voice often stifles creativity. Pressures like regular pay increases, evaluations, and not being tagged a team player can pressure people to focus externally rather than internally. Only when the external world rewards creativity will the inner voice surface. Yet, such circumstances are rare for most people who are very likely hired to do just what they were hired for and nothing more. Sometimes, however, the inner voice can become the worst enemy of creativity if we can become our own worst critic by not suspending judgment to explore ideas.[34] By suspending judgment and exploring an idea further, we increase the chance of appreciating and realizing an idea's potential.[35] From a creativity perspective, here are some ways to counter the affect and effect of not listening to one's inner voice:

- Bring on board a mix of left- and right-brain thinkers.
- Encourage greater use of right-brain thinking on problems and issues.
- Encourage the solicitation of feedback involving both logic and feelings of team members.

Taking on Only What Is Known

Creativity, by its very nature, requires embracing the unknown. By tackling the unknown, a chance of failure, often with a high likelihood, occurs along with all its undesirable consequences. So a natural inclination is to embrace what is known, such as patterns of behavior; and if it involves creativity, then it will be incremental change at best. Naturally, the unknown is scary, but it can pay big dividends if, and only if, it succeeds. But many organizations squash any tolerance for tackling the unknown. The focus in most organizations is working on ideas or problems determined by others, which encourages very little emotional involvement or ownership by an individual or team tackling them, thereby decreasing the likelihood of coming up with anything creative.[36] Organizations, in order to encourage and embrace a culture of creativity, are recognizing the need to break patterns of behavior on a personal and organizational level, according to Allan et al., as people find themselves working on topics that they would not ordinarily address or like to do so.[37] From a creativity perspective, here are some ways to counter the affect and effect of taking on only what is known:

- Encourage people to take on problems, issues, and so on with little available information.
- Encourage team members to embrace ambiguity.
- Encourage team members to experiment with new tools, techniques, and procedures.
- Have team members visit other projects to see how other tools and techniques are applied differently.
- Identify anomalous results and have people investigate the cause to learn different ways to perform responsibilities.

- Perform benchmarking to obtain new ideas.
- Recognize and reward risk taking.
- Visit other projects and organizations to learn new ideas and processes.

Management's Lack of Responsiveness

Nothing can kill creativity in an organization more quickly than management's attitude of "we don't care." Management may go through the motions of talking about creativity but not bother to do anything regarding the topic, thereby hurting its credibility. People, either individually or as a team, will be reluctant to continue to offer creative solutions because management simply gives lip service to the topic. After a while, creative thinking stops or creative people go elsewhere. Management needs to demonstrate its commitment to creativity if it hopes to flourish in an organization. As Allan et al. observe, senior management sets the tone for acceptance or rejection of highly creative ideas through how and what it says. Even the bravest can feel intimidated if senior management sets the wrong tone.[38] From a creativity perspective, here are some ways to counter the affect and effect of management's lack of responsiveness:

- Communicate continuously about the project to key members of management.
- Invite key members of management to attend team meetings.
- Invite key members of management to participate in important decisions.

Success

At first, it is difficult to understand how success can inhibit creativity. After all, success frees one from worry and other negative concerns. Yet success also breeds comfort and even arrogance, leading to a decline in creativity simply because the incentives for creating are no longer there. Creativity requires some degree of anxiety and discomfort either internally or externally. Otherwise, many people would simply be satisfied with the status quo and see no reason to change. Success must be accompanied by failure for creativity to occur continuously. As Eugene Raudsepp says, experience and failure go hand in hand as a consequence of bad judgment. In other words, failure becomes a means of growth as much as success does.[39] Also, both success and failure are required for an individual to attain self-fulfillment by enlarging his or her experiences and obtaining a sense of accomplishment.[40] From a creativity perspective, here are some ways to counter the affect and effect of success:

- Bring on board team members who question the status quo.
- Encourage team members to embrace ambiguity by tackling tasks with little or no data or information.
- Pollinate the team from time to time with new team members with different knowledge and experience.
- Recognize and reward failure as well as success.

Too Many Positive and Negative Incentives

Too many positive incentives can hinder creativity. They can entice people to create only if they receive something in return. People can reach a threshold point of satiation in which they find that positive incentives no longer motivate them to create. As Ross Perot reportedly once said, the hardest part of motivating people is after you've made them millionaires. Having too many negative incentives is just as inhibiting to creativity. Every time something goes awry, which invariably it does when creating, and people get slapped by management (e.g., a negative performance review), then creativity will quickly decline and they will become very risk-averse. Eugene Raudsepp observes that change, as a result of creation and innovation, can be detrimental to one's career, such as a loss of status or position.[41] They will see, or perceive, that taking a chance by being creative costs more than it gains. Regardless of using positive or negative incentives, motivation, or more specifically demotivation, becomes the critical issue because the environment lacks the stimulation necessary to motivate people to be creative.[42] To a large degree, corporations encourage this consequence, add Allan et al., due to a lack of intimacy with the individual that is often found in small groups. Instead, salary and promotions eclipse strong emotional commitment by the individual.[43] From a creativity perspective, here are some ways to counter the affect and effect of too many positive and negative incentives:

- Develop clear standards of performance.
- Provide an equitable distribution of awards, balancing individual and group ones.

Team Composition Imbalance

Nothing can kill creativity on a team more quickly than having too many people of the same psychological profile as members. They all think and act alike; they perceive the world in the same way; and everyone gets along like one big happy family. The problem with this scenario is that it can wreak havoc on creativity. No one questions to any other team member, or the questions are not very challenging because they all think the same. Few if any think outside the box, being locked into the same paradigm. Everyone may work together and share tools, knowledge, data, and so on, but the likelihood of creative thinking will be low simply because no one is available to challenge the dominant thinking style.

From a creativity perspective, here are some ways to counter the affect and effect of team composition imbalance:

- Bring on board a diverse group of people varying in skills, knowledge, experience, and personality.
- Provide training that focuses on improving the skills and knowledge that individuals lack.
- Solicit input from outside experts, either from other projects or outside the organization.

Dominance of Brain Thinking

Management often wants creative, right-brain thinkers, but the hiring and incentives are for left-brain thinkers. Right-brain thinking is less rigorous and emphasizes the emotional, intuitive side of work. Left-brain thinking focuses more on rationality, structure, and so on. While you need both in the work environment, most firms prefer to hire left-brain thinkers. Right-brain qualities are predominantly taught in schools, especially after grade school, in the United States. This adherence to the left brain is a cultural preference. According to William Sonnenschein, the display of emotion is unacceptable despite the fact that emotions are instrumental in the shaping of insights, ideas, perspectives, and clarifications, which in turn help form strong relationships.[44] Not surprisingly, activities like daydreaming are discouraged.[45] The right-brain qualities are harder to define and assess, although most people agree that they can make or break an organization. Too many left-brain people inhibit creativity by emphasizing rules, procedures, and so on. Too many right-brain people and no one follows the rules, procedures, and so on. A balance of both is required if creative output is to result in innovation.

From a creativity perspective, here are some ways to counter the affect and effect of brain thinking dominance:

- Assign a devil's advocate.
- Bring on board a diverse group of people, varying in personality, for example, thinking styles.
- Hire contractors and consultants from time to time to shake up thinking and offer different perspectives.
- Provide a personality assessment of existing team members so they can determine similarities and differences in thinking styles.

Infighting

A quarrelsome team will only lead to people dividing themselves into groups of similar thinkers. It will not produce any degree of creative thinking other than that of sabotaging competing groups. Few, if any, will have the moxie to take chances and create for fear of being mentally or, hopefully not, physically attacked. Intimidation, not creativity, runs high in an environment replete with infighting. The fear of conflict can smother any creativity; Allan et al. observe that people often do not experience the nonanalytical side of the human experience at work, and hence do not hesitate to jump to judgment, resulting in frustration and defensiveness by everyone involved and the circumstance continues to worsen. Conflict is a means for countering another scourge of creativity, complacency. It serves as a vehicle, so to speak, in moving an organization to a future state.[46]

From a creativity perspective, here are some ways to counter the affect and effect of infighting:

- Assign tasks that require team members to work jointly.
- Confront negative differences up front in a project's life cycle.
- Clearly define roles, responsibilities, and authorities.
- Encourage people to share data, information, and insights.
- Establish a conflict resolution process.
- Provide a personality assessment of team members.

CONCLUSION

The bottom line is that one or even several of the aforementioned challenges and constraints in the work environment do not inhibit creativity. In some circumstances, their existence may actually enhance creativity, albeit rarely. The danger is that any of these circumstances can become extreme, increasing the likelihood of inhibiting creativity. Project managers need to be aware of their existence and determine how to best deal with them so that individuals and the entire team can be as creative as they can be in ultimately achieving the vision, goals, and objectives of their projects.

Getting Started Checklist

Question	Yes	No
1. Select the applicable challenges and constraints facing your project with regard to creativity:		
Groupthink		
Mores, Beliefs, Values		
Fear		
Mismatch		
Lack of Tools		
Lack of Data and Information		
Too Much and Too Little Training		
Starting and Stopping Workflow		
Impatience		
Specialization		
Craving for Predictability		
Inability to Adapt		
Poor Communications		
Poor Coordination		
Leaping to Judgment		
Faster, Better, Cheaper Philosophy		
Stretching Resources Too Thin		
Silos		
Focusing on the Past or Present, Not the Future		
Lack of Sharing		
Compliant Workforce		
Hierarchy		
Not Listening to Inner Voice		
Taking Only What Is Known		
Management's Lack of Responsiveness		
Success		

Getting Started Checklist

Question	Yes	No
Too Many Positive and Negative Incentives		
Team Composition Imbalance		
Dominance of Brain Thinking		
Infighting		

2. Which specific actions can you take for the challenges and constraints that you selected above?

Groupthink:

- Bring on board people with different backgrounds, knowledge, experience, and personalities.
- Encourage questioning of proposals, ideas, thoughts, and so on.
- Reassign teaming relationships.
- Other(s):

Mores, Beliefs, Values:

- Assign people whose mores, beliefs, and values are different from the prevalent ones in the group.
- Assign someone the role of being a devil's advocate.
- Investigate other projects' ways of doing business.
- Other(s):

Fear:

- Assign two or more people to a task.
- Encourage team members to share their thoughts and experiences with others on the team.
- Keep all key stakeholders engaged in the outcome of creative tasks.
- Provide frequent one-on-one sessions with the more fearful team members.
- Provide training on relevant tasks.
- Provide training that enhances competence and confidence.
- Use a buddy system (e.g., two or more people assigned to a difficult task).
- Encourage team members to stretch the limits of rules, procedures, and so on.
- Perform benchmarking to expose team members to new ideas, processes, and so on.
- Recognize and reward team members who take risks.
- Other(s):

Mismatch:

- Allow people to identify or choose tasks on which to work.
- Assign people to tasks after having them take a personality assessment.

(Continued)

Getting Started Checklist

Question	Yes	No
• Have periodic one-on-one sessions with individuals to assess task performance.		
• Other(s):		
Lack of Tools:		
• Have people increase their awareness of technological advancements in their profession.		
• Have the latest professional journals available for reference by team members.		
• Provide training on technology related to doing work on the project.		
• Other(s):		
Lack of Data and Information:		
• Adopt a policy of sharing data and information.		
• Encourage access to other sources of data and information beyond the confines of the project.		
• Provide the infrastructure (e.g., a common repository) to enable sharing of data and information.		
• Use tools that follow common standards to enable sharing of data and information.		
• Other(s):		
Too Much and Too Little Training:		
• Identify relevant training for the project.		
• Provide cascade training, e.g., people sharing their knowledge gained from training elsewhere.		
• Tailor training to the specific needs of individuals.		
• Other(s):		
Start and Stop Workflow:		
• Attempt to protect team members from nonproductive requests and activities.		
• Avoid continuously changing priorities.		
• Keep assignments consistent as much as possible.		
• Other(s):		
Impatience:		
• Allow time for relaxation.		
• Allow time to generate ideas.		
• Keep the major goals and objectives in the forefront of team members' minds.		
• Other(s):		
Specialization:		
• Allow for training outside of one's specialization.		
• Provide cross-training.		

Getting Started Checklist

Question	Yes	No

- Provide opportunities for job enrichment.
- Reassign responsibilities whenever possible to broaden knowledge.
- Other(s):

Craving for Predictability:
- Engage stakeholders in developing plans and their management.
- Establish and maintain effective communications.
- Institute good change management discipline.
- Perform risk management.
- Other(s):

Inability to Adapt:
- Allow for open sharing of data and information.
- Be flexible in applying tools, techniques, and procedures.
- Encourage critical thinking.
- Provide cross-training.
- Provide training.
- Other(s):

Poor Communications:
- Allow for open sharing of data, information, and ideas (e.g., team meetings).
- Apply effective listening skills on individual team levels.
- Encourage cross-checking of output as a means to acquire feedback.
- Encourage participating in the planning and management of the project.
- Establish a dispute resolution process.
- Other(s):

Poor Coordination:
- Clesrly define roles, responsibilities, and authorities.
- Develop reliable plans involving the participation of key stakeholders.
- Encourage greater integration and interdependence among team members.
- Provide training on team building.
- Other(s):

Leaping to Judgment:
- Apply brainstorming and other creativity techniques.
- Apply effective listening skills.
- Define problems prior to developing solutions.
- Encourage giving and receiving feedback.
- Practice critical thinking.

(Continued)

Getting Started Checklist

Question	Yes	No

- Seek outside perspectives.
- Other(s):

Faster, Better, Cheaper Philosophy:
- Emphasize the importance of addressing the cause and not the symptoms of a problem or issue.
- Encourage team members to consult peers on key issues, concerns, and problems.
- Implement change management.
- Take time to define problems prior to developing solutions.
- Other(s):

Stretching Resources Too Thin:
- Apply resource leveling to have more efficient and effective usage.
- Determine priorities.
- Encourage sharing of knowledge, experience, and expertise.
- Other(s):

Silos:
- Address conflict early on and directly.
- Communicate continuously with stakeholders.
- Encourage greater integration and interdependence among key stakeholders.
- Other(s):

Focus on the Past or Present, Not the Future:
- Conduct planning with team members.
- Perform contingency planning with team members.
- Perform risk management with team members.
- Perform visioning with team members.
- Other(s):

Lack of Sharing:
- Build a common data repository.
- Encourage sharing of data, information, knowledge, and experiences.
- Provide a common set of tools.
- Use media, such as file shares and email, to share data, information, knowledge, and experiences.
- Other(s):

Compliant Workforce:
- Allow for flexibility when applying standards, procedures, and techniques.
- Encourage team members to think outside the box.

Getting Started Checklist

Question	Yes	No

- Recognize and reward people who initiate taking risks, regardless of outcome.
- Select a diverse team of people, from personality to experience.
- Other(s):

Hierarchy:
- Allow some team members to assume project management responsibilities.
- Apply job enlargement for team members.
- Have project manager and leads assume some of the responsibilities that other team members have.
- Increase span of control for project manager and leads.
- Provide opportunities for cross-training.
- Other(s):

Not Listening to Inner Voice:
- Bring on board a mix of left- and right-brain thinkers.
- Encourage greater use of right-brain thinking on problems, issues, and so on.
- Encourage the solicitation of feedback involving both logic and feelings of team members.
- Other(s):

Taking on Only What Is Known:
- Encourage people to take on problems, issues, and so on with little available information.
- Encourage team members to embrace ambiguity.
- Perform benchmarking to obtain new ideas.
- Recognize and reward risk taking.
- Visit other projects and organizations to learn new ideas and processes.
- Other(s):

Management's Lack of Responsiveness:
- Communicate continuously about the project to key members of management.
- Invite key members of management to attend team meetings.
- Invite key members of management to participate in important decisions.
- Other(s):

Success:
- Bring on board team members who question the status quo.
- Encourage team members to embrace ambiguity by tackling tasks with little or no data or information.

(Continued)

Getting Started Checklist

Question	Yes	No
• Pollinate the team from time to time with new team members with different knowledge and experience.		
• Recognize and reward failure as well as success.		
• Other(s):		
Too Many Positive and Negative Incentives:		
• Develop clear standards of performance.		
• Provide an equitable distribution of awards, balancing individual and group ones.		
• Other(s):		
Team Composition Imbalance:		
• Bring on board a diverse group of people varying in skills, knowledge, experience, and personality.		
• Provide training that focuses on improving the skills and knowledge that individuals lack.		
• Solicit input from outside experts, either from other projects or outside the organization.		
• Other(s):		
Dominance of Brain Thinking		
• Assign a devil's advocate.		
• Bring on board a diverse group of people, varying in personality (e.g., thinking styles).		
• Hire contractors and consultants from time to time to shake up thinking and offer different perspectives.		
• Provide a personality assessment of existing team members so they can determine similarities and differences in thinking styles.		
• Other(s):		
Infighting:		
• Assign tasks that require team members to work jointly.		
• Confront negative differences up front in a project's life cycle.		
• Clearly define roles, responsibilities, and authorities.		
• Encourage people to share data, information, and insights.		
• Establish a conflict resolution process.		
• Provide a personality assessment of team members.		
• Other(s):		

ENDNOTES

1. William Sonnenschein, *The Diversity Toolkit* (Lincoln Wood, IL: Contemporary Books, 1999).
2. Eugene Raudsepp, *How Creative Are You?* (New York: Perigee Books, 1981), p. 61.

3. Raudsepp, *How Creative Are You?* p. 61.
4. Roger von Oech, *A Whack on the Side of the Head* (New York: Warner Books, Inc., 1990), p. 10.
5. Sonnenschein, *The Diversity Toolkit*, p. 35.
6. Dave Allan et al., *What If?* (Oxford: Capstone Publishing Limited, 1999), 56.
7. von Oech, *A Whack on the Side of the Head*, p. 170.
8. Raudsepp, *How Creative Are You?* p. 50.
9. Allan et al., *What If?*, p. 210.
10. Raudsepp, *How Creative Are You?* p. 49.
11. Raudsepp, *How Creative Are You?* p. 94.
12. Brown, *Inventors at Work* (Redmond, WA: Tempus Books, 1988), p. 343.
13. Allan et al., *What If?* p. 142.
14. Raudsepp, *How Creative Are You?* p. 74.
15. Raudsepp, *How Creative Are You?* p. 74.
16. von Oech, *A Whack on the Side of the Head*, p. 11.
17. Thomas S. Kuhn, *The Structure of Scientific Revolutions*, 2nd ed. (Chicago: University of Chicago, 1970), p. 24.
18. Allan et al., *What If?* p. 12.
19. James L. Adams, *Conceptual Blockbusting*, 2nd ed. (New York: W. W. Norton & Company, 1979), p. 81.
20. Raudsepp, *How Creative Are You?* p. 71.
21. Raudsepp, *How Creative Are You?* p. 96.
22. Raudsepp, *How Creative Are You?* p. 71.
23. Allan et al., *What If?* p. 55.
24. Raudsepp, *How Creative Are You?* p. 90.
25. Raudsepp, *How Creative Are You?* pp. 88–89.
26. von Oech, *A Whack on the Side of the Head*, p. 10.
27. Raudsepp, *How Creative Are You?* p. 82.
28. Peter Senge et al., *The Dance of Change* (New York: Currency, 1999), p. 16.
29. Raudsepp, *How Creative Are You?* pp. 83–84.
30. Allan et al., *What If?* p. 26.
31. Kuhn, *The Structure of Scientific Revolutions*, p. 68.
32. Raudsepp, *How Creative Are You?* p. 75.
33. Raudsepp, *How Creative Are You?* p. 95.
34. Raudsepp, *How Creative Are You?* p. 26.
35. Raudsepp, *How Creative Are You?* p. 77.
36. Raudsepp, *How Creative Are You?* p. 92.
37. Allan et al., *What If?* p. 40.
38. Allan et al., *What If?* p. 224.
39. Raudsepp, *How Creative Are You?* p. 49.
40. Raudsepp, *How Creative Are You?* p. 52.
41. Raudsepp, *How Creative Are You?* p. 26.
42. Raudsepp, *How Creative Are You?* p. 81.
43. Allan et al., *What If?* p. 137
44. Sonnenschein, *The Diversity Toolkit*, p. 122.
45. Raudsepp, *How Creative Are You?* p. 92.
46. Sonnenschein, *The Diversity Toolkit*, p. 122.

5

Laying the Groundwork for a Creative Environment

INTRODUCTION

Creativity can occur in just about any type of environment. Some of the most inhospitable work environments can sometimes encourage creativity to blossom. Some other environments can, quite frankly, kill any chance of creativity arising. Generally, the best approach is to understand what is required to engender creativity rather than wait for circumstances to allow it to percolate to the surface on a project. Armed with that understanding, project managers can take the necessary actions.

NECESSARY ACTIONS

Creativity sometimes just happens; but more often than not, project managers have to set up conditions in the environment to further its occurrence. Here are some actions that you can take:

- Establish a receptive audience.
- Make training available.
- Grant necessary access to data and tools.
- Concentrate creative energy.
- Encourage a certain degree of anxiety and tension.
- Establish priorities.
- Encourage diversity.
- Build and maintain trust.
- Support people's growth.

- Encourage ownership.
- Stress communications.
- Emphasize coordination.
- Relax rules, procedures, and so on.
- Align individual and organizational goals and objectives.
- Allow for risk taking.
- Allow time for problem or issue definition.
- Provide opportunities to create.
- Broaden people's knowledge and experience.
- Counter groupthink.
- Encourage transformational leadership.

Establish a Receptive Audience

Being creative, by its very nature, challenges the status quo in which many people have a vested interest and the last thing they want is to be challenged. Naturally, finding a receptive audience is difficult under such circumstances. Without one, creativity will likely be shut down and creative people will go elsewhere. To avoid this situation, opportunities must be available for creative people. One of the first steps is to engender an open environment for people to express their insights without fear of physical or psychological retaliation. Novel ideas that are frequently discounted in the beginning, may lead people to go elsewhere. This sometimes means going to or becoming a competitor.[1] Here are some ways to establish a receptive audience to further creativity:

- Apply stakeholder management; for example, understand interests, concerns, and so on.
- Communicate continuously about key activities on the project.
- Encourage participation by key stakeholders on activities involving creativity.
- Share information about the progress of creative endeavors.

Make Training Available

Creativity requires an increased awareness of what is occurring in the immediate and greater environment. It also requires being up to speed on the latest tools and techniques. Training is the vehicle for allowing that to happen. Regardless of the training medium, making training available can enhance creativity; otherwise, people may become stale, only inhibiting their creativity. This is especially the case in high-technology environments where the pace of technological change and knowledge is furious at times.[2]

Here are some ways to make training available to further creativity:

- Apply the buddy system to work on activities requiring some transfer of skills and knowledge.
- Communicate best practices from other organizations.
- Exploit the use of all training media, for example, CD-ROM training.
- Provide cross-training.
- Share lessons learned from creative activities on other projects.

Grant Necessary Access to Data and Tools

With the exception of proprietary data, creativity requires data to convert into information. Having the data and information then allows creativity to flourish as an enabler of people to experiment freely, combine and recombine the content to gain new insights, and encourage a greater exchange of ideas. Data and information fuel creativity, especially in highly specialized environments.[3] However, having too much access to information can result in paralysis, whether in decision making or creating. Dietrich Dorner, author of *The Logic of Failure*, observes that too much information can be as detrimental as having too little. Sometimes, ignorance breeds simplicity, giving a person a better view of reality. Ironically, the more we know, the less we do.[4] Creativity also requires having the best tools available for much the same reasons as having open access to data and information. Having the necessary tools allows people to experiment, see the impact of their ideas much more quickly, and build confidence. Tools are the engines fueled by data and information, again in specialized environments.

Here are some ways to grant access to data and tools to further creativity:

- Conduct frequent data-sharing sessions.
- Establish a repository of data to which team members have open access.
- Provide people with the tools to access applicable data.
- Provide tools adhering to common standards.
- Provide tools with the most current capabilities.

- Pursue cross-training on using tools.
- Reduce the number of controls restricting access to data.
- Reduce the number of controls restricting the use of tools other than for private application.

Concentrate Creative Energy

The common misperception about creativity is that it is something wild that lacks focus and encourages people to run amuck. Nothing could be further from the truth. For creativity to lead to innovation, it needs to be focused in laser-light fashion, but broad enough to be like high-beam lights on a car. Successful creativity is not unbridled; rather, it is concentrated. It is true that creativity left unbridled may dissipate energy and resources. However, creativity and focus must be aligned to achieve results. Creativity, therefore, requires just enough discipline for people with vision to achieve.

Here are some ways to concentrate creative energy to further creativity:

- Ask continually at meetings whether the topic under discussion helps further the goals of the project.
- Have team members participate in defining and planning the project.
- Have team members ask for creative insights from others on how to address a problem or issue.
- Review the goals of the project at team meetings.

Encourage a Certain Degree of Anxiety and Tension

Complacency is one of the greatest threats to creativity. They do not get along. David Whyte, author of *The Heart Aroused*, says that creativity and its expression serve as a volatile combination that sets everything alight.[5] By providing defined goals and objectives that cause people to stretch but not break, people will experience the necessary degree of anxiety and tension. Too much, however, over a sustained period can prove counterproductive, leading to dysfunctions like burnout and scapegoating. Sometimes, periods of relaxation following high-stress situations that fail to produce creative results can actually encourage greater creativity by allowing the subconscious to work on a problem or issue. It is not uncommon for people to have a creative idea when driving a car, taking a shower, walking in the woods, shaving, or taking a trip. Just the right degree of anxiety and tension will allow for greater awareness, alertness, and directed energy to complete activities. David Whyte likens creativity to fire, bringing great warmth and fear at the same time. A creative fire builds but it can result, sometimes, in getting burned, especially in the workplace.[6] One of the key ways to do that, of course, is to take the comfort level out of being too compliant with the existing way of doing business or hiding behind the rules, referred to by Dietrich Dorner as "crippling conservatism," which restricts one's options.[7] Here are some ways to encourage a certain degree of anxiety and tension to further creativity:

- Give visibility about the project's progress by reviewing repeatedly one or two key metrics at every meeting.
- Have other team members serve as devil's advocates to question prevailing thinking.
- Have people become responsible for complete deliverables.
- Mention at meetings any potential problems or issues looming in the background that could negatively affect the project.

Establish Priorities

Priority setting provides an excellent means to accomplish both concentration along with anxiety and tension. Priorities tell the team where to focus; they also provide high drama by demonstrating impacts if they fail to achieve them. Of course, the priorities must be realistic, based upon constraints, such as time and money. Setting deadlines for those priorities more often than not builds anxiety and tension in a meaningful, constructive manner. However, unrealistic deadlines imposed from elsewhere will inhibit creativity, and the same goes for vague ones. A balance is necessary. Dietrich Dorner says that the propensity to solve a problem sooner rather than later leads to making incremental mistakes that accumulate. This behavior is reflective of not setting specific goals, that is, being too broad.[8] Consequently, a vague goal or goals serve as criteria that make it difficult to assess progress.[9]

Here are some ways to establish priorities to further creativity:

- Have team members participate in determining and assessing priorities.
- Provide continual feedback on achieving priorities.

- Show the relationship of project activities to the higher organization's activities at team meetings.

Encourage Diversity

Most people mistakenly believe that diversity centers on race and religion. This perception is shortsighted. Diversity also includes peoples' different thinking styles. Why is this important? Different thinking styles encourage dialog, assuming everyone feels free to express themselves; helps in raising questions or issues people have seldom, if ever, thought about due to different perspectives; and helps to overcome groupthink. In other words, diversity can cause people to think outside the box by providing perspectives, even if they seem out of this world. The best way to achieve diversity is to enhance creativity by avoiding too many people of the same personality being on the team and then determining the other personality types needed to provide a balance on a team.[10]

The best approach to encourage diversity in thinking is to bring on board people with fresh knowledge and experience. All too often, leaders pick people like themselves, from similar looks to the same ways of thinking. While such selection criteria may make cooperation and communication easier, the reality is that creativity gets hurt simply because people will find it difficult to think outside the box, making it unlikely for someone to raise questions challenging basic assumptions, thoughts, approaches, and so on. People with fresh knowledge and experience can upset this tendency. Their knowledge and experience can shake up the modus operandi by asking, perhaps indirectly, "Why are we doing it this way?" New knowledge and experiences serve as catalysts for creative thinking by shaking up the thinking gene pool.

Here are some ways to encourage diversity to further creativity:

- Change working relationships among team members from time to time.
- Have people from outside the organization join the project team.
- Mix and match personality types on various tasks and deliverables.
- Seek people for their expertise to participate on the project on an ad hoc basis.
- Seek people with varied backgrounds from outside the project to participate to give a different perspective.

- Seek speakers to come in to address topics that are tangentially related to problems and issues occurring on the project.
- Use personality assessment tools to determine different personality types needed on the project.

Build and Maintain Trust

Trust is essential for creativity. When trust is broken, either with peers or superiors, then all else breaks down, for example, communications, esprit de corps, and collaboration. People will resist sharing their ideas for discussion because some others might use them as tools to ridicule or embarrass. People might also be resistant to sharing their ideas because of the fear that someone might take credit for their ideas. Trust in a creative environment is best engendered and maintained when management overtly recognizes and rewards creativity. This also includes whether or not the creative project is successful. Being creative takes considerable courage and risk, and when breaching trust, creativity quickly goes to the wayside. The pressure is so intense in the corporate world, observes David Whyte, that saying "yes" can become career limiting even though "no" may be the right answer.[11]

Here are some ways to build and maintain trust to further creativity:

- Be accessible to team members at all times.
- Emphasize the need to share information, issues, and expertise.
- Encourage people to seek help if they have a problem.
- Share recognition.

Support People's Growth

It is human nature that, after a while, people become restless. They become dissatisfied with their environment and themselves for many reasons. They have to grow. Keeping the status quo may make some people happy; with others it doesn't. David Whyte cites how the famous John Sculley of Apple Computer asked employees to unleash their creative energy in exchange for a corporate contract that provides material comfort. Whyte sees danger in this perspective because it requires one to submit to another person or organization's dreams unless the former can become in sync with the latter. Otherwise, a person submits to the desire of the system in exchange for giving up one's own dreams.[12] Hardly a situation that allows people to grow in a free, open environment. The trade-off becomes one of security and innovation.[13] Creativity involves people of a restless nature. They want to have new experiences to keep their minds and spirit alive. People who are not creative or deemphasize creativity cannot understand this restlessness. To keep creative people engaged and willing to remain, they require opportunities for growth, especially in the form of creative endeavors. They often need more mental stimulus, that is, giving them greater challenges sparks their creativity. They need that feeling of continuous growth; otherwise, stagnation occurs and they will move on.[14] Here are some ways to support people's growth to further creativity:

- Allow individuals to experiment more frequently to address a problem or issue.
- Allow people to attend training sessions relevant to the project.
- Enable people to come up their own solutions to problems or issues.
- Encourage cross-training.
- Remove or lessen the impact of bureaucratic controls on individuals and the entire team.

Encourage Ownership

This requirement covers not only the project, but also its deliverables. Without a sense of ownership, people will be likely not to fully engage because the work is too extraneous; in other words, it lacks the personal touch. It feels like someone else's work, not theirs. There must be that emotional component if that emotional commitment becomes a reality. If the emotional component lies dormant, it can cloud our spirit and judgment.[15] Large projects tend to reflect this situation; the product is so immense in size and complexity that even a major contribution to its success can seem miniscule, even meaningless. Even under this circumstance, it is important to encourage ownership so people feel compelled to apply their creativity. If they invest their own time, energy, and emotion, the chances increase for creative contributions because of a sense of ownership.

Here are some ways to encourage ownership to further creativity:

- Have individuals report on performance for their respective responsibilities.
- Have people plan their own responsibilities' dates of completion.
- Have team members participate in the overall planning of a project.

Stress Communications

This requirement is more than just talking or sending emails; it is an exchange of ideas in a way that encourages further discussion. People begin to ask for feedback as well as insights on how to improve their creative output. Others feel comfortable giving feedback. The exchange occurs up and down the hierarchy as well as laterally among peers. Ongoing communications also help to identify flaws and explore different ways to improve as long as, of course, people can keep their egos in check.

Here are some ways to stress communications to further creativity:

- Communicate frequently on performance status.
- Encourage greater sharing of information, problems, issues, and so on.
- Encourage participation in the development and review of reports and other project documents.
- Encourage team members to reach out to peers for insights on addressing problems or issues.
- Provide templates for sharing information, for example, reports.
- Provide the tools to enable sharing locally and with team members at remote locations.

Emphasize Coordination

Most organizations today require applying multiple skills to roll out a product or service. Due to the growth of technology and expansion of our knowledge in many different fields, coordination among all specialties becomes absolutely critical in a creative environment. While exceptions exist, most creative endeavors involve people participating with different technical skills that necessitate working together to deliver a product or service. The effectiveness of coordination and communication can make the difference between success and failure. Therefore, creativity requires people working together as a team, contrary to the frequent perception that creative people must always work alone.[16] Complexity is associated with the number of interdependent variables involved. This complexity, observes Dietrich Dorner, makes it difficult to act independently, especially in a complex system, because the variables are interrelated to a degree, causing side effects that have consequences that must be dealt with at different levels of abstraction, for example, subsystems and the entire system.[17]

Here are some ways to emphasize coordination to further creativity:

- Assign people to work jointly on a set of tasks or deliverables.
- Conduct meetings requiring people to interact with others to address a problem or issue.
- Publish weekly and two-week look-ahead reports so stakeholders can see what is and will be happening.

Relax Rules and Procedures

Nothing can stifle creativity more than burdensome bureaucratic rules and procedures. Creativity requires freedom to experiment and think, meaning not being unimpeded by constraints from bureaucratic overhead. While rules, procedures, and so on are necessary, they often become a hindrance rather than an aid when it comes to creativity. David Goleman, in *The Creative Spirit*, discusses the work of Dr. Amabile on the topic of "creative killers" in children. Some of these killers include surveillance, overcontrol, and restricting choice, which often exist in the work environment.[18] Too much bureaucracy cannot help but stifle creativity, says David Whyte, likening corporations to acting as a parent controlling and providing everything through rules and procedures.[19] Creative conditions necessitate judicial application of rules, procedures, and so on. Short of doing something illegal or unethical, applying rules and procedures should depend upon enabling creativity while simultaneously ensuring some consistent behavior with the parent organization. The result may be looser managerial oversight so creativity can flourish.

Here are some ways to relax rules and procedures to further creativity:

- Distinguish between what rules, procedures, and so on are more important than others.
- Place most emphasis on completing the project over satisfying administrative requirements.
- Shield team members from complying with administrative requests.

Align Individual and Organizational Goals and Objectives

Because creative people and groups thrive on independence, a tendency may arise that is something akin to an unaligned two-layered cake; in other words, the top layer does not line up with the bottom layer.

Creativity can result in people doing activities that fail to further the goals and objectives of the parent organization. To ensure alignment, creative activities should further the goals and objectives of the parent organization. Otherwise, creative talents and energies will be dissipated and creative activities will not likely add value.[20] A systems perspective works best to understand how everything relates in an organization because the world, according to Dietrich Dorner, consists of many systems with interrelationships.[21]

Here are some ways to align individual and organizational goals and objectives to further creativity:

- Allow individuals to select activities on which to work.
- Have team members participate in planning.
- Hold one-on-one sessions with team members to ascertain whether their motivational needs are being met jointly with that of the project.

Allow for Risk Taking

Creativity requires taking calculated chances against the status quo. The odds often favor the status quo, not creativity. Nothing changes unless an allowance for risk taking exists. If everyone is expected to follow orders, comply with rules, and maintain routine behavior, then creativity will likely have a low priority. Leadership needs to permit risk taking in the hope that the organization adapts and survives changing circumstances. Risk taking, in other words, creates new products and services that allow organizations to continue to survive.[22] But taking a risk requires setting the environment to enable creativity to happen; otherwise, people may be reluctant to take a risk simply because of the ramifications. As mentioned earlier, the warmth of creative risk can result in an unintended consequence—getting burned.[23] Risk taking must not only be allowed; it must also be rewarded. Rewards should exist for success and failure to communicate to everyone that risk taking is an important value in any organization. These rewards, of course, are positive, not negative, such as punishment. By rewarding risk taking, leadership is communicating to everyone that it embraces taking calculated chances. Otherwise, people will avoid it.[24] The consequence can cool the fire in the belly without the same assurance of protection. In other words, it may mean losing our protective cover when being creative.[25] The potential for failure can be real or imagined, which can cause people to become conservative to the point of doing nothing risky and creativity stagnating. Our sense of mastery becomes shattered because of our limited knowledge, which in turn makes us fearful of our limitations. Failure can result due to our limitations in understanding circumstances, in turn causing us to proceed cautiously.[26]

Here are some ways to allow for and reward risk taking to further creativity:

- Demonstrate support for failure; for example, congratulate people for tackling a tough activity and failing.
- Give visibility to any risk-taking efforts on the project, such as giving presentations on progress at team meetings.
- Perform a lessons-learned session after each high-risk activity is completed.
- Protect risk takers using positive incentives on the project, for example, presentations on progress before team members and senior management.
- Recognize risk taking, whether successful or unsuccessful.
- Remove any administrative obstacles impeding risk taking.

Allow Time for Problem or Issue Definition

According to Western tradition, say scholars, the emphasis is on providing a solution as quickly as possible. While it may fix a problem in the short term, such a solution is often not well thought out and may actually worsen the problem in the long run. Whether called a patch, a fix, or band-aid, a short-term approach is reactive and may appear creative, when in reality it is not.

It makes greater sense, from a creativity perspective, to spend more time up front to define a problem and to really understand its causes. Most problems and issues do not present an immediate threat unless they deal with life safety. Goal setting enables reducing complexity by focusing on what we hope to achieve.[27] Then the opportunity arises to allow developing truly creative solutions that address the source of a problem or issue rather than its symptoms. The challenge, of course, is for people to patiently work to define a problem or issue when creating because of the fun and tangible feedback when developing the solution. Considerable willpower is required, whether by one person or an entire team, to spend time up front to perform good problem definition.

Here are some ways to allow time for problem or issue definition to further creativity:

- Involve more than one person in defining a problem or issue to ensure a wider perspective.
- Provide time for defining a problem or issue.
- Revisit the definition frequently to avoid having it be the focus of activities occurring on the project.
- Seek consensus over the definition of a problem or issue before determining any solution.

Provide Opportunities to Create

Opportunities to create are small and incremental in scope. The big-bang type of creative opportunities are the most challenging and rewarding experiences. Such opportunities are usually filled with high drama. Most creative people will naturally gravitate to such opportunities. Unfortunately, many organizations do not screen people to assign them to such endeavors. Many creative people, even with the requisite skills, are left to sit on the sidelines because management has its own pet problems or issues. The result is that creative people take flight, leaving behind others whose skills are more aligned with trouble fixing and other maintenance orientations. Organizations must identify the truly creative people and provide them with opportunities to tackle highly creative projects.[28] Here are some ways to provide opportunities to create that will further additional creativity:

- Allow team members to broaden their knowledge and experience to discover more creative ways to perform project work.
- Encourage people to look for opportunities to be creative rather than wait.
- Identify and highlight problems or issues to address and ask for volunteers.
- Provide some downtime to allow the subconscious to work.

Broaden People's Knowledge and Experience

Studies have demonstrated that one of the most prevalent characteristics of creative people is their broad knowledge base and wide range of many different experiences. These people use that background to come up with truly creative solutions. A major reason is that they do not have what some people refer to as *hardening of the synapses*. These people keep their mind open to different stimulations and recognize that one size does not fit all. The best way to encourage open-mindedness is to encourage people to expand their knowledge and experiences in a way that encourages developing creative solutions to problems and issues.[29] David Whyte quotes William Blake in a way that demonstrates the importance of overcoming a narrow perspective:

> If the doors of perception were cleansed everything would appear to man as it is, infinite.
>
> For man has closed himself up, till he sees all things thro' chinks of his narrow cavern.[30]

Dietrich Dorner warns against the danger of nervously reducing the operations of a system to what he refers to as "reductive hypothesis." He observes that such a hypothesis may result in incomplete assessments that could be proven incorrect.[31] He also notes that many people do what they can to further support a reductive hypothesis by disregarding information not in line with its assumptions, thereby giving a false sense of superiority.[32]

Here are some ways to broaden people's knowledge and experience to further creativity:

- Conduct cross-training.
- Encourage people to look at other projects that have handled similar problems or issues.
- Encourage people to share knowledge and experiences on the existing and other projects.
- Have two or more people who have a diversified background work jointly on a task.
- Provide broad-based training.

Counter Groupthink

One of the biggest challenges to creativity is groupthink. People are as much social animals as they are individualists; sometimes the former can smother the latter, causing them to subordinate their thoughts and opinions to get along with others. People then begin to think alike, even to deny reality. While it is important for everyone to get along, creativity can suffer as people suspend their critical judgment and subordinate their ideas to avoid punishment. Every effort should be made to diversify people on the team based upon knowledge and experiences, and counter the dominance of certain personalities. Not an easy task, as Dietrich Dorner observes, because experts tend to reinforce each other's thinking, which can result in conformance in thought and suppression of criticism, also known as groupthink.[33] Here are some ways to counter groupthink to further creativity:

- Bring in consultants from outside the project team.
- Have every decision identify potential pitfalls that accompany it.
- Hire people with diversified backgrounds, including personality types.
- Select someone at team meetings to play the devil's advocate.

Encourage Transformational Leadership

Everyone on a team has the potential to be a leader. Under most circumstances, certain individuals will emerge as leaders while previous ones become followers for the good of the group. Truly creative groups allow everyone the opportunity to lead their members. This leadership can be either transactional or transformational. *Transactional leadership* is doing the routine tasks that keep the group performing; their tasks are managerial in nature. *Transformational leadership* is taking risks that involve change; these tasks deal more with chance and are often associated with creativity simply because they challenge the status quo. Creative teams, however, need both types of leadership. Transactional leadership keeps the team functioning; transformational leadership does the creative work. The challenge is ensuring that transactional and transformational leadership work together, not operating at cross-purposes.[34] Here are some ways to encourage transformational leadership to further creativity:

- Acknowledge that every project requires both types of leadership.
- Make the distinction between transformational and transactional activities.
- Recognize publicly that transformational leadership has an inherent risk that transactional leadership does not.

CONCLUSION

A good body of knowledge exists on what it takes to set the stage in a work environment to allow creativity to blossom. Unfortunately, a lot of understanding exists but very little action is taken. There seem to be more pressing concerns. Everyone agrees that creativity is important and, in the meantime, other concerns or issues seem to eclipse it in importance. It is small wonder that creativity remains in short supply despite everyone embracing it. Project managers must take the initiative to set the stage for creativity, and ultimately innovation, to become a major focus of their projects or its probability will be low.

Getting Started Checklist

Question	Yes	No
1. Have you determined which of the following actions (or all) you will do to engender a creative environment for your project?		
Establish a receptive audience.		
Make training available.		
Grant necessary access to data and tools.		
Concentrate creative energy.		
Encourage a certain degree of anxiety and tension.		
Establish priorities.		
Encourage diversity.		
Build and maintain trust.		
Bring on board people with fresh knowledge and experience.		
Support people's growth.		
Encourage ownership.		
Stress communications.		
Emphasize coordination.		
Relax rules, procedures, and so on.		
Align individual and organizational goals and objectives.		
Allow for risk taking.		
Reward risk taking.		
Allow time for problem or issue definition.		
Provide opportunities to create.		
Broaden people's knowledge and experience.		
Counter groupthink.		
Encourage transformational leadership.		
Establish a receptive audience.		
Make training available.		

Getting Started Checklist

Question	Yes	No
Grant access to do their job.		
Grant access to the necessary tools.		
Concentrate energy.		
Encourage a certain degree of anxiety and tension.		
Establish priorities.		
Encourage diversity.		
Build and maintain trust.		
Support people's growth.		
Encourage ownership.		
Stress communications.		
Emphasize coordination.		
Relax rules, procedures, and so on.		
Align individual and organizational goals and objectives.		
Allow for risk taking.		
Allow time for problem or issue definition.		
Provide opportunities to create.		
Broaden people's knowledge and experience.		
Counter groupthink.		
Encourage transformational leadership.		

2. If applicable, select the specific action you will take to accomplish the following:

Establish a receptive audience:

- Apply stakeholder management (e.g., understand interests, concerns, and so on).
- Communicate continuously about key activities on the project.
- Encourage participation by key stakeholders on activities involving creativity.
- Share information about progress of creative endeavors.
- Other:

Make training available:

- Apply the buddy system to work on activities requiring some transfer of skills and knowledge.
- Communicate best practices from other organizations.
- Exploit the use of all training media, e.g., CD-ROM training.
- Provide cross-training.
- Share lessons learned from creative activities on other projects.
- Other:

Grant access to data to do their job

- Conduct frequent data-sharing sessions.

(Continued)

Getting Started Checklist

Question	Yes	No

- Establish a repository of data to which team members have open access.
- Provide people with the tools to access applicable data.
- Reduce the number of controls restricting access to data.
- Other:

Grant access to necessary tools
- Provide tools adhering to common standards.
- Provide tools with the most current capabilities.
- Pursue cross-training on using tools.
- Reduce the number of controls restricting the use of tools other than for private application.
- Other:

Concentrate creative energy
- Ask continually at meetings whether the topic under discussion helps further the goals of the project.
- Have team members participate in defining and planning the project.
- Have team members ask for creative insights from others on how to address a problem or issue.
- Review the goals of the project at team meetings.

Encourage a certain degree of anxiety and tension
- Give visibility about the project's progress by reviewing repeatedly one or two key metrics at every meeting.
- Have other team members serve as a devil's advocate to question prevailing thinking.
- Have people become responsible for complete deliverables.
- Mention at meetings potential problems or issues looming in the background that could negatively affect the project.
- Other:

Establish priorities
- Have team members participate in determining and assessing priorities.
- Provide continual feedback on achieving priorities.
- Show the relationship of project activities to the activities of the higher organization at team meetings.
- Other:

Encourage diversity
- Change working relationships among team members from time to time.
- Mix and match personality types on various tasks and deliverables.
- Seek people for their expertise to participate on the project on an ad hoc basis.

Getting Started Checklist

Question	Yes	No

- Seek people with varied backgrounds from outside the project to participate to give a different perspective.
- Seek speakers to come in to address topics that are tangentially related to problems and issues occurring on the project.
- Use personality assessment tools to determine different personality types needed on the project.
- Have people from outside the organization join the project team.
- Other:

Build and maintain trust

- Be accessible to team members at all times.
- Emphasize the need to share information, issues, and expertise.
- Encourage people to seek help if they have a problem.
- Share recognition.
- Other(s):

Support people's growth

- Allow individuals to experiment more frequently to address a problem or issue.
- Allow people to attend training sessions relevant to the project.
- Enable people to come up their own solutions to problems or issues.
- Encourage cross-training.
- Remove or lessen the impact of bureaucratic controls on individuals and the entire team.
- Other:

Encourage ownership

- Have individuals report on performance for their respective responsibilities.
- Have people plan their own responsibilities' dates of completion.
- Have team members participate in the overall planning of a project.
- Other:

Stress communications

- Communicate frequently on performance status.
- Encourage greater sharing of information, problems, issues, and so on.
- Encourage participation in the development and review of reports and other project documents.
- Encourage team members to reach out to peers for insights on addressing problems or issues.

(Continued)

Getting Started Checklist

Question	Yes	No
• Provide templates for sharing information (e.g., reports).		
• Provide the tools to enable sharing locally and with team members at remote locations.		
• Other:		
Emphasize coordination		
• Assign people to work jointly on a set of tasks or deliverables.		
• Conduct meetings requiring people to interact with others to address a problem or issue.		
• Publish weekly and two-week look-ahead reports so stakeholders can see what is and will be happening.		
• Other:		
Relax rules, procedures, and so on		
• Distinguish between which rules and procedures are more important than others.		
• Place more emphasis on completing the project rather than satisfying administrative requirements.		
• Shield team members from complying with administrative requests.		
• Other:		
Align individual and organizational goals and objectives		
• Allow individuals to select activities on which to work.		
• Have team members participate in planning.		
• Hold one-on-one sessions with team members to ascertain whether their motivational needs are being met jointly with that of the project.		
• Other:		
Allow for risk taking		
• Demonstrate support for failure (e.g., congratulate people for tackling a tough activity and failing).		
• Give visibility to any risk-taking efforts on the project, such as giving presentations on progress at team meetings.		
• Perform a lessons-learned session after each high-risk activity completes.		
• Remove any administrative obstacles impeding risk taking.		
• Protect risk takers using positive incentives on the project (e.g., presentations on progress before team members and senior management).		
• Recognize risk taking, whether successful or unsuccessful.		
• Other:		
Allow time for problem or issue definition		
• Involve more than one person in defining a problem or issue to ensure a wider perspective.		

Getting Started Checklist

Question	Yes	No
• Provide time for defining a problem or issue.		
• Revisit the definition frequently to avoid having it be the focus of activities occurring on the project.		
• Seek consensus over the definition of a problem or issue before determining any solution.		
• Other:		
Provide opportunities to create		
• Allow team members to broaden their knowledge and experience to discover more creative ways to perform project work.		
• Encourage people to look for opportunities to be creative rather than wait.		
• Identify and highlight problems or issues to address and ask for volunteers.		
• Provide some downtime to allow the subconscious to work.		
• Other:		
Broaden people's knowledge and experience		
• Conduct cross-training.		
• Encourage people to look at other projects that have handled similar problems or issues.		
• Encourage people to share knowledge and experiences on the existing and other projects.		
• Have two or more people who have a diversified background work jointly on a task.		
• Provide broad-based training.		
• Other:		
Counter groupthink		
• Bring in consultants from outside the project team.		
• Have every decision identify potential pitfalls that accompany it.		
• Hire people with a diversified background, including personality types.		
• Select someone at team meetings to play the devil's advocate.		
• Other:		
Encourage transformational leadership		
• Acknowledge that every project requires both types of leadership.		
• Make the distinction between transformational and transactional activities.		
• Recognize publicly that transformational leadership has an inherent risk that transactional leadership does not.		
• Other:		

ENDNOTES

1. Daniel Goleman, Paul Kaufman, and Michael Ray, *The Creative Spirit* (New York: Dutton, 1992), p. 130.
2. James M. Higgins, *Innovate or Evaporate* (Winter Park, FL: The New Management Publishing Company, 1995), p. 269.
3. Goleman, Kaufman, and Ray, *The Creative Spirit*, p.107–110, 306.
4. Dietrich Dorner, *The Logic of Failure* (Cambridge, MA: Perseus Books, 1996), p. 99.
5. David Whyte, *The Heart Aroused* (New York: Doubleday, 1994), p. 96.
6. Whyte, *The Heart Aroused*, p. 76.
7. Dorner, *The Logic of Failure*, p. 45.
8. Dorner, *The Logic of Failure*, p. 7.
9. Dorner, *The Logic of Failure*, p. 61.
10. Goleman, Kaufman, and Ray, *The Creative Spirit*, p.127.
11. Whyte, *The Heart Aroused*, p. 143.
12. Whyte, *The Heart Aroused*, p. 78.
13. Whyte, *The Heart Aroused*, p. 79.
14. Goleman, Kaufman, and Ray, *The Creative Spirit*, p.140.
15. Whyte, *The Heart Aroused*, p. 92.
16. Goleman, Kaufman, and Ray, *The Creative Spirit*, p.121.
17. Dorner, *The Logic of Failure*, p. 76.
18. Goleman, Kaufman, and Ray, *The Creative Spirit*, p. 61–62.
19. Whyte, *The Heart Aroused*, p. 83.
20. Higgins, *Innovate or Evaporate*, p. 256.
21. Dorner, *The Logic of Failure*, p. 5.
22. Higgins, *Innovate or Evaporate*, p. 302.
23. Whyte, *The Heart Aroused*, p. 76.
24. Higgins, *Innovate or Evaporate*, pp. 261, 304.
25. Whyte, *The Heart Aroused*, p. 85.
26. Dorner, *The Logic of Failure*, p. 69.
27. Dorner, *The Logic of Failure*, p. 43.
28. Goleman, Kaufman, and Ray, *The Creative Spirit*, p. 106.
29. Higgins, *Innovate or Evaporate*, p. 307.
30. Whyte, *The Heart Aroused*, p. 131.
31. Dorner, *The Logic of Failure*, p. 90.
32. Dorner, *The Logic of Failure*, p. 92.
33. Dorner, *The Logic of Failure*, pp. 33–34.
34. Higgins, *Innovate or Evaporate*, p. 241.

6

Common Creativity Tools and Techniques

INTRODUCTION

There are literally hundreds of techniques for enabling teams and individuals to create in their work when supporting projects. In this chapter, some of the more common ones are covered in one of three categories: individual, group, or combination.

Before discussing each technique or approach, keep the following points in mind:

- First, the techniques and approaches described do not make anyone creative. They simply serve as enablers or catalysts for people to create. Creativity comes from the individual, not the technique or tool.
- Second, applying the techniques often requires several attempts before creative ideas begin to flow. Often, there is a learning curve with the techniques before a comfort level settles. With experience comes the opportunity to employ an approach or technique more efficiently and effectively.
- Third, people will find that they are more comfortable with one technique or approach over another because their personality is more conducive to it. This situation may be the case even though two or more techniques can generate the same results.
- Fourth, applying a technique or approach should be easy. An individual or group should not have to worry more about following the rules, so to speak, than being creative. The technique or approach should focus on producing creative results, not how to satisfy its requirements.

- Finally, people have preferential modes for processing data and information and generating creative, innovative results. These four modes are visual (right), auditory (hearing), tactile (touch, also known as haptics), kinesthetic (body movement), and multisensory (e.g., tactile and auditory). A person's preferred mode is likely to determine the technique or approach selected.

COMMON APPROACHES AND TECHNIQUES

Brainstorming

This technique serves as a basis for many other similar techniques and is commonly used to generate ideas in a group. Brainstorming is a facilitated group session that encourages the free generation of creative ideas to solve a problem or provide alternative solutions. This technique has been around for quite a while. Nonetheless, it has been misinterpreted and abused.

Brainstorming offers two main benefits. One benefit is that it can generate many ideas in a relatively short period of time. Another one is that it allows piggybacking one idea off another to generate more. Yet another is that it is a great technique to build esprit de corps.

Unfortunately, brainstorming can also have huge negative results if not conducted correctly. One downside is that, if not facilitated well, group-think and other group dysfunctions can inhibit group discussion, thereby affecting the number and quality of ideas generated. Finally, if facilitated incorrectly, a few individuals can dominate a session. Others may yield to them by not being fully engaged or accepting responsibility for the results.

Keep in mind the following when employing brainstorming:

1. Restrict the size of the group to a manageable level. Ideally, the size should be restricted to three to ten people; it is best around five to seven people. Too many people, that is, more than ten for example, can make it difficult for some individuals to overcome their fear of group pressure.
2. Remember that a group discussion, such as a staff meeting, is not a good venue for brainstorming. A senior manager running a meeting who wants ideas generated will only cause people to mimic the boss or restrict, consciously or subconsciously, their ideas, or "massage" them to reduce value or impact.

3. Restrict the length of time for generating ideas. For example, a four-hour marathon brainstorming session will only jade people. It is better to have shorter sessions for brainstorming, such as two or three thirty- to forty-minute sessions on a topic rather than one long two- to four-hour session.

4. Assign roles. Assign a facilitator and a scribe. The facilitator should be someone who does not have a vested interest in the outcome of the brainstorming session. This person should have good interpersonal skills, such as effective listening and presentation. The scribe should have good communication skills, such as listening and writing, but should not need to participate during the session.

5. Obtain group agreement on the topic to address. The best way is to write the topic on a black or white board or easel pad. Periodically review the description to keep the team focused and able to generate ownership. The best description is one that is open-ended to avoid restricting the flow of ideas.

6. Use an idea to generate subsequent ones. This process is called *piggybacking*. It increases the quantity of ideas but enables leveraging one idea to generate a better one.

7. Compile the ideas and group them, if possible. Then, have the group determine a way to eliminate ideas considered irrelevant.[1]

Some ways to use brainstorming on a project include:

- Determining responses to a specific risk
- Developing potential solutions to a problem, for example, inaccurate reports
- Generating an activity listing
- Identifying risks
- Identifying stakeholders
- Looking for opportunities to improve processes

Role Playing

Role playing is an excellent technique to understand another person's perspective and to acquire new insights. It involves putting a person in another person's "shoes;" understanding the thoughts, emotions, values, beliefs, and so on; and then using that information to attain greater insight into the way a person thinks.

Keep the following in mind when applying role playing:

1. Determine the strategy and goals of the role-playing exercise. Do the same for each role. Both need direction if role playing is to demonstrate value to the project and the individual.
2. As the role playing progresses, have someone capture notes. It is very difficult to capture notes while simultaneously participating in a role. The key is to focus on executing the strategy and achieving the goals of role playing. Running the camera, for example, and acting usually does not go well when the person is doing both tasks.
3. Determine the approach to take when role playing. Contrary to popular belief, participants do not have to *act* the part. They simply have to *think* it. For instance, people can sit around a conference table and discuss a problem or issue from the perspective of a specific role.[2]

Some ways to use role playing on a project include:

- Building a communications matrix
- Conducting an impact analysis for process improvements
- Developing meaningful metrics for reports
- Generating a responsibility matrix
- Identifying ways to improve individual and team performance
- Identifying who should review and approve specific deliverables
- Understanding stakeholder perspectives, needs, and expectations

Tree Diagram

A tree, or hierarchy diagram, is a quality tool to display data and information at various levels of abstraction. Some levels consist of more detail at lower levels than at higher levels. Remember that a tree diagram will not make anyone creative; it is just a way to organize data in a grouping or hierarchy. Arranging the data and information enables greater understanding of a problem or issue and then deriving one or more creative ideas from what they see in the tree diagram.

Keep the following in mind when using a tree diagram:

1. A hierarchy chart helps to display data and information in a way that shows different levels of abstraction; that is, the top level is more modular in scope and summarizes the entries below it. This

arrangement forces a pattern of perception that may constrain creative thinking because it displays information in a particular order.

2. The construction of the tree diagram can do the opposite—encourage creativity. By going through the exercise of creating the diagram, people will generate ideas that they may not have thought of earlier.[3] The subconscious seems to work frequently in the background and generates a creative idea while a person is consciously doing something else, whether related or unrelated.[4]

Some ways to use a tree diagram on a project include:

- Building an organization chart
- Building an organizational breakdown structure
- Developing a work breakdown structure
- Grouping issues into categories
- Grouping risks into categories
- Performing product analysis

Delphi Technique

The Delphi technique was developed by the Rand Corporation. It is predicated on the notion that consensus can be achieved via independent experts using a submitted questionnaire and then mailing it repeatedly after collecting responses each time until consensus is achieved. Although a creativity technique, it is an even more excellent way to select one creative idea among several.

Keep the following in mind when applying the Delphi technique:

1. The experts do not talk with each other. Allowing them to do so will skew results. The process must remain noninteractive. The goal is to encourage people to think independently, while at the same time achieving consensus.

2. Be patient. It takes effort and time to apply the Delphi technique. The compilation, summarization, and number of iterations can prove burdensome, even frustrating. Some respondents may change their minds entirely while remaining unyielding.

3. Carefully select the experts. The membership in the pool can make a big difference in the results. If membership in the pool is not diversified, biases of members can influence results, often not particularly creatively.[5]

Some ways to use the Delphi technique on a project include:

- Assessing the impact of cost, schedule, and technical constraints
- Estimating probabilities and impacts of risks
- Identifying and evaluating contingency plan
- Identifying and evaluating issues
- Identifying and evaluating risks
- Prioritizing requirements

Fishbone Diagram

Also known as the Ishikawa diagram, this tool is used to determine the sources of a problem, which can lay the groundwork for developing creative ideas. As you would suspect, the fishbone diagram is laid out in the shape of a fish with the problem defined at its head. Along the spine, trailing behind the head, are bones representing each category of contributing issues: materials, manpower, methods, and machines. Using all four categories, the source of the problem can be easily identified. Then, the individual or team can develop ideas to resolve the problem.

Keep in mind the following when developing a fishbone diagram:

1. The fishbone diagram is more for defining the cause of a problem, not generating ideas. However, once the source of a problem is identified, it becomes easier to generate creative ideas to fix it.
2. Be careful not to overanalyze a problem. Fishbone diagrams can easily become elaborate and actually make it more difficult to determine the source of a problem and may actually hinder coming up with creative solutions.[6]

Some ways to use fishbone diagramming on a project include:

- Determining the contributors to poor quality, such as defects
- Identifying causes of deliverable changes
- Identifying the root causes of a process bottleneck
- Performing value analysis
- Removing roadblocks that impede the progress of a project

Brainwriting

This technique is essentially for the faint-hearted who do not want to, or prefer not to participate in a spontaneous group session. Everyone is different in how they approach creating, and brainwriting is another way to accommodate a person's unique style. Brainwriting is just as the name implies. Each person records their ideas on a sheet of paper and then passes it on to the next person for additions or other input. The idea is that one person's thoughts lay the groundwork on which the next person can expand.[7]

Keep the following in mind when applying brainwriting:

1. As mentioned earlier, this approach accommodates people who may not like traditional brainstorming. However, there are others who do. Just be aware of this point. Some people enjoy working alone, for example, while others thrive in a teaming environment.
2. Set a time limit for a person to provide their input on paper. The originator of an idea often takes less time than the subsequent contributors.
3. Ideas must be made public for evaluation. Paper recording can only go so far. Sooner or later, the person who prefers not to participate in group sessions has to do so.

Some ways to use brainwriting on a project include identifying:

- Contents and layout of a war room
- Corrective actions to address a schedule slide
- Cost and schedule metrics
- Key issues
- Opportunities for improving cost and schedule performance
- Potential threats and corresponding strategies for responding to them

Affinity Diagramming

This technique, like many other quality management methods, is useful for logically grouping a wide number of items having similar characteristics. By logically grouping a pile of ideas, it becomes easier to use the diagram to develop creative ideas. For example, it might be easier to identify some patterns that enable developing creative theories about the data; these theories then lend themselves to testing.

Keep in mind the following when using affinity diagrams:

1. Recognize that whatever groupings are used, they are constructs that may not necessarily represent reality. Keep in mind that just about everything in nature is not logically grouped; grouping everything is a judgment call. However, groupings might reveal clues about reality because it has become more understandable.
2. The affinity diagram does not guarantee creativity. The user of the affinity diagram still has to come up with creative ideas based upon the data. It provides order to what may seem like a mess, thereby enabling some creative thinking to occur.
3. Use the affinity diagram as a communications technique among the stakeholders. It will help in looking at the data and information and to start exchanging ideas about what stakeholders see.[8]

Some ways to use affinity diagramming on a project include:

- Categorizing issues recorded in an Issues Log
- Categorizing requirements
- Grouping elements in a work breakdown structure
- Placing risks into appropriate categories

Trend Chart

A trend chart, also known as a run chart, plots data over time to reveal a pattern of behavior that could also indicate anomalous behavior. These anomalies may provide fruit for creative thinking. A spike or dip in a trend may indicate that something unique has happened, requiring further investigation.

Keep in mind the following when using a trend chart:

1. The span of time to track data will affect the ease of spotting anomalies. Usually, the longer the time continuum to track, the greater the opportunity to discover an anomaly requiring investigation.
2. Some anomalies are good; the inverse is also true. In the manufacturing environment, an anomaly often threatens productivity and adds costs. In creative environments, an anomaly often serves as a springboard to develop ideas.

3. Compare the spike or dip with a baseline having a normal pattern of behavior. The differences may reveal clues to come up with a creative idea that could improve the overall pattern of behavior.[9]

Some ways to use a trend chart on a project include:

- Identifying whether certain threats are rising or declining over time
- Plotting the number of change requests over time
- Tracking the number of defects over time
- Tracking earned value, such as schedule performance index over time
- Tracking the number of missed milestones over time

Statistical Process Control Chart

Also referred to as an SPC chart, the statistical process control chart is another quality technique that can help enable creativity. Like the trend chart discussed in this chapter, the key is to focus on anomalous data points to provide clues for creative ideas. The SPC chart treats anomalies as something requiring further investigation, often resulting in corrective action. The SPC chart has an upper and lower control limit, and a range above and below the mean. Over time, plots of discrete data points occur. Ideally, these plots all fall around the mean. However, sometimes plots go above or below the range, indicating an anomaly; sometimes seven or more successive plots on either side of the mean exist, also indicating anomalies. These are anomalies that may provide an opportunity to develop creative ideas rather than treating them as "defects."

Keep in mind the following when using SPC charts:

1. Like the trend chart, the span of time is important. Too short of a time span and the opportunity to discover an anomaly is gone. The span of time is a judgment call.
2. Remember that anomalies can be good, but not all are. They simply provide the basis for creative thinking.[10]

Some ways to use a statistical process control chart on a project include:

- Assessing the stability of a specific process
- Recording quality of deliverables to identify anomalous results

- Tracking costs
- Tracking discrete values, such as cost performance index, to determine if expected results are being achieved consistently
- Tracking the effectiveness of a change

Offsite

The offsite is a technique to get a group away from the normal work environment, often for a day or two. It is a way to build esprit de corps; it also allows for people to "let down" and free their creative powers to rise as they tackle burning problems and issues, whether on an intra- or interorganizational level. Teams and subteams work on problems and issues with the purpose of coming up with recommendations, many of which are creative.

Keep in mind the following when conducting an offsite:

1. Define the goals and objectives to achieve at the offsite. The attendees can further define them either before or at the beginning of the offsite.
2. Leave laptops, cell phones, and modern communications media behind. The goal is to remove people from their environment to allow them physical and, just as importantly, mental freedom. If people bring such technology, allocate a certain break time to allow them to return calls or respond to emails. Then, have them turn off the equipment.
3. Be sure to take good notes and publish them. Subsequent meetings should be held to plan and execute recommendations so that the offsite becomes more than a get-together.

Some ways to use an offsite on a project include:

- Engendering greater team building
- Enhancing communications among stakeholders
- Isolating the team from external influences when making key decisions
- Providing a comfortable environment for sharing knowledge, experiences, and insights to address key issues and concerns
- Providing training opportunities

Force Field Analysis

This technique assumes that for every action, one or more counter-actions exist. Using this technique, an idea can be evaluated by the forces that will enhance, as opposed to resist, its implementation. The value of force field analysis is that it helps determine which creative idea has a likelihood of acceptance and what potential constraining or restraining forces need to be dealt with when implementing in the real world.

Keep in mind the following when apply force field analysis:

1. For each idea brainstorm, either alone or with a group, be mindful of the forces or pressures that drive the idea and the counter forces that make implementation a challenge or impossible.
2. If an idea is selected, determine the strategy to make it a reality. Essentially, three strategies exist: (1) enhance the forces to implement an idea, (2) decrease or weaken the counter forces, or (3) combine strategies 1 and 2.
3. Diagram the analysis. Various options are available. The two most common approaches are to develop a T-Table, similar to tables used by accountants, or build a systems diagram showing the relationships between the forces and counter forces.[11]

Some ways to use force field analysis on a project include identifying the forces for and against:

- Adopting a certain risk strategy
- Changing a cost or schedule baseline
- Hiring a consultant
- Implementing a solution to address a specific issue
- Making a process change

Pareto Chart

This chart is used to identify the major causes of problems. The notion is that you can distinguish between what is and is not significant. With that information, identifying the cause of a significant number of problems becomes easier. From a creativity standpoint, the benefit of the technique is that it identifies major problems and then enables developing one or more creative ideas to solve it.

Keep in mind the following when using a Pareto chart:

1. Take an objective approach when collecting data. Avoid the tendency to throw away data that does not meet expectations; to do so will only skew the results. This situation can easily happen inadvertently when scrubbing the data that is used in a Pareto chart.
2. Develop a histogram showing the results. It is easier to see where most of the problems occur. Then, focus on determining the cause of a selected problem and develop creative ideas to solve it.[12]
3. Test the creative idea to see if the problem disappears. The best way to do that is to collect more data after implementing the idea.

Some ways to use a Pareto chart on a project include:

- Determining the major contributors to poor quality, such as defects
- Identifying causes of a change in the specifications
- Identifying roadblocks that impede the progress of a project
- Identifying the root cause of a process bottleneck

Benchmarking

This technique can enhance creativity by comparing the performance of a process to another one to determine its effectiveness and efficiency relative to different organizations. It determines how well your process works in comparison with what is considered best in class. The basis for that comparison is a standard or measure. From a creativity standpoint, it helps identify whether a change is necessary, and if so, what can be learned from other processes that can be adopted.

Keep in mind the following when benchmarking:

1. Determine a population against which to compare data. Often, these are cohorts similar to your organization. Data for similar organizations can be obtained from sources such as the Mayflower Group. While no grouping will be exactly alike, selecting one that is similar to one's own makes the comparison much easier.
2. Determine the standard or measure to conduct the evaluation. Strive to have a quantifiable standard. If qualitative only, then consider using a definitive criterion that everyone can support.

3. Conduct the comparison, looking for opportunities to generate creative ideas. Gaps indicate opportunities to apply creativity that will result in a meaningful change.
4. Apply creativity to improve performance by acting on the identified opportunities to develop creative ideas to improve products or processes, for example.
5. Develop an implementation plan for new ideas. Be sure to include monitoring to determine how well the creative solutions improve performance according to the acceptable standard and adjust accordingly.[13]

Some ways to use benchmarking on a project include:

- Compiling lessons learned and other insights from other projects
- Establishing a baseline or standard to evaluate the performance of the project relative to others
- Identifying better ways to improve processes, such as collecting data and reporting
- Identifying opportunities to reuse part or all of the project management deliverables developed on other projects

Nominal Group Technique

Also referred to as NGT, this technique is a variant of brainstorming. The principal difference is the approach taken. NGT is more structured and is methodical when evaluating ideas. The technique allows a group to generate ideas. Then, the group develops criteria for evaluation and votes for and against ideas based on the criteria.

Keep in mind the following when applying NGT:

1. Make every effort to facilitate the free flow of concepts when conducting NGT. Try to prevent biases, preconceived notions, and other prejudices from influencing the generation of ideas.
2. Determine the agreed-upon criteria to determine which ideas to combine, revise, or remove. The criteria should strive for objectivity. A common method is to have the group determine the criteria. Then the group applies the criteria to the list of ideas via priority voting. The results are then tabulated; only the highest-scoring ideas are chosen.

3. As in brainstorming, select a facilitator and a scribe. They should have the same qualities as outlined in the brainstorming section.[14]

Some ways to use the nominal group technique on a project include:

- Developing and selecting potential solutions to a problem
- Generating and choosing an activity listing
- Identifying and selecting opportunities
- Identifying and selecting threats and strategies for responding to them

Modeling

This technique is used to capture an idea in physical (e.g., prototype) or graphical (e.g., diagram) form. A typical model consists of components, relationships, states (or conditions), signals, and roles that make the idea much more understandable and tangible to the person creating it, and to others. In addition, a model helps identify flaws in an idea, as well as leverage or expand on good ideas.

Keep in mind the following when building models:

1. Consider using other techniques, such as mind mapping, to generate the content of a model. A model takes information from other techniques and creates a more organized view of the idea.
2. Remember that a model is rarely complete. It is a construct that tries to mimic what people know at the time, including what they think are facts and assumptions. By its very nature, a model will never be complete, whether representing something in the real world or a vision. As a model is built, make adjustments, if necessary, as content is confirmed via reviews and evaluations.
3. Try to determine the rules and symbols for the model in advance; however, it is also okay to determine some rules and symbols as the model is being built. Adding other variables to the model may require refining or updating it.
4. Models can take many forms. They can be graphical, such as systems diagrams; prototypes, such as miniversion of a new plane; or mathematical, such as a ratio of radioactive elements in a nuclear explosion. Regardless of form, remember that the model should further understanding and communication.

5. Models can be logical, physical, or both. A logical model is an ideal abstraction of something and mainly represents how the components, relationships, and so on work together. A physical model often reflects the real-world equivalent and eventual implementation of the logical model. Often, only one logical model exists, but multiple physical models can exist to represent different options. The physical model that is eventually chosen is then implemented along with any additional refinements to reflect reality.[15]

Some ways to use modeling on a project include:

- Analyzing bottlenecks in a process
- Building a network diagram
- Conducting what-if analyses
- Documenting processes and procedures
- Performing a quantitative risk analysis
- Visualizing as-is and to-be processes

Mind Mapping

Advocated by Tony Buzan, mind mapping is a technique to identify relationships among concepts. It uses the associative capabilities of the human brain to determine the details of a specific idea. The brain is a neural network of cells; mind mapping capitalizes on that structure to determine linkages among the components that make up an idea.

Keep the following in mind when mind mapping:

1. Select a place that is free of all distractions and is equipped with an easel pad, blackboard, or white board. Also, make sure that multiple color markers are available to draw the mind map.
2. Try to visualize in the mind's eye the subject to address. Be specific enough to be tangible, but not so much so that it restricts the free flow of ideas.
3. Start by drawing a circle in the center of the board or paper. Inside the circle, record the idea with a very short description. Let the mind freely record concepts based upon the central idea, and then link these concepts. Using markers of different colors, identify related concepts and connect them to show relationships. Add descriptions

in the circles and on the connections. The important point is to let the concepts and their relationships flow.

4. Avoid the biggest danger with mind mapping: flow of control. Thinking in terms of flow of control, such as a programming flow chart, will restrict free thinking, which will be reflected in the quality and quantity of concepts and their relationships.

5. Whether doing mind mapping as an individual or group, remember to encourage further concepts using piggybacking or leapfrogging on other concepts. This action will help increase the number of concepts and relationships, which in turn make the idea more thorough and tangible.[16]

Some ways to use mind mapping on a project include:

- Analyzing issues recorded in an issues log
- Collecting ideas and displaying their relationship to solve a scheduling problem
- Identifying all the elements of a work breakdown structure and their relationships to each other
- Identifying and documenting ideas for specific management plans before drafting the plans

Imagineering

Also known as visualization, imagineering is using one's imagination to describe an ideal state for an idea. This ideal state consists of components and their relationships. People can generate different versions or models of this ideal state.

Keep in mind the following when using imagineering:

1. It is one thing to mentally visualize the idea; it is another to write it down. Putting it on paper solidifies the vision and allows for better communication about it. In other words, it becomes tangible.

2. Free the mind, if possible, of all preconceptions, assumptions, and so on that inhibit the ability to imagine something very creative. Doing so is not easy because it requires stepping outside of oneself, so to speak, and seeing the vision in a way that would never seem possible. Repeat: writing it on paper helps one see if the assumptions and preconceptions have surfaced.

3. Try to use imagineering to generate different versions of an idea. Perhaps, for example, change a component's size or purpose or alter some of the relationships and see the effects.

4. As a creative idea is placed into the real world, compare the actual results with the anticipated ones using imagineering. Such action may reveal that an idea was erroneous to some degree or completely out of touch with reality. Modifications may then be necessary.

5. Remember that imagineering works with other techniques. These techniques include modeling, such as prototyping.[17] The other techniques enable using the imagination and churning the vision into something tangible.

Some ways to use imagineering on a project include:

- Capturing the to-be state of a process
- Formulating an ideal response strategy to a high-probability and high-impact risk, should it occur
- Picturing what a deliverable should ideally look like
- Visualizing the outcome of an executive-level status presentation

Lateral Thinking

Edward de Bono is the creator of this approach. It is predicated on the notion that people normally use patterned thinking, which is linear and analytical in orientation. In contrast, lateral thinking encourages the breaking of patterns through synthesis (e.g., combining and recombining to determine different alternatives).

Keep the following in mind when employing lateral thinking:

1. Look for evidence of patterned thinking, such as assumptions treated as facts and adherence to a paradigm or model already in use. Such evidence reveals a person's preferences on how he or she interprets and responds in the real world.

2. Identify any shortcomings. These are opportunities to generate creative solutions. They are usually gaps in patterned thinking.

3. Look at a problem from different angles or perspectives. Do the same with alternatives.

4. Try to break, or step outside, the boundaries of the prevailing mindset that people often follow even without really thinking about it.

Provoke the paradigm by issuing mental challenges (e.g., provocative questions) to its most sacred beliefs, assumptions, and so on.

5. Recognize that the world is mostly shades of gray, not black and white. Gray thinking recognizes that there is no one right answer but multiple ones. The cookie-cutter approach only restricts thinking and, consequently, limits options.

6. Lateral thinking serves as an excellent approach to use with different techniques. For example, lateral thinking can work well with imagineering and modeling.[18]

Some ways to use lateral thinking on a project include taking a cross-functional or interdisciplinary perspective to:

- Improve a process described in a management plan
- Overcome an obstacle impacting cost and schedule performance
- Respond to a risk

Workflow Analysis

This technique entails reviewing a process to determine key elements of information and primary controls regulating its behavior. This analysis helps ascertain opportunities to generate creative solutions that optimize the effectiveness and efficiency of a process. Workflow analysis is essentially, then, a tool to develop creative ideas to enhance process performance.

Keep in mind the following when performing workflow analysis:

1. Document the as-is process. This documentation provides a means to identify opportunities for improvement, such as in the area of time constraints, rules, roles, responsibilities, and cycle time.

2. Use symbols that everyone understands and keep the number to a minimum. A complicated diagram often reflects a lack of true understanding of fundamental issues or represents an opportunity for creative thinking to improve a process. Keep it simple, unless the purpose is to demonstrate that reducing complexity is necessary.

3. After documenting the as-is and determining opportunities for creative thinking, develop the to-be process. Any gaps will reflect differences, and just as importantly the benefits, of a new process over the old.[19]

Some ways to use workflow analysis on a project include determining:

- At what points in a project to hire consultants
- Process bottlenecks
- The source of defects
- Under what circumstances senior management should become involved in approving a change

Matrices

These techniques help capture relationships among different variables. These relationships can be between two or more variables. A matrix helps capture considerable data in a compact table and records the different relationships. From a creativity perspective, a matrix helps capture creative solutions under varying circumstances, such as using a design experiment to show that certain conditions in a test will have expected results.

Keep the following in mind when using a matrix:

1. Identify the variables that have a causal or correlative relationship. Each relationship should have a result with some degree of confidence of occurring.
2. Keep the contents of the matrix current. Data in the matrix is often time dependent and circumstances change. Dated contents lessen the value of a matrix during experimentation with the relationships of different variables. In fact, the matrix may have to be revised as tests reveal results that are different than expected.
3. Remember that a matrix represents a known finite universe. It may not capture all the results of a bi- or multivariable relationship.[20]

Some ways to use matrices on a project include:

- Building a communications plan
- Building a responsibility assignment chart
- Comparing expected and actual cost performance results
- Implementing contingency plans under specific circumstances
- Performing a qualitative risk assessment
- Preparing a requirements traceability matrix

Reengineering

This is an approach that seeks to come up with a more efficient and effective process than currently exists. It involves discarding an old process and replacing it with a new one. In theory, it enables breakthrough results in performance.

Keep in mind the following when reengineering:

1. Document the as-is process. Then, collect as much data and information as necessary about the existing process. This data and information will serve as a baseline to compare how the new process enhances efficiency and effectiveness. Also, look for non-value-added areas in an existing process, such as delays, which may reveal opportunities to improve performance.
2. Document the to-be process. Then compare the as-is and to-be processes to ensure actual capture of the improvements as a result of the latter. The to-be processes must demonstrate improvements that replace the status quo of doing business. Keep in mind that significant changes in improvement to warrant the new to-be process will arise. Here is where creativity applies. Using other tools and techniques enables coming up with highly creative, innovative solutions.
3. Conduct the implementation of the to-be process. Expect resistance from some individuals and organizations threatened by the loss of the as-is process. They have probably invested considerable time and effort into building and sustaining the as-is process, which, if it went away, would also threaten them. Often individuals and organizations may exhibit cautionary acceptance, contingent upon the benefits gained by the to-be process.
4. During the implementation of the to-be process, expect to make revisions along the way. Reality will necessitate revisions to the new process as the need to adapt arises. These revisions will be likely to lessen the advantages of the to-be process. Be cognizant of these impacts to address concerns by people who subscribe to the as-is process.

Technically, reengineering is not a creativity technique. However, it provides the opportunity to use several techniques to identify and implement creative ideas that can dramatically change the status quo.[21] Some ways to use reengineering on a project include discarding inefficient or ineffective:

- Processes in management plans and replacing them with completely new ones
- Tools and techniques and replacing them with new ones that enable better performance of existing processes

PDCA Cycle

The Plan-Do-Check-Act (PDCA) cycle, also known as the Deming Wheel, is an approach for solving problems. Its major focus is on incremental continuous improvement. However, it is also useful for implementing new ideas resulting in substantial change. *Plan* is determining the objective; *Do* is executing the plan supporting the objective; *Check* is measuring performance; and *Act* is analyzing results and determining improvements. This cycle continues and is iterative. The PDCA cycle is an excellent approach to determine the effectiveness of a new idea while being implemented in the real world.

Keep in mind the following when applying the PDCA cycle:

1. Define the idea as clearly as possible. It serves as a baseline for how well the idea is implemented.
2. Use the PDCA cycle with other techniques (e.g., force field analysis) to effectively implement an idea.
3. Consistently apply the cycle. Avoid applying it only once. Oftentimes, problems and challenges associated with a new idea do not surface right away. Creative ideas often have long-term consequences, some anticipated and some not.
4. Involve the people who have to implement a new idea. Have them participate in the PDCA cycle. Doing so helps offset resistance that may be directed toward a new idea. When developing a creative idea, a sense of ownership generated during its implementation also proves useful.[22]

Some ways to use the PDCA cycle on a project include evaluating the effectiveness of the following:

- Change to a process
- Risk response
- Scope change
- Solution to resolve a dispute

Scatter Gram

This technique reflects the result of a relationship between two variables. The result is plotted on a graph, demonstrating the causal or correlative relationship between an independent and a dependent variable. To show the measure of central tendency, a line is drawn through the middle of a cluster, indicating the average. While not directly a creativity tool, it does help flag anomalies that provide fruit for creative thinking.

Keep in mind the following when using a scatter gram:

1. Determine a meaningful population. Be sure to make a reasonably intelligent guess when identifying two variables, preferably one being an independent variable and the other a dependent variable. It should be anticipated that the independent and dependent variables have a relationship. During tests, record the results on the graph.
2. Look at the measure of central tendency and draw a line through the clustering. Then look for anomalies, that is, those considerably below or above the measure of central tendency. Such anomalies have the potential to provide insight into new areas.
3. Of course, verify through further testing that a true relationship exists between the two variables. What may appear as a relationship may really be due to an unknown third variable.[23]

Some ways to use a scatter gram on a project include:

- Ascertaining if training on a subject has reduced a learning curve
- Determining the impact of a change in cost and schedule baselines
- Identifying the relationship of two variables involved in making a change to a process

Crawford Slip Technique

This technique is another brainstorming method used to develop creative ideas to solve a problem. Rather than initially having everyone generate ideas as a group, the participants, with the aid of a facilitator, first define a problem. Using a well-defined problem statement, each person records ideas and other supporting thoughts on a slip of paper or note card. Each description should be clear and concise. Then, the slips or cards are compiled, grouped, and summarized to reduce the number of categories. The results are incorporated in a final report.

Keep in mind the following when using the Crawford slip technique:

1. Make sure the problem statement is well defined. If so, people can focus their thoughts; if not, their thinking can go way beyond what was intended.
2. As with other group techniques, select the right people. The right people will encourage greater participation and enable them to focus on a problem.
3. Make sure that everyone records their ideas the same way. Consistency and uniformity will ensure ease of categorizing and summarizing input.[24]

Some ways to use the Crawford slip technique on a project include:

- Defining the cause of a key milestone slide in a schedule and then compiling input from others on ways to take corrective action
- Defining the potential cause of a threat and compiling suggestions for responding to it
- Defining the problem related to a process and then compiling potential improvements

Hypothetical Scenario

Like role playing and contingency planning, hypothetical scenarios can encourage creativity about how to deal with someone or something potentially occurring in the future. One goal is to identify the major facts and data of a situation and determine the possible courses of action to pursue.

Keep in mind the following when using the hypothetical scenario technique:

1. Make the scenario as realistic as possible. A sense of realism prepares participants for a real-life situation, should it occur. Be sure to capture people's thoughts while participating in the scenario, because many creative ideas will be likely to deal with not only future situations, but possibly the current way of doing business.
2. Give people enough latitude and freedom to learn more doing the scenario. Too specific, and it will be difficult for them to exercise their imagination; too general, and they will find it almost too vague a

challenge to address. Encourage team members to generate assumptions and assimilate facts on how they would respond to a scenario.
3. Conduct a lessons-learned session at the conclusion of the scenario.
A lessons-learned session should discuss how they came up with creative ideas as well as what problems or challenges they faced during
the scenario.

Some ways to use a hypothetical scenario technique on a project include:

- Determining the circumstances under which to take corrective
action as opposed to replanning
- Determining the circumstances under which to withdraw funds
from the management reserve
- Identifying contingency plans to respond to events
- Identifying responses to specific risks

Synectics

This technique uses analogies to develop creative ideas. Like brainstorming, it requires suspending judgment, but it also provides a way to select a
solution to a problem or issue.
Keep in mind the following when using synectics:

1. Engage the team members and other stakeholders in the process. This
engagement requires stating a problem clearly and concisely. Multiple
problem statements may be developed until the right one is defined.
2. Stakeholders develop a list of solutions to address a problem. This is
a difficult point in time because people must *want* to suspend their
judgments. After several iterations, the customer chooses the solution.
3. They identify any reservations. The entire process repeats itself, only
to end once the customer is satisfied with the results.
4. Have a list of different analogies available to define the problem and
generate solutions. Analogies can be personal, symbolic, or highly
abstract. The analogy is a key tool in synectics to encourage creative
thinking.
5. Keep the session short, emotional, and rational. During an approximately one-hour session, emotion plays a key role in selecting a
solution, for example, in terms of its characteristics and values.
Criticism is highly encouraged by the session leader, while at the
same time keeping minds positive about a proposed solution.[25]

Some ways to use synectics on a project include:

- Improving cost performance
- Improving performance reporting
- Improving schedule performance
- Resolving issues more quickly and effectively

Storyboarding

This brainstorming technique is useful for generating a list of ideas and evaluating them. The whole notion of storyboarding is to see the interconnectedness of ideas to solve complex problems and enable piggybacking or hitchhiking on ideas. All thinking is captured on paper with columns to record thoughts as they relate to the topic and purpose. Capturing information on paper serves as a basis to create at least four storyboards: (1) for capturing significant ideas to solve the problem; (2) for coming up with subtopics for ideas; (3) for addressing questions related to who, what, and when; and (4) and for communicating, by also answering who, what, and where. Storyboards can be used for multiple purposes: creative thinking to come up with new ideas and critical thinking to evaluate ideas.

Keep in mind the following when using storyboarding:

1. Limit the use of storyboarding. It is an effective yet time-consuming technique. Reserve its use for big problems.
2. Assign roles during the storyboard session. One role is the facilitator, who ensures that the group progresses; another is the scribe, who records results and other group output; and of course, the team itself, which should not exceed eight people.
3. Storyboarding requires a lot of work and effort to apply it successfully. Considerable upfront planning is necessary to ensure that success occurs downstream. Prepare as much as possible prior to conducting this type of session so that people can focus on thinking creatively and critically.[26]

Some ways to use storyboarding on a project include:

- Enhancing the quality of deliverables in a manner that reduces the number of defects

- Identifying and implementing an idea for overcoming potential showstoppers caused by cost and schedule constraints
- Improving processes described in management plans, such as reducing cycle time

Problem Solving

In project management, problem solving is an ongoing process. In many respects, problem solving is the major reason for a project. It often requires coming up with a creative solution. It entails coming up with a targeted, unambiguous solution to a problem or issue.

Keep the following in mind when performing problem solving:

1. Define a problem as clearly as possible before embarking on a solution. This part of problem solving is often overlooked. Too many projects start without a clear idea of what to achieve. Instead, due to management pressure or something else, a project pops up without any real idea of what to fix. If it does fix something, often the result is incomplete or requires rework.
2. Record the assumptions behind the problem being solved. For example, what are the potential causes vis-à-vis the symptoms? What was the event that made everyone aware that a problem existed that needed resolution?
3. After defining the problem, develop a list of potential solutions. Generating solutions can be as creative as defining a problem. Sometimes no one solution can adequately address a problem, but several innovative solutions may do the job.
4. Whether defining a problem or identifying multiple solutions, make every effort to rely on facts and data to come up with results. Frequently, whether intentionally or not, prejudices or biases can influence outcome. Make every effort to avoid such influences when coming up with a creative solution.
5. Develop an implementation plan. A plan is necessary even if nothing happens right away. The plan should follow something similar to the PDCA (Plan-Do-Check-Act) cycle that quality experts often follow. *Plan* is determining what solution to implement; *Do* is implementing a plan to make it a reality; *Check* is measuring the effectiveness of the new solution; and *Act* is taking the data to determine whether improvements are needed.[27]

Some ways to use problem solving on a project include identifying and implementing a solution to the following:

- Process problem
- Reoccurring defect repair
- Schedule performance problem
- Workaround

Compare and Contrast

Not necessarily a technique for generating ideas, it is however an excellent way to choose and evaluate ideas. Whether in a T-format or a matrix, comparing and contrasting ideas allow seeing the pluses and minuses. The key is to take a systematic approach toward weighing the pros and cons.

Keep the following in mind when comparing and contrasting ideas:

1. Establish a weighting criterion to determine which ideas can help in solving, for example, a problem or issue. The criteria will also help minimize the tendency to allow biases to influence selecting an idea.
2. Have an outside person or group review the results. Outside reviews help ensure that nothing is overlooked in the weighting and that any biases are caught.

Some ways to use compare and contrast on a project include:

- Comparing cost and schedule baselines to actual performance
- Conducting a lessons-learned session using examples from other projects
- Looking at other projects to see how to improve their execution
- Matching success criteria at a specific point in time with that identified in the project charter
- Reviewing the schedule performance of other projects to assess the project's current performance at a specific point in time

Analogies, Metaphors, and Similes Thinking

The use of analogies, metaphors, and similes are excellent techniques to generate creative ideas. An *analogy* compares dissimilar ideas, problems, things, and so on that share a common feature or characteristic. *Similes* compare dissimilar ideas, problems, things, and so on, but include the use of the words *like* or *as*. *Metaphors* combine descriptions with an idea, problem, thing, and so on that seem unrelated, too, and may really have no connection. Analogies, metaphors, and similes are excellent for sparking imagination in visualizing problems or issues and for developing creative solutions.

Keep the following in mind when using analogies, similes, and metaphors:

1. Thinking in terms of analogies, similes, and metaphors capitalizes on the power of the right hemisphere of the human brain. It requires the mind to use its associative and connotative powers to make connections. Therefore, recognize that sometimes such thinking requires loosening the rules and other constraints associated with the left side of the brain.
2. Let the team come up with analogies, similes, and metaphors. The diversity of minds coupled with the opportunity to generate many analogies, similes, and metaphors can lead to creative ideas originating from thinking outside the box. It also builds ownership in an idea.

Some ways to use analogies, metaphors, and similes on a project include:

- Viewing a project as something akin to an event that occurred in another industry
- Viewing a project as something that occurred in an organization's past and identifies some opportunities for improvement
- Viewing a threat to a project as something that was faced by another project elsewhere to learn what can be done

Literature Reviews

This technique involves researching the Internet or going to the library. Additional data and information are collected about an idea to determine its validity. Primary sources, such as raw data and interview notes, and secondary sources, such as articles and books, can provide additional information and guidance. They can also help support and dispel assumptions about an idea.

Keep the following in mind when conducting literature reviews:

1. Look at a wide array of sources, ranging from raw data to video presentations on the Internet. Use as many sources as possible. The information gathered will provide the basis for doing additional research. It will also help support or disclaim other information gathered from the literature review.
2. Always consider the source of the information. Just because something is published by an organization does not mean it is unbiased; some organizations fill their presentation with facts and data with a slant. It is always good to find multiple sources that take a different or contrarian view of a topic.
3. Look at multiple sources. Relying on one organization may not broaden perspective. Coverage may not be biased but narrowly focused, such as in a specialized field. Conducting a literature overview on an idea appearing in different fields may provide a broader perspective.

Some ways to use literature reviews on a project include reviewing:

- Articles in trade publications about projects of a similar nature in other environments
- Case studies provided by professional organizations to learn from the experiences of projects of a similar nature
- Technical journals on the latest advancements in technology that could improve the quality of deliverables

Devil's Advocate

This technique involves having someone take an opposite stance on an idea with the specific purpose of identifying flaws. The basic premise behind this technique is that contrary thinking can reveal shortcomings regarding an idea, which can be modified or discarded. The objective is to uncover a false positive, which is something that appears true but is, in reality, incorrect.

Keep the following in mind when applying the devil's advocate approach:

1. The person chosen to play the role of the devil's advocate should have good interpersonal skills. The exchange of viewpoints about an idea can quickly turn personal, if uncontrolled.

2. Capture both the pros and cons of an idea. Just because an idea has a flaw does not automatically mean discarding it. An idea may be salvageable after a few changes.

3. If an exchange does get overheated, act before it gets out of hand. Some ways to cool it down include tabling discussion or changing the person's degree of involvement in the exchange.

Some ways to use a devil's advocate on a project include assigning someone to:

- Challenge a decision to improve a process described in a management plan
- Disrupt prevalent thinking about how to go about managing a project
- Question the validity and reliability of a solution to a schedule performance problem
- Question the validity of a key performance metric

Checklists

Checklists are not, of themselves, a creativity technique. However, they can help further creativity if used to help remember key concepts, data, and so on, which in turn can lead to creative ideas. Checklists, therefore, serve as a vehicle to encourage greater thinking. Checklists offer at least two advantages. They can help avoid oversight of key information. They can also encourage further thinking using an element in a checklist to encourage creative thinking; in other words, piggybacking from an element to generate a creative idea.

Keep the following in mind when using checklists:

1. The contents of a checklist should relate to each other in some way, such as a specific topic. Too broad a scope will make it difficult to come up with a tangible, creative idea.

2. The checklist need not be exhaustive. In fact, too many elements in a checklist may confuse more than help. Approximately ten elements will often suffice.

3. Keep in mind that a checklist is an aid. It is not exhaustive, and it should help to expand boundaries in thinking, not constrain it.[28]

Some ways to use checklist on a project include listing:

- Different scenarios for performing what-if analysis in a scheduling tool
- Performance reports
- Potential solutions to a process problem
- Potential threats
- Roles and responsibilities of contractors
- Stakeholders

Observation

Observation is an excellent technique for coming up with new ideas. It can open people's perspective on new ways to do business. Observations, of course, should be varied to expose the observer to new phenomena. It entails someone visiting and watching an individual or organization execute its activities to learn about or enhance creative ideas.

Keep the following in mind when using observation:

1. Apply the guidelines for good observation. These include keeping one's physical and emotional distance, suspending biases and prejudices as best as possible, and applying effective listening skills.
2. Collect facts and data about the observation, such as the who, what, when, where, why, and how. Facts and data help evaluate any creative ideas arising out of the observation.
3. Document thoughts about observations. Take some time to reflect on the observations. Such thinking will encourage coming up with insights that could not possibly arise had time not been available for reflection. Consider reflection as soon as possible after an observation to avoid memory loss.

Some ways to use observation on a project include:

- Observing team meetings to identify opportunities for improvement
- Visiting other organizations having projects of a similar nature to see how they deal with replanning
- Visiting other projects of a similar nature to see how to establish a war room

- Watching another project team performing similar activities to learn process and procedural improvements

Interviewing

Interviewing is an excellent technique to uncover creative ideas. It involves, through question and answer, obtaining data, information, or ideas to address a problem or issue. Through interviews, questions can serve as a means to challenge the thinking of interviewees. This interchange between the interviewer and interviewee can result in a dynamic exchange of thoughts that can generate creative thinking.

Keep the following in mind when using interviewing techniques:

1. Use a combination of closed and open-ended questions. Closed questions are very specific, requiring a precise answer. Open-ended questions are broad, leaving room for considerable flexibility in thinking. These type of questions encourage "blue skying," that is, exploring thoughts that can lead to creative ideas.
2. Take notes. Ideas can fade as quickly as they arise. By writing interview notes, any creative ideas can become more crystallized in the minds of interviewees and interviewers alike.
3. Find a good location to conduct the interview. It should be free from distractions. Just as importantly, it should allow for a degree of privacy for the interviewee to express ideas needing to be kept confidential.

Some ways to use interviewing on a project include:

- Asking individual stakeholders about their expectations for the project
- Asking individuals in private sessions how to improve schedule and cost performance
- Asking key stakeholders on the customer side to suggest ways to improve satisfaction
- Asking individual team members how to improve the morale and esprit de corps
- Asking other project managers how they dealt with a showstopper that is looming on the horizon

Field Trip

A field trip is a great technique to generate creative ideas or at least acquire them from other places. It involves traveling to different places to observe and collect facts and data that can be used to broaden one's perspective and come up with creative ideas. A field trip exposes people in ways that broaden their perspectives. Such exposure challenges their biases and assumptions, causing them to think differently, which in turn encourages coming up with creative, innovative ideas. Field trips may include a trip to another company or going on a retreat.

Keep in mind the following when encouraging field trips:

1. Determine up front the purpose of the trip. The field trip should further the goals and objectives of a project.
2. Keep the entourage relatively small. Too big a group on a field trip will lessen the likelihood of people engaging in fulfilling the goals and objectives of a project.
3. Provide a written or oral report about the outcome of the field trip. Members of the entourage should share their insights, observations, and information so that others not attending can use that experience to generate even more new ideas.

Some ways to use a field trip on a project include:

- Attending conferences and seminars with the intent to learn how other organizations manage projects of a similar nature
- Taking select team members to another organization to learn different ways to execute a project of a similar nature
- Taking the team members to the customer's location to learn about how it does its business

Idea Bulletin Board

The idea bulletin board is a technique to capture ideas as they arise over a certain time period. The idea board can be placed above a water cooler, in a conference room, in a cafeteria, or at any other location where people can readily access it. As people come up with ideas, they simply record, on a small card or paper, a creative idea that comes to mind to improve performance, product, or service. People can then choose whether to sign their names or add information (e.g., suggestions for implementation) to the card or paper.

The idea bulletin board offers several benefits. One benefit is that it recognizes people are just not creative at the same time and all the time. Many ideas arise in an ad hoc manner, and the board is a convenient place to record them before becoming lost or stolen. The other advantage is that it shows that an organization encourages creativity and takes it seriously.

Keep the following in mind when using an idea bulletin board:

1. Visit the board periodically to collect the ideas. Boards, containing ideas for months on end without being reviewed, indicates a lack of seriousness about the importance of creativity.
2. If reviewing the board, management should provide feedback on any idea after conducting an initial evaluation. This evaluation should include an approval or disapproval decision and any accompanying explanations about the conclusions.
3. If an idea has been accepted, an implementation plan should be developed. This action will demonstrate the degree of importance attributed to an idea. Naturally, assigning resources demonstrates commitment to making any idea a reality.[29]

Some ways to use an idea bulletin board on a project include:

- Capturing issues related to morale and esprit de corps
- Capturing potential threats
- Collecting ideas on improving processes described in management plans
- Collecting ideas on overcoming a potential showstopper

CONCLUSION

Obviously, the approaches and techniques described above are not exhaustive. They are a just a sample of hundreds that project managers can use on their projects. It is important to stress that the right approach and technique depends on the circumstances in terms of effort, time, place, and culture. Some of the approaches and techniques require considerable time and effort to apply, whereas in some circumstances, little time and other resources are available to apply. It is important, therefore, to consider all the trade-offs before selecting and applying an approach or technique.

Getting Started Checklist

Question	Yes	No
1. For your project, which of the creativity approaches and techniques have you decided to employ, and how would you use the ones selected (e.g., build a work breakdown structure)?		
Affinity Diagramming		
Use:		
Brainwriting		
Use:		
Brainstorming		
Use:		
Checklists		
Use:		
Compare and Contrast		
Use:		
Crawford Slip Technique		
Use:		
Delphi Technique		
Use:		
Devil's Advocate		
Use:		
Field Trip		
Use:		
Fishbone Diagram		
Use:		
Force Field Analysis		
Use:		
Hypothetical Scenario		
Use:		
Idea Bulletin Board		
Use:		
Imagineering		
Use:		
Interviewing		
Use:		
Lateral Thinking		
Use:		
Matrices		
Use:		
Mind Mapping		
Use:		
Modeling		

(Continued)

Getting Started Checklist

Question	Yes	No
Use:		
Nominal Group Technique		
Use:		
Observation		
Use:		
Offsite		
Use:		
Pareto Chart		
Use:		
PDCA Cycle		
Use:		
Problem Solving		
Use:		
Reengineering		
Use:		
Role Playing		
Use:		
Scatter Gram		
Use:		
Statistical Process Control		
Use:		
Storyboarding		
Use:		
Synectics		
Use:		
Tree Diagram		
Use:		
Trend Chart		
Use:		
Workflow Analysis		
Use:		

ENDNOTES

1. Ralph L. Kliem, *The Project Manager's Emergency Kit* (Boca Raton, FL: St. Lucie Press, 2003), pp. 7–8.
2. Robert W. Pike, *Creative Training Techniques Handbook* (Minneapolis, MN: Lakewood Books, 1989), pp. 82–84.
3. Michael Brassard, *The Jogger Memory Plus+* (Methuen, MA: Goal/QPC, 1989), pp. 73–98.

4. Brassard, *The Memory Jogger Plus+*, pp. 73–98.
5. James M. Higgins, *101 Creative Problem Solving Techniques* (New York: The New Management, 1994), pp. 135–136.
6. Ralph L. Kliem and Irwin S. Ludin, *Tools and Tips for Today's Project Manager* (Newtown Square, PA: Project Management Institute, 1999), p. 54.
7. Higgins, *101 Creative Problem Solving Techniques*, pp. 125–126.
8. Kliem, *The Project Manager's Emergency Kit*, p. 2.
9. Brassard, *The Memory Jogger Plus+*, p. 11.
10. Kliem, *The Project Manager's Emergency Kit*, pp. 166–167.
11. Michael Michalko, *Cracking Creativity* (Berkeley, CA: Ten Speed Press, 2001), pp. 75–79.
12. Kliem, *The Project Manager's Emergency Kit*, pp. 112–113.
13. Kliem, *The Project Manager's Emergency Kit*, p. 6.
14. Kliem, *The Project Manager's Emergency Kit*, p. 103.
15. Kliem, *The Project Manager's Emergency Kit*, pp. 95–96.
16. Kliem, *The Project Manager's Emergency Kit*, pp. 94–95.
17. Kliem and Ludin, *Tools and Tips for Today's Project Manager*, p. 71.
18. Kliem, *The Project Manager's Emergency Kit*, pp. 70–71.
19. Kliem, *The Project Manager's Emergency Kit*, pp. 198–199.
20. Kliem and Ludin. *Tools and Tips for Today's Project Manager*, p. 88.
21. Kliem, *The Project Manager's Emergency Kit*, p. 141.
22. Kliem and Ludin, *Tools and Tips for Today's Project Manager*, p. 42.
23. Kliem and Ludin, *Tools and Tips for Today's Project Manager*, p. 164.
24. Higgins, *101 Creative Problem Solving Techniques*, pp. 132–135.
25. Gerard I. Nierenberg, *The Art of Creative Thinking* (New York: Cornerstone Library, 1982), pp. 197–199.
26. Higgins, *101 Creative Problem Solving Techniques*, pp. 161–176.
27. Kliem, *The Project Manager's Emergency Kit*, pp. 125–126.
28. Higgins, *101 Creative Problem Solving Techniques*, p. 40.
29. Higgins, *101 Creative Problem Solving Techniques*, p. 142.

7

Creativity Life Cycle Models

INTRODUCTION

Contrary to popular belief, creativity requires having some type of discipline in place to allow it to be further exercised and result in something that is understandable and meaningful to others. Without some kind of rigor, creative energy is dissipated and its effectiveness becomes less than optimal. The following models are just a few of the ones that can blend well with the project life cycle and its defining, organizing, planning, executing, monitoring and controlling, and closing processes.

MODELS

These models exist to manage creativity:

- Imagination, illumination, and stage gates
- Creative problem solving
- Behavioral
- Traditional creativity life cycle

Incubation, Illumination, and Stage Gates

Daniel Goleman identifies essentially two main stages (see Figure 7.1) applicable to the creative process. The Incubation Stage is the first one. This stage involves letting the unconscious part of the mind go to work. It does so by allowing the mind to float freely rather than controlling and censoring thoughts. Judgment is suspended through emotion, intuition, daydreaming, and imagery. The Illumination Stage is the

FIGURE 7.1
Two-stage creativity process.

second one. The creative idea seems to originate from a void and then provides the groundwork for innovation.[1] To ensure that the creative process generates ideas of value, James Higgins recommends employing a stage gate system to ensure that ideas are evaluated for their innovativeness. The first series of stages involves allowing the creative process to flow; the latter phases allow for the "rational" mind to take over. The gates are threefold: (1) conduct preliminary investigation, (2) perform a business case to determine practicality, and (3) develop and implement a plan.[2]

Creative Problem Solving Model

Arthur VanGunder provides an in-depth model known as creative problem solving (see Figure 7.2). He identifies the following eight essential processes:

- Understand the environment by analyzing it to determine if a problem needs attention.[3] Not all problems are equal; some are more important than others.
- Increase your awareness about the existence of the problem.[4] In other words, understand what the problem is about. Problem definition is absolutely critical at this point.
- Gather information about the problem.[5] Collect information surrounding the who, what, where, when, why, and how of the problem. Of course, use judgment to distinguish the critical from the insignificant elements.
- Generate assumptions about the circumstances or conditions that contributed to the problem.[6] These assumptions will, of course, be challenged as you know more about the problem and what contributed to it. Remember that assumptions are considered facts by most people—until proven otherwise.
- Determine different alternatives, also known as options, to address the problem.[7] No limit exists as to the number of options, and they

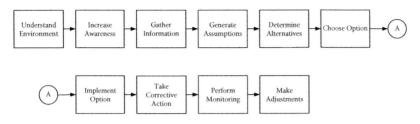

FIGURE 7.2
Creative problem-solving diagram.

can vary in effectiveness. Avoid closing the mind when generating options. It is best to suspend judgment until completing the list.

- Choose one of the options after careful review.[8] Determine the criteria for making the choice and apply it objectively. Define the criteria clearly. Ideally, it will fix the problem and not the symptoms.
- Implement the option by developing and deploying a plan.[9] Good project management works well here; its application is a matter of scale.
- Ascertain what was implemented effectively and, if necessary, take any corrective action to ensure the option does the job of fixing the problem.[10] Very few things in life turn out as planned. Implementing a solution to a problem or addressing an issue requires ongoing monitoring that will be likely to involve making adjustments to the plan.

Behavioral Model

Dave Allan et al. developed an extensive creativity process involving six behaviors (referred to as the behavioral model) that conveniently flow in a series: freshness, greenhousing, realness, momentum, signaling, and bravery.

Freshness entails looking at a problem from different perspectives. It requires holding back on accepting assumptions as facts and not using them to provide a solution based upon current reality and previous experience. Freshness, that is, taking a different approach to viewing a problem, is stimulating. It means describing a problem or issue in an alternative way, challenging rules and assumptions, and making seemingly random linkages among different facts and data. Freshness, in others words, centers on reexpression of the issue or problem to be addressed.[11]

Greenhousing involves laying the groundwork for ideas to blossom by suspending judgment. Analysis often results in exercising judgment too soon. Under greenhousing, people restrain their analytical side and take a more exploratory view of a problem or issue. They contrast this environment with what they call the emergency-room environment, whereby swift judgment and action allow little flexibility or time to explore. They also note the logical, scientific approach, which, with its pursuit of the right answer, does not allow ideas to take root. They note that greenhouse behavior is exhibited or prohibited in one of two ways. The acronym SUN is used to describe a method that encourages creative behavior through suspension (S) of judgment, understanding (U) via empathy and open questioning, and nurturing (N) by providing a supportive environment. RAIN, as you might suspect, inhibits creative thinking by reacting (R) in a rush to judgment; assuming (A) through the use of uncertain, unverified assumptions that are viewed as facts; and insisting (IN), by attacking an idea right from the beginning. Greenhousing, therefore, allows ideas to grow rather than be attacked the minute they arise.[12]

Realness entails turning an idea into reality through various ways of expressing it. The key is to overcome the tendency to be consumed by a bias toward a way of expressing ideas, verbally or graphically for example, or by developing a prototype. A prototype allows ideas to manifest a sense of being tangible, that is, a sense of realness that has as much an emotional as a logical flavor to it that words and pictures have difficulty eliciting.[13] However, team members should be open to new ideas for changing a prototype.

Momentum turns an idea into reality. It started with the prototype, but now involves putting it in the real world with urgency and direction. It is taking action by eliminating barriers, such as bureaucracy, and having people no longer bar coding, which starts and stops work when managing several tasks. Both are examples of creating inertia, not momentum. According to the authors, one of the best ways to encourage momentum is to ensure that all energy is aligned toward achieving common goals and objectives, whether organizational or personal.[14]

Signaling is about preparing to turn the creation into reality. The purpose is to bridge the difference between analysis and creativity because, as mentioned earlier, a gap often exists here in so many ways. The former is logical, efficient, and judgmental; the latter is open, free flowing, and effective. With signaling, emphasis is on language as a way to bridge the gap. Just as importantly, signaling communicates as much emotion as the logic behind a creative idea and does so in verbal, visual, and kinesthetic ways. Signaling is, therefore, a matter of doing the psychological work to introduce a new idea.[15]

Bravery, the final behavior, entails turning an idea into reality. It means that creative people must courageously face all the hardships associated with implementing change. Like all change, positive and negative aspects are associated with taking on the status quo. The slings and arrows of change often inhibit the best creative ideas from being implemented. In addition, overanalysis of an idea and its consequences can be substantially negative when implementing change. Not surprisingly, creative ideas often die during implementation because they become so incremental that they no longer result in any substantive change. True bravery, therefore, requires considerable courage and self-confidence. The forces can be so strong as to seem overwhelming, allowing fear to take over, versus the comfort of the status quo of habitual behavior. With bravery, people often need to step out of the comfort zone by taking action and facing the consequences—intended and unintended—to make an idea a reality through techniques like visualization.[16]

Traditional Creativity Model

A more traditional model (see Figure 7.3), and one more frequently cited, consists of five phases that flow in this order: preparation, concentration, incubation, illumination, and verification and production. The *preparation phase* is doing the groundwork to create. It requires learning as much as possible about a certain topic (e.g., issue, problem, concept). It involves obtaining the necessary background, such as common principles, data, problems, and techniques, on a topic. Preparation, therefore, is building a foundation.[17]

The *concentration phase* is centered on focusing on a problem or issue by defining exactly what the problem or issue is and determining what is and is not relevant. The result, hopefully, is a well-defined issue. Essentially, it enables focusing on a problem or issue when using creativity.[18]

The *incubation* phase is where the focus is least on the conscious level by allowing the subconscious to work and the mind to rest. The mind releases the reigns of concentration and runs free, so to speak. The solution to the issue slowly percolates from the depth of the mind, enabling the next phase to occur.[19]

The *illumination* phase is perhaps the shortest of all phases, but by no means the least important. In fact, it is the reason for creativity. This phase allows the creative thought to percolate to the surface. It is what causes

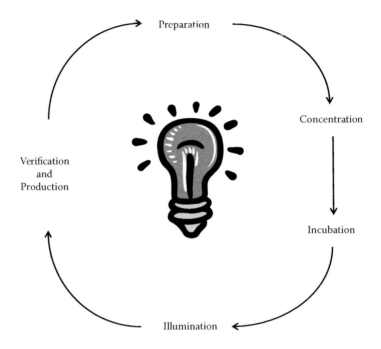

FIGURE 7.3
Traditional creative life cycle.

one to scream, oftentimes figuratively but sometimes literally, "Eureka!" or Aha!" A sort of euphoric feeling consumes the creator.[20]

Verification and production is the final phase. Now the test of an idea occurs from a practicality standpoint. Technical complications and organizational resistance are just two examples where reality can make or break a creative idea, that is, get it accepted and implemented or rejected.[21]

CONCLUSION

Creativity requires some discipline if it is to contribute to the success of a project. Unfortunately, the perception is often that creativity is something that must lack discipline (e.g., no processes or rules) to enable it to blossom. Nothing could be further from the truth. While occasionally undisciplined, creative people must direct their efforts in a focused and disciplined manner to deliver something that is not only creative, but innovative.

The traditional model of creativity is preferred by the author simply because it has been used extensively in different industries, is the most familiar to people, and has proven to be most effective. The following chapters discuss how the traditional model can be applied with each of the project management processes of defining, organizing, planning, executing, monitoring and controlling, and closing.

Getting Started Checklist

Question	Yes	No
1. Have you decided to follow one or a combination of the following creative processes?		
Creative problem-solving process as described by Arthur VanGundy		
Imagination, illumination, and stage gates as described by James Higgins		
Six behaviors of creativity as described by Dave Allen et al.		
Traditional model as described by David Campbell		
Other(s):		
2. Whichever process is chosen, list some ways to apply the processes on your project (e.g., training):		
Way(s):		

ENDNOTES

1. Daniel Goleman, Paul Kaufman, and Michael Ray, *The Creative Spirit* (New York: Dutton, 1992), pp. 19–22.
2. James M. Higgins, *Innovate or Evaporate* (Winter Park, FL: The New Management Publishing Co., 1995), p. 214.
3. Arthur B. VanGundy, *Creative Problem Solving* (Westport, CT: Greenwood Press, Inc., 1987), pp. 61–65.
4. VanGundy, *Creative Problem Solving*, pp. 61–65.
5. VanGundy, *Creative Problem Solving*, pp. 61–65.
6. VanGundy, *Creative Problem Solving*, pp. 61–65.
7. VanGundy, *Creative Problem Solving*, pp. 61–65.
8. VanGundy, *Creative Problem Solving*, pp. 61–65.
9. VanGundy, *Creative Problem Solving*, pp. 61–65.
10. VanGundy, *Creative Problem Solving*, pp. 61–65.
11. Dave Allan et al., *What If?* (Oxford: Capstone Publishing Limited, 1999), pp. 7–17.
12. Allan et al., *What If?* pp. 54–93.
13. Allan et al., *What If?* pp. 95–123.
14. Allan et al., *What If?* pp. 127–169.
15. Allan et al., *What If?* pp. 171–205.
16. Allan et al., *What If?* pp. 208–237.

17. David Campbell, *Take the Road to Creativity and Get Off Your Dead End* (Niles, IL: Argus Communications, 1977), pp. 30–33.

18. Campbell, *Take the Road to Creativity and Get Off Your Dead End*, pp. 33–36.

19. Campbell, *Take the Road to Creativity and Get Off Your Dead End*, pp. 36–38.

20. Campbell, *Take the Road to Creativity and Get Off Your Dead End*, pp. 39–40.

21. Campbell, *Take the Road to Creativity and Get Off Your Dead End*, pp. 40–41.

8

Creativity and the Defining Process

INTRODUCTION

The defining process is the first of six processes and the only one that is theoretically completed before all the other ones are applied. It defines, at a high level, the answers to who, what, when, where, why, and how.

BENEFITS

Many benefits are attributed to the defining process. It helps define the scope, identify key stakeholders and their interests, garners support, obtains early commitment, initiates communications, and provides overall parameters for a project.

CONSEQUENCES OF FAILURE

Studies have shown that, unfortunately, failure to perform this process has a tremendous impact downstream on a project, especially during the executing, and monitoring and controlling processes. Failure occurs frequently on information technology projects and is reflected in a cartoon whereby the project manager tells the team to start coding while he goes upstairs to see what the customer wants. In the end, the failure to properly execute the defining process leads to rework, negative relationships, and overall poor performance.

DELIVERABLES

The defining process (see Figure 8.1) has several project management deliverables, including:

- Business case
- Project charter
- Requirements documentation
- Scope definition
- Stakeholder analysis
- Statement of work

IDEAL STATE

Ideally, the business case and the project charter are complete before project managers come on board. Project managers need to understand

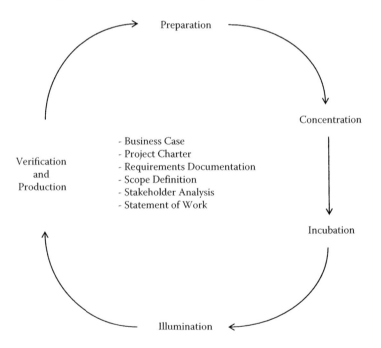

FIGURE 8.1
Defining process and deliverables.

both the deliverables and concentrate on producing a statement of work, performing stakeholder analysis, defining the scope more clearly, and producing requirements documentation.

Realistically, perhaps more so than not, the opposite exists. The business case is either nonexistent or partially complete, and the same goes for the project charter. The scope definition and requirements may be vague, and the onus is on project managers to pursue the necessary definitiveness required to produce a product or deliver a service. As for stakeholders, project managers have to seek out stakeholders beyond the one or two that are already probably identified. This circumstance confronting project managers often provides, ironically, an opportunity to exercise creativity right away.

CONTEXT

There are several contextual factors that project managers often face when they are assigned during the defining process. Here are just a few:

Quite frequently, the project sponsor or customer (who may or may not be one and the same) never bothers to develop even a straw horse of any of the deliverables. The project manager assumes the responsibility of ensuring that defined deliverables are created.

Additionally, the context of the project may affect how much time and effort went into producing the deliverables. Contextual factors, such as potential budget cuts, management instability, managerial indecisiveness, bureaucracy, lack of clarity of goals and objectives, unavailability of information and data, and just plain fear in the ranks can all impact the quality of the project management deliverables for this process and, indeed, for all subsequent processes and phases in the project and product life cycles, respectively.

CHALLENGES AND CONSTRAINTS

Considerable ambiguity and vagueness often occur in the defining process. A project is often, if at all, little defined and the stakeholders are not clearly identified. In addition, some potential stakeholders may just not like the idea of a project because it invades their turf or they do not find it compatible with the beliefs or values embraced by the organization in general, or the leadership in particular. Other stakeholders may not want to communicate or coordinate with each other due to issues unrelated to the project. Others may be fearful of the consequences of participating on a project and would rather sit on the sidelines until they see who supports it and how well it progresses.

Another challenge and constraint is obtaining clarity in project scope. All too often, customers only have a vague idea of what they want, let alone what they need. Customer confusion can lead to frustration on everyone's part, especially for members of the project team. In the end, of course, it boils down to communication among the customer, sponsor, and the project manager.

Some common creative challenges and constraints that may be present during this process for a project are shown in Table 8.1.

TABLE 8.1

Defining Process Challenges and Constraints

Creative Challenge and Constraint	Example
Faster, better, cheaper philosophy	Stakeholder desire to see results quickly
Fear	Feeling, by some stakeholders, that they might lose power and influence as a result of a project
Groupthink	Stakeholders, such as a management team, subscribes to a set of beliefs that may not embrace a project despite its economic advantages
Hierarchy	Senior management dictates what types of projects are included in an organization's portfolio
Lack of sharing	Information that could impact a decision about a project is not shared by key stakeholders
Management's lack of responsiveness	Certain stakeholders, specifically management, does not participate in defining key elements of a project
Mores, beliefs, values	A perception by certain stakeholders that a particular project is not the type embraced historically by an organization, regardless of the business case
Poor communications	Jargon used by certain categories of stakeholders, making it difficult to share and understand information
Poor coordination	A stakeholder's perception that a project is the sole province of a specific organization
Silos	Stakeholders not wanting to participate in the defining process because of another stakeholder (e.g., Engineering not working with Sales and Marketing)

CREATIVE ABILITIES

Project managers will have to be highly creative in this process, especially when it comes to obtaining information for the vision of a project, as well as receiving buy-in from significant stakeholders. Failure to achieve both will result in radiating problems throughout the entire life cycle of the project and even beyond (e.g., operations and maintenance).

Some of the relevant creative abilities that project managers may find useful for this process are shown in Table 8.2.

GROUNDWORK FOR CREATIVE ENVIRONMENT

Project managers, during this process, will often find themselves having to take the initiative to complete the necessary project management deliverables. It will behoove them to develop creative solutions to the challenges and constraints presented in the execution of this process. They must encourage interaction among potential stakeholders, further information sharing and data, establish what is not important, align the project with organizational interests, and enable the definition of the issues and problems to address.

Some of the possible necessary actions that project managers may have to do to lay the groundwork for a creative environment are shown in Table 8.3.

GROUNDWORK FOR INDIVIDUAL CREATIVITY

For the most part, the number of people on a project is small. The people participating in the process are individuals who have been assigned to the core team, and their participation is somewhat preliminary. Most team members perform the role of a subject matter expert or provide some power or expertise to have a project on everyone's radar by knowing about it and providing the information and approval signatures for significant project management deliverables.

Some actions that project managers can take to allow people to be creative are outlined in Table 8.4.

TABLE 8.2

Defining Process and Creative Abilities

Creative Ability	Example
Being observant	Watching the behavior, such as body language, of certain stakeholders to determine receptivity to a project when seeking project charter acceptance
Conceptualizing	Subscribing to a big-picture perspective about a project, e.g., relationship of a project relative to other projects in a portfolio
Cross-domain thinking	Using both logic and intuition to determine the vision, goals, and objectives for a project
Defining the problem	Pinpointing exactly what the vision, goals, and objectives are for the project
Determining the essence of something	Identifying the fundamental problem or issue to address with a project
Embracing ambiguity	Recognizing during the defining process that a large number of unknowns exists that will be later defined more clearly
Generalization	Trying to derive some patterns of thinking among key stakeholders about a project
Intuitive	Being attuned to internal feeling about a certain stakeholder's commitment to a project
Looking, from the outside, in	Not allowing one's preferences to tarnish objectivity, such as seeing only one way to execute a project
Reasoning, such as being logical	Concentrating on the facts and data about a potential project, e.g., looking at the results of a business case
Seeing multiple answers	Recognizing that the determination of whether to proceed with a project only rests with one criterion, e.g., return on investment, when other criteria might also justify another project
Shifting between convergent and divergent thinking	Being able to see the *big picture* while simultaneously narrowing down key issues justifying a project
Shifting from analysis to synthesis mode of thinking	Being able to break down elements of a project, such as a business case, and then bringing all the components back together to make a determination whether to proceed with the project
Shifting from linear to nonlinear thinking	Moving from a flow of control rather than an object view of requirements
Shifting perspectives	Attempting to see viewpoints of all key stakeholders when drafting a project charter
Suspending judgment	Avoiding the tendency to jump to conclusions before considering all the data and information compiled in a business case

TABLE 8.3

Defining Process and Groundwork for Creative Environment

Action	Example
Aligning individual goals and objectives with the project's goals and objectives	When building a business case, attempting to demonstrate how the vision, goals, and objectives of a project support key stakeholders' interests
Allowing time for issue or problem definition	Allowing a period for key stakeholders (e.g., management) to reconcile differences of opinion over the definition of a problem or issue that a project will address
Building and maintaining trust	Establishing ongoing rapport and communications with key stakeholders, especially with the sponsor and customers, when developing a statement of work
Emphasizing coordination	Providing opportunities for key stakeholders to work together in drafting a project charter
Encouraging ownership	Seeking participation by key stakeholders in the development of a business case
Establishing a receptive audience	Interviewing key stakeholders about their interests and insights concerning a project
Establishing priorities	Encouraging key stakeholders to set priorities and incorporating their decision in a project charter
Stressing communications	Encouraging stakeholders to share data and information among key stakeholders about a project

TABLE 8.4

Defining Process and Groundwork for Individual Creativity

Action	Example
Be competitive and collaborate at the same time	Recognizing individual and team performances at specific points in the project life cycle
Be conceptualizers	Identifying the major elements (e.g., processes, products, stakeholders, etc.) and analyzing them to understand the context of a project when performing a business case
Have a diverse background	Using a wide range of knowledge and experience to draft a charter or business case for a project
See outside the box	Taking a different perspective that is contrary to the one subscribed to by other stakeholders to overcome disagreements over requirements

TABLE 8.5

Defining Process and Groundwork for Team Creativity

Action	Example
Allow for open discussion and have a tolerance for ideas	Provide everyone the opportunity to speak at team meetings
Build a collegial and nonhierarchical relationship	Assign people to activities that require working other colleagues with varying levels of position, knowledge, and experience
Diversify membership	Hire people on the project team with knowledge and experience that is at least different from others
Know the priorities	Revisit the vision, goals, and objectives at the beginning of every meeting
Seek balance among creating, planning, and implementing	Emphasize the need that ideas are great but they require planning and action to make them a reality
View failure as a learning experience	Require a lessons-learned session at the conclusion of every phase and at the end of the project

GROUNDWORK FOR TEAM CREATIVITY

The team is somewhat small. People representing certain stakeholders and others with expertise must achieve consensus and work together to produce the necessary project management deliverables.

Some actions that project managers could take to allow a team to be creative are outlined in Table 8.5.

RELEVANT TOOLS AND TECHNIQUES

The tools and techniques employed for this process should enable achieving several goals. They should help encourage people to express their views and interests, develop with a common vision, achieve consensus over specific deliverables, and enable greater coordination and communication among the significant stakeholders.

Some common creativity tools and techniques that project managers can apply for this process are shown in Table 8.6.

TABLE 8.6

Defining Process and Tools and Techniques

Tool and Technique	Example
Benchmarking	Comparing business cases of similar projects to determine whether to proceed with a project
Interviewing	Conducting one-on-one sessions with each of the key stakeholders to provide information to incorporate in a project charter
Lateral thinking	Reviewing the interests of a functional stakeholder (e.g., Engineering and Finance) to develop a creative solution for overcoming an impasse in producing common requirements
Matrices	Summarizing common and different interests of stakeholder in a matrix when performing stakeholder analysis
Modeling	Capturing requirements using a systemic approach based on, for example, data flow
Nominal group technique	Prioritizing requirements based upon the common and different interests of stakeholders
Offsite	Assembling key stakeholders at a remote location to negotiate a project charter
Problem solving	Holding a brainstorming session to generate different factors, (e.g., return on investment, payback period, etc.) to consider in the evaluation portion of a business case
Reengineering	Throwing out a previous process (the *as-is*) and drawing a *to-be* one that does not consider the former
Role playing	Assuming the position of one or more stakeholders to understand their interests and concerns when conducting stakeholder analysis

TRADITIONAL CREATIVITY LIFE CYCLE MODEL

Within the defining process, project managers can apply the five phases of the creativity life cycle model. Each phase plays an instrumental role in clarifying and resolving an issue or problem.

Preparation Phase

The purpose of the preparation phase is to learn as much information as possible about a topic and to compile any necessary information that will prove useful in coming up with creative ideas. This phase is focused largely on people and product or service.

For example, a project manager is presented with an idea about a project and must build a business case to determine whether or not to proceed. Business management (e.g., financial and accounting data) and strategic considerations are compiled and used to build the business case. The information and data are not easily available or are unavailable. The project manager decides to do some benchmarking, interviewing, and constructing of matrices and charts.

Concentration Phase

The purpose of the concentration phase is to focus on exactly defining a problem or issue to address. Project managers need to distinguish between what is and is not relevant, and just as importantly, what is and is not significant.

Continuing with the use of the business case as an example, the project manager determines what financial data to use and what formulae to apply. He also has to ascertain thresholds and other factors to provide a recommendation about his project.

Incubation Phase

The purpose of the incubation phase is to allow the subconscious part of the mind to work by suspending judgment and avoiding concentration on a conscious level.

Continuing with the use of the business case as an example, a frequent problem is determining what data and information to employ in calculations or how to present the results. The project manager decides to leave the business case alone for a time and work on a different project, thereby freeing his mind to work on the problem or issue.

Illumination Phase

The purpose of the illumination phase is to allow an idea to rise to the conscious level of its creator. This phase involves coming up with solutions to difficulties identified earlier.

Continuing with the use of the business case as an example, the project manager decides on the solution for using specific calculations, and the data and information to perform them come to light. The project manager wrestles over whether to present his work either graphically or orally, or a combination of both. He also decides to present the payback period or net present value, or internal rate of return, or a combination thereof, for instance.

Verification and Production Phase

The purpose of the verification and production phase is to test and implement an idea. It is when thought turns to action.

Continuing the use of the business case as an example, the project manager determines which significant stakeholders must grant approval before proceeding with the project. Revisions, of course, may be necessary once the changes are identified. He then updates the business case and presents it to significant stakeholders for review and approval, and a decision on whether to proceed. Assuming stakeholder approval, he uses the business case to serve as a basis to start building another deliverable for the defining process, the project charter. Of course, working on the charter or any of the other project management deliverables for this process may require additional review and revisions.

CONCLUSION

The defining process lays the basis to perform the work in the subsequent processes throughout the project and product life cycles. The most difficult challenges center on obtaining the necessary information and identifying and engaging key stakeholders. Having people with the requisite creative skills to employ tools and techniques can go a long way for starting projects in the right direction.

Getting Started Checklist

Question	Yes	No
1. During this process, determine the challenges and constraints that could impact the creativity of your project team:		
Faster, better, cheaper philosophy		
Fear		
Groupthink		
Hierarchy		
Lack of sharing		
Management's lack of responsiveness		

(Continued)

Getting Started Checklist

Question	Yes	No
Mores, beliefs, values		
Poor communications		
Poor coordination		
Silos		
Other(s):		
2. Determine the creative abilities that are applicable to this process:		
Being observant		
Conceptualizing		
Cross-domain thinking		
Defining the problem		
Determining the essence of something		
Embracing ambiguity		
Generalization		
Intuitive		
Looking from the outside, in		
Reasoning, such as being logical		
Seeing multiple answers		
Shifting between convergent and divergent thinking		
Shifting from analysis to synthesis mode of thinking		
Shifting from linear to nonlinear thinking		
Shifting perspectives		
Suspending judgment		
Other(s):		
3. Determine the actions that are necessary to lay the groundwork for a creative environment:		
Aligning individual goals and objectives with those of the project		
Allowing time for issue or problem definition		
Building and maintaining trust		
Emphasizing coordination		
Encouraging ownership		
Establishing a receptive audience		
Establishing priorities		
Stressing communications		
Aligning individual goals and objectives with those of the project		
Allowing time for issue or problem definition		
Building and maintaining trust		
Other(s):		
4. Determine the actions to take to improve individual creativity:		
Be competitive and collaborate at the same time		
Be conceptualizers		

Getting Started Checklist

Question	Yes	No
Have a diverse background		
See outside the box		
Other(s):		
5. Determine the actions to take to improve team creativity:		
Allow for open discussion and have a tolerance for ideas		
Build a collegial and hierarchical relationship		
Diversify membership		
Know the priorities		
Seek balance among creating, planning, and implementing		
View failure as a learning experience		
Other(s):		
6. Identify the creativity tools and techniques to use:		
Benchmarking		
Interviewing		
Lateral thinking		
Matrices		
Modeling		
Nominal group technique		
Offsite		
Problem solving		
Reengineering		
Role playing		
Other(s):		

9

Creativity and the Organizing Process

INTRODUCTION

The organizing process involves identifying and setting up the infrastructure to effectively and efficiently manage a project. Its focus is on providing a backbone for a project that ensures communication, coordination, and information occur in a manner enhancing individual and overall performance of a project.

BENEFITS

There are many benefits attributed to the organizing process. It provides a means for all stakeholders to communicate with each other, make tangibles (e.g., supplies) and intangibles (e.g., tribal knowledge, artifacts) available, offer a common operating rhythm for all stakeholders, and enable opportunities to resolve conflict in a manner that minimizes disruption.

CONSEQUENCES OF FAILURE

Failure to perform this process has tremendous impact downstream on a project, especially during the executing, monitoring and controlling, and closing processes. Lack of communication, coordination, and information affects decision making, determining and assessing cost and schedule performance, and satisfying the customer requirements. An inefficient application of resources, for example, increases rework, which often means additional costs and schedule slides. An ineffective application of resources can mean that the deliverables do not meet the customer's wants and needs, which results in dissatisfaction.

DELIVERABLES

The organizing process has several project management deliverables (see Figure 9.1), including:

- Control room
- Forms
- Management plans
- Newsletter
- Organizational structure
- Project manual

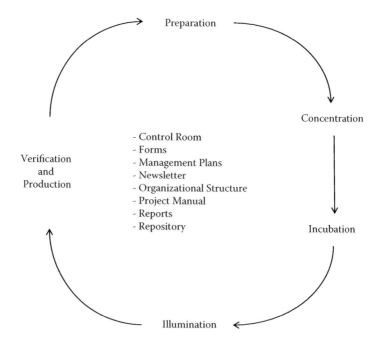

FIGURE 9.1
Organizing process and deliverables.

- Reports
- Repository

IDEAL STATE

Ideally, project managers have carte blanche to set up an infrastructure to complete their project. They have all the financial and in-kind support needed to succeed: sufficient tools and information, latitude to build an organizational structure giving the autonomy they seek, locations to establish a project library, and the opportunity to develop and publish a uniform set of procedures, forms, reports, and other documents to ensure effective communications and coordination.

In reality, however, more often than not, everything in the previous paragraph is a dream for many, if not all, project managers. The norm is not having enough time, money, and support to establish an infrastructure that runs and supports a project efficiently and effectively. The time and effort to set up a good infrastructure is considered, by some stakeholders, wasteful because tangible results are often not readily apparent. Additionally, project managers often have to compete with their colleagues for the very same resources. Not surprisingly, many project managers take a minimalist approach toward building a supporting infrastructure, ironically at great cost.

CONTEXT

There are several contextual factors that project managers face during the organizing process. Here are just a few: The customer and other key stakeholders want to keep the cost baseline for their projects as low as possible to maximize profitability. They view time to build an ideal infrastructure as too costly and as offering marginal return. Due to limited resources, project managers and other key stakeholders find they have to suboptimize, that is, sacrifice certain time, cost, and quality goals and objectives for their project. Under such circumstances, project managers usually have to cut the infrastructure to achieve other goals and objectives, thereby impeding efficiency and effectiveness.

CHALLENGES AND CONSTRAINTS

Most challenges and constraints in this process revolve around time and money. Both time and money are insufficient to put in place an ideal infrastructure. For example, obtaining data and information to populate a repository can entail considerable labor, effort, and expertise that some stakeholders may deem unnecessary or overkill. Additionally, time and money may be initially available, but as the project's performance degrades, which it often does, resources and attention are taken away from the organizing process to concentrate on bringing a project back on track.

Some common creative challenges and constraints confronting this process are shown in Table 9.1.

TABLE 9.1

Organizing Process and Challenges and Constraints

Challenge and Constraint	Example
Hierarchy	Having little autonomy in drafting the content of management plans
Lack of data and information	Not being able to find the necessary data and information to populate a project repository
Lack of sharing	Prevailing sense of suspicion existing among stakeholders, thereby inhibiting a willingness to share anything with anyone else on a project
Lack of tools	Not having the ability to share data, information, and tools due to a lack of common technology standards
Poor communications	Having certain shareholders who refuse to participate in team meetings, especially if a certain person or representation from another organization is present
Poor coordination	Having two or more stakeholders not coordinating with each other when putting together an organization chart for a project
Team composition imbalance	Having too many people from a specific discipline (e.g., engineering) dominating team composition, thereby skewing decision making
Too much and too little training	Offering training on a tool (e.g., project management software) that exceeds the level of competence required to perform work

CREATIVE ABILITIES

At first, creativity does not appear to play an important role in organizing a project. Nothing can be further from the truth. Creative abilities are necessary to come up with the most appropriate organizational structure, deploy resources in a manner that increases effective and efficient performance, and compile and display information to users. Ultimately, creative abilities are necessary to build an infrastructure that enables projects to succeed.

Some relevant creative abilities required for this process are shown in Table 9.2.

GROUNDWORK FOR CREATIVE ENVIRONMENT

Putting in place the groundwork for organizing a project requires understanding the needs and wants of stakeholders, such as a customer, steering committee members, and the project team. The infrastructure should enable project performance, not the other way around (i.e., stakeholders participating to serve the infrastructure). Some project managers often forget this important point.

Some actions that project managers may take to lay the groundwork for a creative environment are shown in Table 9.3.

TABLE 9.2

Organizing Process and Creative Abilities

Creative Ability	Example
Being a linear thinker	Developing process flowcharts to incorporate in the management plans for a project
Being precise	Detailing the exact content required to complete forms, requesting tools, data, etc.
Synthesizing components	Integrating all tools and the repository for reporting purposes on the project
Verbalizing	Producing narrative reports to describe progress
Visualizing	Producing report templates with graphics (e.g., trend chart) to reflect status to specific stakeholders

TABLE 9.3

Organizing Process and Groundwork for Creative Environment

Action	Example
Aligning individual and project goals and objectives	Arranging team organization in a way that brings people's goals and objectives in line with those of a project
Allowing time for issue definition	Taking the time to define differences of opinion, such as the content of reports, before trying to come up with a solution
Bringing people on board with fresh knowledge and experience	Assigning people on a team who have a wide background entailing a breadth of experience working on different projects
Broadening people's knowledge and experience	Grouping people on a team in a manner that causes them to share knowledge, expertise, and experience with others having different backgrounds
Countering groupthink	Arranging teams that encourage people with different backgrounds to work together
Emphasizing coordination	Setting up a fully equipped control room that stakeholders can be regularly use to enable them to work together
Establishing a receptive audience	Encouraging stakeholders to contribute articles to a project's newsletter or website
Granting access to data to do their job	Setting up a work area, frequently in a control room, that enables people to use their electronic equipment to obtain the data and information needed to perform their responsibilities
Granting access to necessary tools	Setting up a work area that enables team members to use their tools (e.g., laptops) to access data
Making training available	Using a control room as a learning center to train team members on new tools or processes
Stress communications	Working with key stakeholders to develop a communications plan
Support people's growth	Using a control room as a training center

GROUNDWORK FOR INDIVIDUAL CREATIVITY

The organizing process should result in establishing an infrastructure that enables success. Project managers should seek to minimize bureaucracy and the degree of aggravation that accompanies the organizing process while completing their activities. Hence, the organizing process should center on supporting people operating with little or no oversight.

Some actions that project managers can take to allow people to be creative are outlined in Table 9.4.

TABLE 9.4

Organizing Process and Groundwork for Individual Creativity

Action	Example
Be spontaneous	Granting the people the freedom to express their thoughts and speak frankly without fear of reprisal
Conceptualize	Encouraging people to use their critical thinking to determine how the major components (e.g., processes, inputs, outputs, etc.) fit together
Have a diverse background	Encouraging people to work with others having a background or knowledge different from their own
Have the capacity to "break set"	Providing training opportunities that enhance people's abilities to look at a problem or issue from a different perspective
See outside the box	Providing people with training on creative tools and techniques that encourage looking from the outside, in

GROUNDWORK FOR TEAM CREATIVITY

The organizing process should provide opportunities for people to work as a team by setting up an infrastructure that encourages collaborating, communicating, and sharing of data, information, and other resources.

Some actions that project managers can take to allow a team to be creative are shown in Table 9.5.

RELEVANT TOOLS AND TECHNIQUES

Tools and techniques should assist stakeholders, especially team members, in accomplishing the goals and objectives of their project. The emphasis should not be on reinventing the wheel, so to speak, but using existing supporting infrastructures from a parent organization or identified in lessons learned in other projects.

Some common creativity tools and techniques that project managers can apply for this process are shown in Table 9.6.

TABLE 9.5

Organizing Process and Groundwork for Team Creativity

Action	Example
Avoid noncontributory activities	Reducing the number and frequency of meetings that do not contribute to the deliverable on a project
Emphasize relationship building	Arranging the work area so that people have an opportunity to communicate and coordinate more often
Improve the physical environment but not too much	Providing enough comfort in a work area that frees people from excess noise and other distractions
Keep the team small	Restricting the number of people that are assigned to a project or at least the quantity assigned to a subteam
Obtain diverse membership	Hiring people from different fields and experiences to encourage alternative viewpoints about issues or solutions
Reduce the fear of the unknown	Providing people with training on tools and techniques for developing and evaluating ideas
Seek balance among creating, planning, and implementing	Placing people on the team who have experiences and knowledge in coming up with new ideas, determining what must be done to make them a reality, and finally to put them in the real world
Seek people who are unafraid to push boundaries	Hiring people who have enough courage to challenge people's assumptions and beliefs about a particular topic
Share tangible and intangible assets	Setting up a work area that provides a common set of tools to access data and information residing in a repository

TRADITIONAL CREATIVITY LIFE CYCLE MODEL

Within the organizing process, project managers can apply the five phases of the creativity life cycle model. Each phase plays an instrumental role in clarifying and resolving an issue or problem.

Preparation Phase

The purpose of the preparation phase is to learn as much information as possible about a topic and to compile any necessary information that will prove useful in coming up with creative ideas. This phase is largely focused on people and process.

TABLE 9.6

Organizing Process and Tools and Techniques

Tool and Technique	Example
Checklists	Developing a list of data and information to populate a repository
Field trip	Taking select team members to other locations to see how other projects populate and use their control rooms
Idea bulletin board	Putting up a wall panel in a control room with the purpose of collecting ideas for improving communications on a project
Interviewing	Meeting in one-on-one sessions with key stakeholders to obtain their thoughts about what should go into the management plans
Matrices	Using matrices to capture data and information to populate management plans
Modeling	Developing flowcharts to complement or supplement management plans
Observation	Visiting other projects to see how their work areas are set up, such as a control room
Offsite	Taking team members to a remote location to design the work area for a project
Role playing	Taking the perspective of certain stakeholders to try to understand what they would like to see in a control room

For example, a project manager faces one of the hardest challenges when addressing the communications requirements of a project with a large number of stakeholders. His difficulty is providing all stakeholders with common information, while at the same time meeting their specific needs or wants. Some stakeholders are interested only in financial performance; others in schedule; still others in technical quality. The danger is that providing narrow information, such as only financial, may simply be tunnel vision and may lose participation of other stakeholders. However, putting in information that someone else deems unimportant may have the same effect. The key is balance. The project manager decides to meet with the stakeholders and collect needs and wants regarding project information. He also decides to see what ideas for information distribution currently exist outside his organization or on other projects.

Concentration Phase

The purpose of the concentration phase is to focus on exactly defining a problem or issue to address. Project managers need to distinguish between what is and is not relevant, and just as importantly, what is and is not significant.

Continuing with communications requirements as an example, the project manager realizes he has to define exactly what each stakeholder needs and somehow determine some commonalities among the requests. Then he can determine the specific needs and requirements of each significant stakeholder. He then obtains their answers by going through the information collected during the preparation phase. A lingering question concerns how to record those requirements.

Incubation Phase

The purpose of the incubation phase is to allow the subconscious part of the mind to work by suspending judgment and avoiding concentration on a conscious level.

Continuing with communications requirements as an example, the project manager elects to do something else, such as work on another task or support another project, to free his mind. This available time allows the subconscious to work and also allows time for him to discover other ways to communicate information.

Illumination Phase

The purpose of the illumination phase is to allow an idea to rise to the conscious level of its creator. This phase involves coming up with solutions to difficulties identified earlier.

Continuing with communications requirements as an example, the project manager discusses with core team members what another project team did and then creates what is known as a *communications management plan*. Some core team members offer suggestions on the type of content to include in a communications management plan.

Verification and Production Phase

The purpose of the verification and production phase is to test and implement an idea. It is when thought turns to action.

Continuing with communications requirements as an example, the project manager with the core team prepares a draft of a communications management plan. He prepares a straw horse to review with the core team and then eventually presents it to significant stakeholders for review and approval. Finally, after receiving concurrence, the project manager publishes it.

CONCLUSION

The organizing phase centers on providing key stakeholders with an infrastructure that enables a project to run efficiently and effectively. The most difficult challenge is to separate what is necessary from the superfluous. Failure to do so can inhibit performance by setting up a bureaucracy that becomes the focus of attention rather than helping people to do work. Creativity helps ensure that the elements of the infrastructure work for key stakeholders.

Getting Started Checklist

Question	Yes	No
1. During this process, determine the challenges and constraints that could impact the creativity of your project team:		
Hierarchy		
Lack of data and information		
Lack of sharing		
Lack of tools		
Poor communication		
Poor coordination		
Team composition imbalance		
Too much and too little training		
Other(s):		
2. Determine the creative abilities that are applicable to this process:		
Being a linear thinker		
Being precise		
Synthesizing components		
Verbalizing		
Visualizing		
Other(s):		
3. Determine the actions that are necessary to lay the groundwork for a creative environment:		
Aligning individual and project goals and objectives		
Allowing time for issue definition		
Bringing on board people with fresh knowledge and experience		
Broadening people's knowledge and experience		
Countering groupthink		
Emphasizing coordination		
Establishing a receptive audience		
Granting access to data to do their job		

(Continued)

Getting Started Checklist

Question	Yes	No
Granting access to necessary tools		
Making training available		
Stress communications		
Support people's growth		
Other(s):		
4. Determine the actions to take to improve individual creativity:		
Be spontaneous		
Conceptualize		
Have a diverse background		
Have the capacity to "break set"		
See outside the box		
Other(s):		
5. Determine the actions to take to improve team creativity:		
Avoid noncontributory activities		
Emphasize relationship building		
Improve the physical environment, but not too much		
Keep the team small		
Obtain diverse membership		
Reduce the fear of the unknown		
Seek balance among creating, planning, and implementing		
Seek people who are unafraid to push boundaries		
Share tangible and intangible assets		
Other(s):		
6. Identify the creativity tools and techniques to use:		
Checklists		
Field trip		
Idea bulletin board		
Interviewing		
Matrices		
Modeling		
Observation		
Offsite		
Role playing		
Other(s):		

10

Creativity and the Planning Process

INTRODUCTION

The planning process involves determining the roadmap to achieve the goals and objectives of a project and provides the details for the output identified from the defining process. It provides specificity in addressing the who, what, when, why, where, and how that is often lacking in the output of the defining process.

BENEFITS

There are many benefits attributed to the planning process. Perhaps most importantly, it provides a roadmap to achieve the vision, goals, and objectives for projects. It also encourages greater communication and coordination among stakeholders, enhances one's ability to perform proactively rather than reactively, and instills confidence among the stakeholders that the project manager knows what he or she is doing and where the project is going.

CONSEQUENCES OF FAILURE

Failure to perform this process has tremendous impact downstream on a project, especially during the executing, monitoring and controlling, and closing processes. A considerable number of problems that occur in subsequent processes and the latter part of the project life cycle manifest shortcomings in the planning process. A poorly defined work breakdown structure, an unrealistic schedule, unreliable cost and time estimates, and no risk assessment are just a few common shortcomings that occur in the planning process and permeate the latter processes and phases of a project. Ultimately, such shortcomings impact cost, schedule, and quality performance.

DELIVERABLES

The planning process has several project management deliverables (see Figure 10.1), including:

- Cost and time estimates
- Issue management
- Management plans
- Network diagram

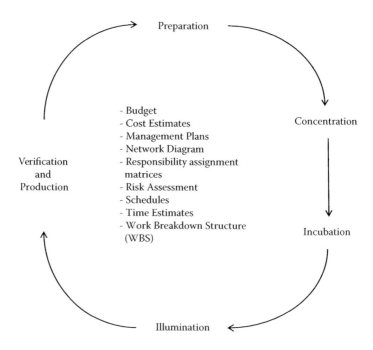

FIGURE 10.1
Planning process and deliverables.

- Responsibility assignment matrices
- Risk assessment
- Schedules (e.g., milestone chart, bar chart, precedence diagram)
- Work breakdown structure

IDEAL STATE

Ideally, project managers would like to have all the deliverables from the defining process complete and available. Using the output from the defining process, project managers have just the right amount of time and resources. Enough time is available to determine the details to achieve the vision, goals, and objectives of a project. Resources, which often include time, provide the knowledge, expertise, and experience needed. Project managers would also like to have the tangible and intangible support to develop meaningful plans. Tangible support might include money, for example; intangible support might include being a champion for a project. Project managers also have the latitude to work independently with the team and other stakeholders to come up with the best possible plan.

As usual, the reality often prevails over the ideal state. Sufficient time and resources are unavailable; if they are, they may be inadequate (e.g., stakeholders lacking the requisite knowledge, expertise, or experience to plan adequately). Not all significant stakeholders may be supportive and, in fact, may be hostile to the project or offer tepid support at best. Some important stakeholders may not care about a project. Stakeholders providing oversight may not give project managers the latitude to work with the team to plan the project and may impose unrealistic constraints that lay the groundwork for failure.

CONTEXT

There are several contextual factors that project managers often face during the planning process. Here are just a few: The environment in which a project finds itself is often in flux. Changes in stakeholders and financial conditions can impact the planning process. The output of the defining process may be subject to change too, resulting in it soon being partially or totally irrelevant to the project. For technology projects, such environmental conditions can often be the case due to competitive pressures and market conditions. Budgeting can change due to a dynamic environment. Issues like funding reconciliation can prove difficult as revenue streams for the parent organization ebb and flow.

Ultimately, the context for planning is one of an ever-changing reality. Like a new car coming off a dealer's lot, a new plan can quickly lose its value, and therefore must be reconditioned to reflect reality.

CHALLENGES AND CONSTRAINTS

Of all the project management processes, the one facing the most challenges and constraints is the planning process.

Planning takes considerable time, energy, and other resources that few people have the wherewithal to apply to overcome challenges and constraints confronting this process. Some key stakeholders want action right away and think too much time and effort spent in planning is a waste. Others take the opposite view and see extreme detail as reflecting solid thinking. Some stakeholders view the insights, values, and so on of others as not as significant if coming from another discipline. Still others prefer to "wing it" and leap to judgment rather than do much planning at all.

Some common creative challenges and constraints confronting this process are shown in Table 10.1.

CREATIVE ABILITIES

Project managers and their team members must have a wide array of creative abilities to develop deliverables for this process. They must exhibit the abilities at strategic and tactical levels to ensure alignment of the vision, goals, and objectives of their project with the parent organization, while simultaneously creatively transcending accepted modes of business. These creative abilities must capitalize on both capabilities of the brain, that is, left and right. They must be analytical while simultaneously putting

TABLE 10.1

Planning Process and Challenges and Constraints

Creative Challenge and Constraint	Example
Craving for predictability	Lacking confidence in generating time estimates with minimal information
Embrace only what is known	Taking work breakdown structure templates from other projects and tailoring for a project
Fear	Avoiding making time estimates with the possibility of them being unreliable
Focus on the past or future, not the present	Not addressing a problem affecting a project at the moment but rather dealing with ones that have occurred early on and ones that potentially could occur in the future
Groupthink	Experiencing extreme pressure by peers to embrace an unrealistic time estimate
Having a compliant workforce	Following a process that has no relevance to solving a managerial or technical problem
Hierarchy	Having a management that has no interest in sliding a milestone despite a change in scope
Impatience	Not permitting enough time for brainstorming techniques to work
Inability to adapt	Adhering to the contents of a management plan despite the fact that a different approach is better to achieve desired project results
Insecurity	Avoiding making a decision about a key issue for fear of being wrong
Lack of sharing	Not providing key information to complete time estimates for a specific set of activities
Leaping to judgment	Resolving an issue in the Issues Management Log before collecting key facts, data, and approvals
Management's lack of responsiveness	Causing a delay in schedule performance due to management not making a key decision
Methodism	Adhering strictly to accepted procedures for estimating despite their inapplicability to the content of the project
Mismatch	Assigning people to a set of activities not conducive to their knowledge, skills, or abilities without having the appropriate training
Mores, beliefs, values	Subscribing to a managerial style for projects that may be inappropriate for a specific project
Not listening to inner voice	Not seriously considering one's gut feeling about a potential risk that might occur on a project despite evidence to the contrary

(Continued)

TABLE 10.1 (*Continued*)

Planning Process and Challenges and Constraints

Creative Challenge and Constraint	Example
Overemphasizing a by-the-book philosophy	Adhering to a procedure described in a management plan that is counterproductive because "those are the rules"
Poor communications	Not having a communications management plan
Poor coordination	Failing to engage the right people in building a responsibility assignment matrix
Silos	Not encouraging people from other organizations or disciplines to participate in estimating time to perform activities
Specialization	Failing to encourage stakeholders to increase their perspective when building a work breakdown structure
Start and stop flow	Designing the schedule in a manner that will cause people to switch from activity to activity before completing any of them, thereby causing people to take time to reacquaint themselves with the previous work to begin again
Stretching resources too thin	Making assignments that result in relying on a few individuals to perform most of the work for a project
Success	Allowing people to curtail the momentum of a project after successfully completing a major phase or deliverable

all the parts back together to create a new, improved deliverable. Their abilities should encourage stretching, even breaking boundaries by challenging accepted assumptions and rules in an attempt to find new ways to enhance cost, schedule, and quality performance. Project managers and team members exercise both intuition and logic, often at the same time.

Some relevant creative abilities required for this process are shown in Table 10.2.

GROUNDWORK FOR CREATIVE ENVIRONMENT

Creativity is absolutely critical to achieve a successful outcome to the planning process. The context as well as the challenges and constraints necessitate giving importance to creativity. After all, a project entails

TABLE 10.2

Planning Process and Creative Abilities

Creative Ability	Example
Applying reverse thinking	Determining in detail what is not in scope versus what is
Being iconoclastic, even nihilistic	Questioning the fundamental assumptions behind time estimates
Being analytical	Exploding a deliverable into smaller components
Being intuitive	Identifying a potential risk based upon a gut feeling and limited information
Being precise	Calculating a budget down to the last penny
Being self-critical	Questioning one's own assumptions about time estimates
Being serial	Calculating the forward and backward passes in a schedule
Combining intuition and logic	Using the nominal group technique to identify deliverables and selecting the ones for incorporating in the work breakdown structure
Conceptualizing	Drawing a high-level sketch of the logical relationships among deliverables in a work breakdown structure
Embracing ambiguity	Calculating time estimates for activity completion based upon little or no information
Reasoning, such as being logical	Building a network diagram
Seeing multiple answers	Performing Monte Carlo simulations
Shifting between convergent and divergent thinking	Building a work breakdown structure by starting at the bottom and working up to more abstract (higher) levels in the tree
Shifting from analysis to synthesis mode of thinking	Taking a random list of activities and grouping them according to some common criteria (e.g., deliverable)
Shifting perspectives	Reviewing a work breakdown structure from different functional areas (e.g., finance, information technology, etc.)
Suspending judgment	Avoiding the tendency to generate a time estimate to complete an activity before considering additional information
Unlearning and relearning	Shifting from a single-point estimating technique to a three-point estimating technique
Using cross-domain thinking	Applying both intuition and logic when estimating time for one or more activities
Using linear thinking	Constructing a network diagram

(Continued)

TABLE 10.2 (*Continued*)

Planning Process and Creative Abilities

Creative Ability	Example
Using nonlinear thinking	Drawing data flow diagrams to reflect the flow of data for executing a process described in a management plan
Using synthesis	Tying together the work packages of a WBS into a logical sequence (reflected in a network diagram)
Visualizing	Drawing a Gantt or bar chart

TABLE 10.3

Planning Process and Groundwork for Creative Environment

Action	Example
Align individual and team goals and objectives	Providing opportunities for team members to work on activities that they want to do
Build and maintain trust	Not attacking a stakeholder for communicating shortcomings and risks associated with a schedule resulting from a planning session
Concentrate creative energy	Focusing a team's effort to resolve a potentially severe risk affecting the quality of a deliverable
Emphasize coordination	Building a responsibility assignment matrix that reflects multidisciplinary cooperation in completing activities
Encourage ownership	Having people with responsibilities to complete activities to estimate the time to perform the work
Establish priorities	Working with key stakeholders to verify priorities (e.g., goals and objectives) so the team can plan accordingly
Make training available	Providing traditional and alternative approaches for training prior to performing assignments
Stress communications	Encouraging ongoing sharing of data and information about a project to develop meaningful plans

going into unprecedented territory and so does creativity. For the latter to enable the former, project managers must establish an atmosphere in which people feel comfortable expressing their ideas and channeling their energies into creating something useful for furthering the project. Ownership, trust, and communication are just some ways to further and capitalize on the creativity of individuals and an entire team.

Some actions that project managers can take to lay the groundwork for a creative environment are shown in Table 10.3.

GROUNDWORK FOR INDIVIDUAL CREATIVITY

Individuals are the linchpins for enabling creativity on projects. Project managers, however, need to encourage people to exhibit certain values and behaviors while others simply need to let naturally creative people be themselves. Project managers need to encourage and allow for the right side of the brain to flourish as much as the left. Too often, the left side has emphasis, giving preference to following form and function, for example, at the expense of the capabilities of the right side of the brain, which encourage breaking the rules, taking a different perspective, and liking to experiment. Project managers need to encourage both sides of the brain by seeking a balance and skewing the capabilities of one side of the brain over the other, based on a conscious decision.

Some actions that project managers can take to allow people to be creative are outlined in Table 10.4.

GROUNDWORK FOR TEAM CREATIVITY

Laying the groundwork for individuals to be creative is one half of engendering creativity on a project. Project managers must also make a concerted effort to lay additional groundwork for individuals to work together synergistically. They should focus on reducing oversight, red tape, and non-value-added activities, such as irrelevant meetings. They should also stress taking the cumulative creative energy of a team and directing it toward achieving the common vision, goals, and objectives of the project, but with minimal control.

Some actions that project managers can take to allow a team to be creative are outlined in Table 10.5.

RELEVANT TOOLS AND TECHNIQUES

The tools and techniques employed for the planning process span a wide range simply because of all the project management deliverables to produce. These tools and techniques will require using both sides

TABLE 10.4

Planning Process and Groundwork for Individual Creativity

Action	Example
Be destructive	Continuing to emphasize the importance of challenging assumptions and shattering ones no longer relevant when building a schedule
Be discontented with the status quo	Stressing the need for no longer performing in a manner equivalent to business as usual, such as giving first guess time and cost estimates
Be intuitive	Encouraging team members to express the gut feeling about risks pertaining to probability and impact
Be self-confident	Providing people with the training, tools, and data to perform their activities
Be theoretical and experiential at the same time	Encouraging team members to think about the different types of risks that could impact a project while simultaneously trying out potential mitigation strategies to see if they work
Conceptualize	Keeping the vision of the project in everyone's mind while building a work breakdown structure
Experience pleasure when creating	Allowing team members to select activities that they enjoy performing and reflecting on those experiences in a responsibility assignment matrix
Have a diverse background	Encouraging team members to expand their knowledge and experience by agreeing to work with colleagues on activities requiring multidisciplinary work
Have a strong sense of curiosity	Creating and assigning activities that require obtaining additional knowledge about a topic
Have an interest in the novel	Assigning people to activities that they had no previous knowledge or experience performing
Have the capacity to "break set"	Including in the work breakdown structure activities that challenge basic assumptions about a topic
See outside the box	Encouraging team members to consider other perspectives when building the work breakdown structure

of the brain on individual and group levels. These tools and techniques also require and encourage communication and collaboration with others to further the exchange of information and knowledge to produce creative results that enhance executing the project and product life cycles.

Some common creativity tools and techniques that project managers can apply for this process are shown in Table 10.6.

TABLE 10.5

Planning Process and Groundwork for Team Creativity

Action	Example
Allow everyone a sense of ownership	Holding a team session when building a work breakdown structure
Allow for open discussion and tolerate ideas	Conducting a team working session to identify risks and associated mitigation strategies
Allow the individual and group to coexist	Allowing individuals to come up with risk mitigation strategies and then holding a team discussion on which ones are potentially most effective dealing with risks
Be curious	Assigning a subteam or the entire team to investigate different ways to address a specific issue in the Issues Management Log
Build a collegial and hierarchical relationship	Conducting an offsite for key stakeholders to become familiar with others' interests and style when constructing a schedule
Know the priorities	Having the team constantly keep the vision in the forefront of their minds when building a work breakdown structure
Seek balance among creating, planning, and implementing	Reminding team members during planning sessions to keep the entire project life cycle and creativity life cycle in mind

TRADITIONAL CREATIVITY LIFE CYCLE MODEL

Within the planning process, project managers can apply the five phases of the creativity life cycle model. Each phase plays an instrumental role in clarifying and resolving an issue or problem.

Preparation Phase

The purpose of the preparation phase is to learn as much information as possible about a topic and to compile any necessary information that will prove useful in coming up with creative ideas. This phase focuses on all people, process, and product or service.

For example, a project manager needs to build a work breakdown structure (WBS), which clarifies the scope and content of a project and serves many other purposes. Many different ways exist to design the layout of the WBS by applying certain rules and heuristics to determine

TABLE 10.6

Planning Process and Tools and Techniques

Tool and Technique	Example
Affinity diagramming	Creating an activity listing and then grouping like activities into specific categories
Analogies, metaphors, and similes thinking	Comparing an estimating technique to an event or process that occurs in real life
Brainstorming	Taking key stakeholders in a room and listing all the risks that could occur on a project
Brainwriting	Having each person record ideas for dealing with a risk and passing it on the next person for revision
Checklists	Listing all the steps required to build a schedule and checking off each item as it is completed
Compare and contrast	Comparing two different planning methodologies and identifying the similarities and differences between the two
Crawford slip technique	Assembling a subteam or an entire team to address an issue listed in the Issues Management Log by identifying the problem or issue, generating ideas for dealing with the issue or problem, and then categorizing them
Delphi technique	Seeking to achieve consensus over time and cost estimates for a set of work packages on an entire project
Devil's advocate	Having someone assigned to challenge planning assumptions
Field trip	Visiting other companies to learn different approaches for planning projects of a similar nature
Force field analysis	Evaluating different schedule proposals to complete a project by looking at the forces and counter forces for each one
Hypothetical scenario	Determining what potential circumstances, not risks, could arise and ascertaining their consequences
Idea bulletin board	Setting up an easel pad or white board in a control room for stakeholders to record any ad hoc ideas for making reliable estimates
Imagineering	Visualizing what the perfect control room would look like and then recording it on paper
Interviewing	Holding one-on-one sessions with key stakeholders to identify risks and ideas for mitigation strategies
Lateral thinking	Taking a cross-functional perspective when developing a work breakdown structure
Matrices	Building a responsibility assignment matrix
Mind mapping	Recording, on a large sheet of paper or white board, a high-level approach for planning a project
Modeling	Drawing a network diagram
Nominal group technique	Generating ideas for mitigating a risk, developing criteria for evaluating them, and then having team members vote on each one

TABLE 10.6 (*Continued*)

Planning Process and Tools and Techniques

Tool and Technique	Example
Offsite	Conducting an off-premises planning session with team members
PDCA cycle	Resolving an issue in the Issues Management Log
Role playing	Assuming the perspective of another stakeholder when developing a risk mitigation strategy
Storyboarding	Taking an issue from the Issues Management Log; identifying ideas for addressing it; answering questions related to the who, what, when, where, why, and how for both the issue and resulting idea; and communicating the results
Synectics	Taking an issue from the Issues Management Log and using an analogy that works with the customer to clearly define the issue and develop a solution
Tree diagram	Developing a work breakdown structure
Workflow analysis	Creating a workflow for a scheduling a management plan and identifying areas for improvement in the process (e.g., reducing the number of approvals)

its usefulness as a project management deliverable. The project manager decides to conduct research on different designs and how to best display them. He does so by looking at the work breakdown structures of other projects, interviewing experts on building a work breakdown structure, conducting a literature review, and meeting with other team members.

Concentration Phase

The purpose of the concentration phase is to focus on exactly defining a problem or issue to address. Project managers need to distinguish between what is and is not relevant, and just as importantly, what is and is not significant.

Continuing with the WBS example, the project manager assembles team members to determine, based upon available information, what goes into the content of the work breakdown structure. Using the collected information and scope definition, the team starts to clarify the design and content of the WBS. This phase will likely require revising the scope to reflect unanticipated changes in work or additional information to complete the WBS.

Incubation Phase

The purpose of the incubation phase is to allow the subconscious part of the mind to work by suspending judgment and avoiding concentration on a conscious level.

Continuing with the WBS example, sometimes the approach is not readily apparent to members of the project team. Disagreements arise over the design and content. An impasse results and the project manager suggests, and everyone agrees, to work on something else. It is similar to a cooling-off period following a labor dispute. This allows the subconscious of individuals to work on the issue. When the team reconvenes during the next phase, team members can then share the ideas that percolated deep in their subconscious mind.

Illumination Phase

The purpose of the illumination phase is to allow an idea to rise to the conscious level of its creator. This phase involves coming up with solutions to difficulties identified earlier.

Continuing with the WBS example, team members assemble to resolve issues, especially ones that led to an impasse during the concentration phase. They employ a series of tools and techniques to allow ideas to arise, such as brainstorming or a variation (e.g., nominal group technique) to develop a solution.

Verification and Production Phase

The purpose of the verification and production phase is to test and implement an idea. It is when thought turns into action.

Continuing with the WBS example, assuming the design and content of the WBS are acceptable to the team, this phase requires ensuring that other key stakeholders support its design and content. Having found the WBS acceptable, the project manager and team members build a WBS for the project.

CONCLUSION

The planning process requires creativity more than any other process, with the exception of a situation where a showstopper occurs during the execution process. This process offers more opportunities than any other process to apply creativity. Unfortunately, too many planning sessions have people going through the motions to develop project management deliverables. As a result, opportunities to manage a project more efficiently and effectively are lost. It behooves project managers to encourage stakeholders in general, and team members in particular, to allow creativity to flow in a manner that will improve cost, schedule, and quality performance.

Getting Started Checklist

Question	Yes	No
1. During this process, determine the challenges and constraints that could impact the creativity of your project team:		
Craving for predictability		
Embracing only what is known		
Focusing on the past or future, not the present		
Groupthink		
Having a compliant workforce		
Hierarchy		
Impatience		
Inability to adapt		
Insecurity		
Lack of sharing		
Leaping to judgment		
Management's lack of responsiveness		
Methodism		
Mismatch		
Mores, beliefs, values		
Not listen to the inner voice		
Overemphasizing a by-the-book philosophy		
Poor communications		
Poor coordination		
Silos		
Specialization		
Start and stop of flow		
Stretching resources too thin		
Success		
Other(s):		
2. Determine the creative abilities that are applicable to this process:		
Applying reverse thinking		
Being iconoclastic, even nihilistic		
Being analytical		
Being intuitive		
Being precise		

(Continued)

Getting Started Checklist

Question	Yes	No
Being self-critical		
Being serial		
Combining intuition and logic		
Conceptualizing		
Embracing ambiguity		
Reasoning, such as being logical		
Seeing multiple answers		
Shifting between convergent and divergent thinking		
Shifting from analysis to synthesis mode of thinking		
Shifting perspectives		
Suspending judgment		
Unlearning and relearning		
Using cross-domain thinking		
Using linear thinking		
Using nonlinear thinking		
Using synthesis		
Visualizing		
Other(s):		

3. Determine the actions that are necessary to lay the groundwork for a creative environment:
   Align individual and team goals and objectives
   Build and maintain trust
   Concentrate creative energy
   Emphasize coordination
   Encourage ownership
   Establish priorities
   Make training available
   Stress communications
   Other(s):

4. Determine the actions to take to improve individual creativity:
   Be destructive
   Be discontented with the status quo
   Be intuitive
   Be self-confident
   Be theoretical and experiential at the same time
   Conceptualize
   Experience pleasure when creating
   Have a diverse background
   Have a strong sense of curiosity
   Have an interest in the novel
   Have the capacity to "break set"

Getting Started Checklist

Question	Yes	No
See outside the box		
Other(s):		
5. Determine the actions to take to improve team creativity:		
Allow everyone a sense of ownership		
Allow for open discussion and tolerate ideas		
Allow individual and group to coexist		
Be curious		
Build a collegial and hierarchical relationship		
Know the priorities		
Seek balance among creating, planning, and implementing		
Other(s):		
6. Identify the creativity tools and techniques to use:		
Affinity diagramming		
Analogies, metaphors, and similes thinking		
Brainstorming		
Brainwriting		
Checklists		
Compare and contrast		
Crawford slip technique		
Delphi technique		
Devil's advocate		
Field trip		
Force field analysis		
Hypothetical scenario		
Idea bulletin board		
Imagineering		
Interviewing		
Lateral thinking		
Matrices		
Mind mapping		
Modeling		
Nominal group technique		
Offsite		
PDCA cycle		
Role playing		
Storyboarding		
Synectics		
Tree diagram		
Workflow analysis		
Other(s):		

11

Creativity and the Executing Process

INTRODUCTION

The executing process involves actually applying a plan to achieve the vision, goals, and objectives of a project. It also helps to ensure that the efforts of a project remain focused efficiently and effectively.

BENEFITS

There are many benefits attributed to the executing process. It focuses the efforts on achieving vision, goals, and objectives; requires applying resources cost effectively; and helps keep the project in control by taking a disciplined approach during execution.

CONSEQUENCES OF FAILURE

Failure to perform this process has tremendous impact downstream on a project, especially during the monitoring and controlling, and closing processes. The energy of a team can dissipate. A team can lose sight of its vision, goals, and objectives. Morale and esprit de corps may plummet. Cost and schedule performance can deteriorate. The customer may end up with something that fails to meet expectations, that is, if anything is delivered. Finally, resources may be wasted.

FIGURE 11.1
Executing process and deliverables.

DELIVERABLES

The executing process has several project management deliverables (see Figure 11.1), including:

- Assessments and audits
- Change management
- Conflict resolution
- Issues management
- Meetings
- Product or service

IDEAL STATE

Ideally, project managers want the executing process to occur as smoothly as possible. People clearly focus on the vision, goals, and objectives. They know exactly what they have to do without much difficulty and oversight. Communication and collaboration occur without a flaw. Cost and schedule performance also goes according to baseline. If an issue or change arises, it is handled according to the appropriate management plan. All stakeholders are satisfied with what has happened and is happening.

The reality is, of course, far from the above description. Often, a tendency exists to stray from the plan. Esprit de corps must be maintained. Issues and defects arise that are not always handled according to the applicable management plan (if one even exists). Communication is difficult and collaboration is hindered by a host of constraints; and to add fuel to the fire, actual cost and schedule performance deviates from baselines and corrective action, even replanning, becomes necessary. The customer frequently changes its mind even to the point of dissatisfaction on the part of just about everyone.

CONTEXT

There are several contextual factors that project managers often face during the executing process. Here are just a few: The environment that a project often finds itself in is one of very high intensity. Stakeholders, especially the project manager and the team, are focusing on achieving the vision, goals, and objectives according to plan. Emotions often run high, whether negatively or positively, depending on how well the project is progressing. Problems, issues, and challenges, from people to technical ones, arise; some are anticipated, but more often than not, they are unexpected. Success occurs in some areas while in others, nightmares arise. Some stakeholders are extremely supportive during the executing process while others, quite frankly, sit on the sidelines taking sniper shots. Additionally, decisions external to the project can arise, resulting in a change in requirements, schedule milestones, and budget.

The entire executing process usually consumes the brunt of the resources and effort for a project. It truly is at that point where the project crosses the Rubicon and needs to balance its plan with reality to reach its vision, goals, and objectives. Naturally, this process

214 • *Creative, Efficient, and Effective Project Management*

offers many opportunities to exercise creativity, both on individual and team levels.

CHALLENGES AND CONSTRAINTS

Of all the processes, the executing process poses the greatest opportunity to witness the affects and effects of the challenges and constraints imposed on a project. Usually, the challenges and constraints center on these five areas: people, process, cost, schedule, and quality.

Project managers often do not get the people with the requisite skills, knowledge, and expertise to execute efficiently and effectively. They also do not get people who will work in a way that furthers the performance of the project; personality or cultural differences can constrain the flow of the project.

They may also have to perform according to an ambitious schedule. Key milestones may have been dictated; and while they have a duty to report on the impracticality of such a schedule, project managers may have no choice but to accept it or make a career-limiting decision. Imposed constraints limit the options project managers have at their disposal.

Project managers may also face a cost challenge or constraint. They may have to follow a cost baseline that, quite frankly, is unrealistic. They may have to adapt the best way they can to this circumstance to achieve the vision, goals, and objectives of a project. Again, project managers have a theoretical duty to report the impracticality of such constraints on projects, but often have no other choice but to accept it.

While people, time, and money are the usual constraints, having to follow a process to meet a specific qualitative or quantitative criterion can present challenges and constraints to a project. A process can actually be unrealistic by not being scalable to a project, thereby adding an administrative burden that deflects people from actually producing a deliverable.

Whether facing a challenge or constraint related to people, process, cost, schedule, or quality, a project will need individuals and a team that have some very highly creative abilities in its pursuit toward achieving vision, goals, and objectives.

Some common creative challenges and constraints confronting this process are shown in Table 11.1.

TABLE 11.1

Executing Process and Challenges and Constraints

Challenge and Constraint	Example
Compliant workforce	Having an unwillingness on the part of some team members to raise an issue at a team meeting
Dominance of brain thinking	Not considering how all the components of a project are impacted by a change
Faster, better, cheaper philosophy	Allowing the tendency to circumvent the change management process
Fear	Lacking the willingness or courage to address a conflict over an issue due to groupthink
Focus on the past or future, not the present	Applying a past successful approach for resolving an issue that may not work under contemporary conditions
Groupthink	Allowing peer pressure that results in pretending a problem or issue concerning a project is nonexistent
Impatience	Having an unwillingness to collect the facts and data about an issue before implementing a solution
Inability to adapt	Refusing to modify the schedule because of a scope change
Infighting	Allowing constant bickering to persist over a minor issue due to personality conflicts
Insecurity	Allowing an impasse over a critical issue to fester "below the radar" due to fear of conflict
Lack of data and information	Not having the necessary access to data and information to make a key decision about an important issue
Lack of sharing	Failing to impart knowledge or experience for the benefit of the team
Lack of tools	Not having tools to build a component of the product or service being delivered
Leaping to judgment	Jumping to conclusions about a change before collecting the necessary facts and data
Management's lack of responsiveness	Giving up on the need to continue to push management for a key decision or approval regarding a change
Methodism	Going through the motions to generate time estimates for implementing a change without really analyzing assumptions
Mismatch	Having someone work on an activity for which they are not suited and allowing the activity to slide
Mores, beliefs, values	Not challenging certain people's beliefs about how a project should be managed
Not listening to inner voice	Discounting one's gut feeling that an undetected risk has become an issue and impacts a project's performance

(Continued)

TABLE 11.1 (*Continued*)

Executing Process and Challenges and Constraints

Challenge and Constraint	Example
Overemphasis on by-the-book philosophy	Following a change management plan despite the fact that a need exists to remove certain approvals to improve performance
Poor communications	Failing to inform key stakeholders that an important change has been implemented
Poor coordination	Not involving key stakeholders (identified in a responsibility assignment matrix) while performing certain activities
Silos	Allowing different functional organizations to work independently on activities when they should be performing jointly
Specialization	Allowing different disciplines to work independently on activities when they should be performing jointly
Start and stop flow	Moving people from one activity to another before making any progress on the former
Stretching resources too thin	Performing two or more concurrent activities located on the critical path of a schedule
Success	Allowing the tendency to relax too long after the successful completion of a major milestone, leading to a slide in activities for the next delivery
Take on only what is known	Avoiding activities in the work breakdown structure that have little information, but can have high payback if executed successfully
Team composition imbalance	Having too many individuals with the same specialized background working on a work package when a balanced multidisciplinary composition works better
Too many positive and negative incentives	Giving out too many positive rewards, including rewards for meaningless work, so that the incentive to do an outstanding job is worthless
Too much and too little training	Sending people off to training who do not need it, at the expense of performing actual work for a project

CREATIVE ABILITIES

Creative abilities are absolutely critical during the executing process. As a planning process, this one provides several opportunities to exercise creativity on individual and team levels.

To a large extent, most opportunities arise when a challenge, issue, or problem impacts progress. A defect or change or potential showstopper is a typical example. Often, the most desired creative ability centers on taking a different perspective and then determining a precise solution that fixes the cause, not the symptom. Logic and intuition both play a role as well as a need to take a risk and learn from failure. Considerable analytical work is needed too, along with an ability to put the components back together in a manner that enhances performance.

Some creative abilities required for this process are shown in Table 11.2.

GROUNDWORK FOR CREATIVE ENVIRONMENT

Naturally, project managers must at least set the stage for creative abilities to blossom forth—not an easy task when a project is going full speed ahead toward achieving its vision, goals, and objectives. Creativity requires some break in the momentum of a project and many times people have little tolerance for taking the necessary time to apply creative abilities. Project managers, therefore, can play a key role in encouraging stakeholders, especially team members, to take the necessary time to use their creative abilities. They can also encourage stakeholders to share their resources to help others develop creative solutions. Key elements for enabling this to happen are building trust, encouraging openness, and allowing risk taking.

Some actions that project managers can take to lay the groundwork for a creative environment are shown in Table 11.3.

GROUNDWORK FOR INDIVIDUAL CREATIVITY

From an individual perspective, project managers need to ensure that the social and political environment allows the freedom to think creatively and take risks by thinking differently, using both logic and intuition. At the same time, they must encourage such thinking in a way that does not upset teaming because creative ideas often require the acceptance and collaboration of others to implement. Project managers must communicate their confidence and trust by providing the time and resources to generate creative solutions as well as provide an environment wherein other people can seriously consider individual contributions.

Some actions that project managers can take to allow people to be creative are outlined in Table 11.4.

TABLE 11.2

Executing Process and Creative Abilities

Creative Ability	Example
Applying reverse thinking	Evaluating the cause of a technical issue identified in the Issues Management Log by taking the opposite view of what is happening, thereby identifying the source of the problem
Applying synthesis	Decomposing a problem into understandable components (e.g., technical, personnel, etc.) and then putting them together to come up with a complete understanding of what is happening
Being iconoclastic, even nihilistic	Ruthlessly attacking the assumptions about a request for a change
Being analytical	Decomposing a problem into fundamental parts to enhance understanding of what has been, and is, occurring
Being observant	Watching team members performing their activities to determine whether a revised management plan is necessary for using tools
Being precise	Identifying the exact cause of a problem, such as a slide on a critical path in a schedule
Being self-critical	Questioning one's own assumptions to the point of reversing a decision about responding to an issue in the Issues Management Log
Combining intuition and logic	Acting on a technical or general problem where the information is inadequate but requires action soon before it negatively impacts a project
Determining the essence of something	Taking time with the team to analyze the cause of a change request
Embracing ambiguity	Acting on a problem where the cause is difficult to determine and the consequences of a fix will be hard to anticipate
Having fun	Holding a party for a team to relieve stress, build esprit de corps, and celebrate successes to date
Listening to your intuition	Operating on a gut feeling about a problem when facts and data are hard to find
Looking from the outside, in	Extricating yourself and others from a problem, which increases objectivity and independence when evaluating a change request
Reasoning	Evaluating a change request from a purely cost perspective
Shifting between convergent and divergent thinking	Evaluating the impact of a potential change from a contextual perspective and also from a detailed one (e.g., macro and micro levels)
Shifting from analysis to synthesis mode of thinking	Decomposing an issue into fundamental elements, and then putting the components back together in a way to determine their relationships and the cause for the issue
Shifting perspectives	Evaluating a change from multifunctional, multidisciplinary perspectives

TABLE 11.2 (*Continued*)

Executing Process and Creative Abilities

Creative Ability	Example
Suspending judgment	Waiting for all the schedule, cost, and quality facts and data about an issue to be in before making a decision about a change request
Tinkering	Experimenting with a change to the schedule to see the impact on the project end date
Uncovering patterns	Reviewing schedule data to determine patterns with the performance involving certain team members
Unlearning and relearning	Quitting making revised single-point estimates and performing the three-point estimate technique
Using linear thinking	Replanning by drawing a revised network diagram
Using nonlinear thinking	Drawing data flow diagrams to reflect interaction among revised contents within a cost management plan

GROUNDWORK FOR TEAM CREATIVITY

Project managers must also set the environment to encourage creativity on a team level. Again, the social and political environment plays a crucial role in helping creativity to blossom forth. Key in this respect is ensuring that the team tolerates new ideas; project managers should, for example, counter the potential for groupthink. They must, at the same time, ensure the team capitalizes on its synergistic capabilities by encouraging greater relationship building; providing facilitating as a directing role; keeping everyone focused on the vision, goals, and objectives; and engendering a learning, sharing, and collating environment, all coupled with ongoing communication.

Some actions that project managers can take to allow teams to be creative are outlined in Table 11.5.

RELEVANT TOOLS AND TECHNIQUES

The tools and techniques for the executing process are more focused on developing creative solutions to resolve problems or issues. If a project runs smoothly, then applied rather than critical thinking has a prevalent role. If a project is like many others, then unforeseen problems or issues

TABLE 11.3

Executing Process and Groundwork for a Creative Environment

Action	Example
Allow for risk taking	Giving support to team members to take a different technical approach that has a high chance of failure but, if it succeeds, will improve cost and schedule performance
Allow time for issue definition	Setting aside sufficient time for analysis of a change request
Build and maintain trust	Continuously communicate both positive and negative information
Concentrate creative energy	Allowing noncritical activities to slide by shifting people to work on activities that are slipping on the critical path in the schedule
Counter groupthink	Assigning new people on the project who do not have a vested interest in what was done in the past
Emphasize coordination	Encouraging people from different disciplines to work together to resolve an issue identified in the Issues Management Log
Encourage a certain degree of anxiety and tension	Keeping approaching milestones in the forefront of the minds of key stakeholders
Encourage ownership	Giving people an opportunity to present the outcome of their efforts to the rest of the project team and other key stakeholders
Encourage transformational leadership	Pushing people to apply their skills in a way that goes beyond the norm
Establish a receptive audience	Working to keep key stakeholders, especially senior leaders, abreast of what is going on in the project
Grant people access to data to do their job	Removing obstacles that prohibit team members from getting the data needed to do their job
Grant access to necessary tools	Ensuring team members have the necessary software to collect and process data
Make training available	Providing timely training before team members need it, not during or after
Provide opportunities to create	Allowing people some time to experiment with a new tool or technique to see what outcome might occur
Relax rules, procedures, etc.	Reducing the number of required approvals to obtain tools and data
Reward risk taking	Giving people recognition for taking a risk, even if they fail
Stress communications	Constantly emphasizing the need for people to inform others about the results of their work

TABLE 11.4

Executing Process and Groundwork for Individual Creativity

Action	Example
Be competitive and collaborate at the same time	Encouraging individuals to speak their minds but still embrace consensus, meaning they might not agree in total with a decision but will support it nonetheless
Be courageous	Having people who are willing to speak up against the status quo despite it having a long tradition of acceptance by key stakeholders
Be curious	Encouraging individuals to tinker and experiment with new techniques
Be destructive	Encouraging individuals to challenge long-held assumptions and beliefs
Be discontented with the status quo	Having individuals challenging business-as-usual practices to improve schedule performance
Be intuitive	Encouraging individuals to tackle issues that sometimes have very few facts and data and rely on one's gut feeling to take the right action
Be self-confident	Giving individuals the psychological support needed to take on complicated activities
Be spontaneous	Encouraging individuals to be willing to share their thoughts, such as in a brainstorming session, without fear of reprisal by team members
Be theoretical and experiential at the same time	Having individuals draw a conceptual or logical model of a deliverable before actually creating a physical one
Experience pleasure when creating	Continuing to ask individuals whether they are getting burned out, especially during times of sustained activity
Have an interest in the novel	Encouraging individuals to look for new and better tools and techniques to complete their activities
Have self-discipline	Ensuring individuals have the self-control to know that whatever they do on a project contributes to its overall success
Have the ability to be self-critical	Encouraging people to question their own assumptions, such as when replanning
Have the capacity to "break set"	Recognizing that people move from the beaten path to complete their activities
Persevere	Providing support to people who demonstrate an inclination to challenge seemingly overwhelming resistance from key stakeholders
Realize that sooner or later creativity must be implemented	Having people develop new ideas for improving a process or technique to create an accompanying implementation plan

(Continued)

TABLE 11.4 (*Continued*)

Executing Process and Groundwork for Individual Creativity

Action	Example
See outside the box	Encouraging people to take a different perspective in trying to resolve an issue or problem
Take risks	Encouraging people to try a new tool or technique during an activity that could eventually improve the cost performance of the project
Tolerate failure	Encouraging people to accept responsibility for their failures as well as their successes

arise because of the dynamics of the environment, thereby necessitating the application of good creative thinking tools and techniques. These tools and techniques center on defining the problem or issue; coming up with a real solution (meaning fixing the problem and not the symptoms); and then implementing the solution while receiving feedback on its effectiveness followed by corrective action, if necessary.

Some common creativity tools and techniques that project managers can apply for this process are shown in Table 11.6.

TRADITIONAL CREATIVITY LIFE CYCLE MODEL

Within the executing process, project managers can apply the five phases of the creativity life cycle model. Each phase plays an instrumental role in clarifying and resolving an issue or problem.

Preparation Phase

The purpose of the preparation phase is to learn as much information as possible about the topic and to compile any necessary information that will prove useful in coming up with creative ideas. This phase focuses largely on people and process.

For example, the project manager experiences an issue regarding buy-off on a deliverable for the project. Key stakeholders, such as the customer or sponsor, request a change in the requirements that was unanticipated during the early phases of the project life cycle. The customer still insists that schedule commitments must be met and no additional budget is available.

TABLE 11.5

Executing Process and Groundwork for Team Creativity

Action	Example
Act as if on a mission	Keeping the vision, goals, and objectives at the forefront of the team when making collaborative decisions
Allow for open discussion and have a tolerance for ideas	Conducting frequent meetings to share knowledge and experiences on common issues and problems experienced
Allow individual and group to coexist	Giving everyone an opportunity to speak, share thoughts, and contribute at meetings
Avoid noncontributory activities	Sheltering the team from insignificant administrative responsibilities so members can focus on their activities
Be collegial and hierarchical	Encouraging team members to communicate informally as well as formally, both laterally and vertically
Be curious	Providing subteams with opportunities to experiment with new tools and techniques to determine if schedule performance can improve
Be emotional and logical	Building esprit de corps and excitement among team members while simultaneously encouraging people to continue to comply with the schedule
Be small in size	Keeping teams as small as possible and breaking into subteams, if necessary
Be synergistic	Encouraging everyone to work as harmoniously as possible to capitalize on their combined strengths
Be true believers	Reminding everyone constantly of the importance of the team's work in achieving the vision, goals, and objectives of the project
Be unafraid to push boundaries	Encouraging team members to "break set" when executing their responsibilities
Emphasize relationship building	Providing opportunities for team members to work together, addressing problems or issues
Engender facilitative and supportive leadership	Providing the necessary protection from bureaucratic obstacles and interventions from stakeholders who are not directly involved with the project
Have fun	Holding celebrations after delivering a major deliverable or completing a major milestone
Know the priorities	Reminding the team of the vision, goals, and objectives when executing activities
Seek balance among creating, planning, and implementing	Reminding the team that it must be not only creative, but must also implement the ideas
Share tangible and intangible assets	Enabling team members to share information, tools, and knowledge among colleagues
View failure as a learning experience	Reminding everyone on the team that groups, as well as people, do not always succeed, at least as expected, and should use failure as a learning experience

TABLE 11.6

Executing Process and Tools and Techniques

Tool and Technique	Example
Affinity diagramming	Collecting a list of issues and arranging them in categories for greater manageability and determining a pattern
Analogies, metaphors, and similes thinking	Comparing a technical problem to something unrelated to the project to provide insight into a possible solution
Brainstorming	Assembling team members together to develop potential solutions to a technical problem
Brainwriting	Having each person record ideas for dealing with an issue and passing it on the next person for revision
Crawford slip technique	Assembling a subteam or an entire team to address an issue listed in the Issues Management Log by identifying the problem or issue, generating ideas for dealing with the issue or problem, and then categorizing them
Devil's advocate	Assigning someone on the team to question the prevailing thinking when addressing a problem
Fishbone diagram	Having the team do an analysis of a problem to determine the root cause for its existence
Force field analysis	Requiring any suggestion for improvement to identify the forces and counterforces affecting the change before being implemented
Hypothetical scenario	Identifying a potential challenge confronting a project and identifying a contingency plan for dealing with it
Nominal group technique	Generating ideas for solving a problem, developing criteria for evaluating them, and then having team members vote on each one
PDCA cycle	Having all improvements in processes progress through this cycle
Problem solving	Requiring that any solution go through an evaluation predicated on a solid definition of the problem in order for the solution to be selected

Disagreements exist over how to respond to this situation. During this phase of the creativity life cycle, the project manager and team members conduct research to determine how other projects may have successfully dealt with the scenario in dealing with the same customer. They conduct a literature review to determine what possible approaches might exist. Finally, they talk to experts not associated with the project, who may be external or internal to the parent organization. Particularly noteworthy is that the project manager makes every effort during this phase to engage all relevant parties to encourage buy-in of what the final problem is—if not through agreement, then by consensus.

Concentration Phase

The purpose of the concentration phase is to focus on exactly defining the problem or issue to address. Project managers need to distinguish between what is and is not relevant, and just as importantly, what is and is not significant.

Continuing with the deliverable example, team members assemble to address the issue. The results of the preparation phase are shared, and disagreements quickly surface over the solutions proposed, even before the problem has been fully defined. A small number of team members disagree vehemently over what the problem is and every proposed solution. The project manager, after looking at the schedule, determines that some time exists to let the issue rest to give people time to think about what the problem and solutions are.

Incubation Phase

The purpose of the incubation phase is to allow the subconscious part of the mind to work by suspending judgment and avoiding concentration on a conscious level.

Continuing with the deliverable example, team members work on the issue. It also affords them an additional opportunity to conduct some more research on just what the problem is and what the possible solutions are. Some stakeholders realize that the issue is not what they thought it was, and a different approach from what anyone considered is required.

Illumination Phase

The purpose of the illumination phase is to allow an idea to rise to the conscious level of its creator. This phase involves coming up with solutions to difficulties identified earlier.

Continuing with the deliverables example, team members, including representatives from the customer, assemble to share any additional information and offer their thoughts on what the problem is and the possible solutions for resolving it. The team decides to apply the nominal group technique to achieve consensus over the definition of the problem, draw a fishbone diagram to identify its causes, generate potential solutions, and eventually select the most suitable one.

Verification and Production Phase

The purpose of the verification and production phase is to test and implement an idea.

Continuing with the deliverable example, the project manager decides to set up a half-day offsite with the team and other stakeholders, such as representatives from the customer, to develop a roadmap to deploy the accepted change. All participants in the offsite decide that a cost and schedule replanning effort is necessary to achieve the original performance targets for the project.

CONCLUSION

The executing process provides all the opportunities necessary to apply creativity on a project. The chances of something unexpected are high, especially as the complexity and the size of a project increase. Many opportunities center on correcting problems or resolving issues. If good project management disciplines exist, applying the creativity life cycle is fairly straightforward. However, sometimes the difficulty of a problem or issue, and the dynamics of the team members, can make coming up with an agreed-upon definition and an acceptable solution quite challenging in itself. Some of the creativity techniques can go a long way in achieving consensus, if not agreement.

Getting Started Checklist

Question	Yes	No
1. During this process, determine the challenges and constraints that could impact the creativity of your project team:		
Compliant workforce		
Dominance of brain thinking		
Faster, better, cheaper philosophy		
Fear		
Focus on the past or future, not the present		
Groupthink		
Impatience		
Inability to adapt		
Infighting		
Insecurity		
Lack of data and information		

Getting Started Checklist

Question	Yes	No
Lack of sharing		
Lack of tools		
Leaping to judgment		
Management's lack of responsiveness		
Methodism		
Mismatch		
Mores, beliefs, values		
Not listen to the inner voice		
Overemphasis on by-the-book philosophy		
Poor communications		
Poor coordination		
Silos		
Specialization		
Start and stop of flow		
Stretching resources too thin		
Success		
Take on only what is known		
Team composition imbalance		
Too many positive and negative incentives		
Too much and too little training		
Other(s):		
2. Determine the creative abilities that are applicable to this process:		
Apply reverse thinking		
Applying synthesis		
Being iconoclastic, even nihilistic		
Being analytical		
Being observant		
Being precise		
Being self-critical		
Combining intuition and logic		
Determining the essence of something		
Embracing ambiguity		
Having fun		
Listening to your intuition		
Looking from the outside in		
Reasoning		
Shifting between convergent and divergent thinking		
Shifting from analysis to synthesis mode of thinking		
Shifting perspectives		
Suspending judgment		

(Continued)

Getting Started Checklist

Question	Yes	No
Tinkering		
Uncovering patterns		
Unlearning and relearning		
Using linear thinking		
Using nonlinear thinking		
Other(s):		
3. Determine the actions that are necessary to lay the groundwork for a creative environment:		
Allow for risk taking		
Allow time for issue definition		
Build and maintain trust		
Concentrate creative energy		
Counter groupthink		
Emphasize coordination		
Encourage a certain degree of anxiety and tension		
Encourage ownership		
Encourage transformational leadership		
Establish a receptive audience		
Grant access to data to do their job		
Grant access to necessary tools		
Make training available		
Provide opportunities to create		
Relax rules, procedures, and so on		
Reward risk taking		
Stress communications		
Other(s):		
4. Determine the actions to take to improve individual creativity:		
Be competitive and collaborative at the same time		
Be courageous		
Be curious		
Be destructive		
Be discontented with the status quo		
Be intuitive		
Be self-confident		
Be spontaneous		
Be theoretical and experiential at the same time		
Experience pleasure when creating		
Have an interest in the novel		
Have self-discipline		
Have the ability to be self-critical		
Have the capacity to "break set"		

Getting Started Checklist

Question	Yes	No
Persevere		
Realize sooner or later creativity requires being implemented		
See outside the box		
Take risks		
Tolerate failure		
Other(s):		
5. Determine the actions to take to improve team creativity:		
Act as if on a mission		
Allow for open discussion and have a tolerance for ideas		
Allow individual and group to coexist		
Avoid noncontributory activities		
Be collegial and hierarchical		
Be curious		
Be emotional and logical		
Be small in size		
Be synergistic		
Be true believers		
Be unafraid to push boundaries		
Emphasize relationship building		
Engender facilitative and supportive leadership		
Have fun		
Know the priorities		
Seek balance among creating, planning, and implementing		
Share tangible and intangible assets		
View failure as a learning experience		
Other(s):		
6. Identify the creativity tools and techniques to use:		
Affinity diagramming		
Analogies, metaphors, and similes thinking		
Brainstorming		
Brainwriting		
Crawford slip technique		
Devil's advocate		
Fishbone diagram		
Force field analysis		
Hypothetical scenario		
Nominal group technique		
PDCA cycle		
Problem solving		
Other(s):		

12

Creativity and the Monitoring and Controlling Process

INTRODUCTION

The monitoring and controlling process involves collecting and assessing information about the performance of a project and taking the necessary corrective actions to improve that performance. It is closely linked with another project management process, executing.

BENEFITS

There are many benefits attributed to the monitoring and controlling process. It gives cost, schedule, and quality performance feedback on where the project has been, is, and will be; it gives stakeholders a sense of confidence that project managers have a good idea about the state of a project at any given time; it serves as an excellent way to communicate to all applicable stakeholders; and it provides project managers with a way to respond more effectively to circumstances, especially if something unexpected does arise.

CONSEQUENCES OF FAILURE

Failure to perform this process has several consequences. Project managers and other stakeholders will have little or no idea about the current state of their projects or where they will end up. Due to lack of information about status when something does go awry, they react by constantly putting out fires. Communication and collaboration challenges and failures are commonplace. Esprit de corps and morale often deteriorate as people start thinking the worst.

DELIVERABLES

The monitoring and closing process has several project management deliverables (Figure 12.1), including:

- Change request disposition
- Configuration management
- Corrective action
- Management reserve
- Procurements
- Quality control
- Replanning
- Risk response
- Status collection and forecasting

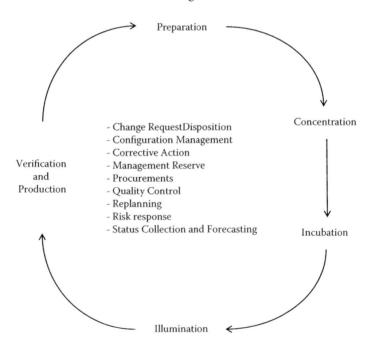

FIGURE 12.1
Monitoring and controlling process and deliverables.

IDEAL STATE

Ideally, project managers have a good communication management plan in place that enables information to flow vertically (e.g., up and down the chain of command) and horizontally (e.g., among peers, cost effectively). All stakeholders identify and receive the information that they need, no more and no less. They have at their disposal the tools to provide status on their activities and deliverables, and can pull any information satisfying their needs or wants. All stakeholders follow the change and configuration management processes and help evaluate the cost and schedule impacts of a change. Everyone attends the necessary meetings and actively participates by sharing information and other insights. Ample time is available to determine and take corrective action and, if necessary, perform replanning.

The reality, of course, is often far from what is described above. Data to generate information is frequently inaccurate and must be scrubbed and verified. Some team members forget or do not want to provide status. Some key stakeholders do not have the time or wherewithal to attend meetings. Some changes are implemented, whether intentionally or inadvertently, after bypassing the change and configuration management disciplines. Time and money are in short supply, which makes analysis and decision making difficult and often results in quick fixes on symptoms rather than focusing on the source of a problem or issue.

CONTEXT

There are several contextual factors that project managers often face during the monitoring and control process. Here are just a few.

The monitoring and controlling process occurs simultaneously with the executing process. This makes the relationship between the two processes a very critical one to ensure that what is occurring in the executing process is reflected in what is produced during the monitoring and controlling process.

As a result, the inputs and outputs of the monitoring and controlling process must be accurate, timely, and useful to the stakeholders. Not an easy responsibility to assume for any fast-moving, highly visible project. In addition to the accuracy, timeliness, and usefulness of the output, the data obtained during this process must be scrubbed to ensure information is not garbage. The larger the project, the greater the need to integrate the two processes (executing and monitoring with controlling).

Also, effort is made, due to the dynamic environment of projects during the executing process, to be proactive rather than reactive. Hence, there exists a need to implement a disciplined approach to manage issues, changes, and risks. Again, communication and information play key roles as well as a need to adhere to management plans.

The entire monitoring and controlling process is viewed by some stakeholders as necessary, while others might see it as red tape or bureaucratic. Depending on the degree of power that project managers possess, this process can operate smoothly or it can be a major headache. If the latter, it can require some creative thinking on how to make the process more efficient, effective, and value-added for all key stakeholders.

CHALLENGES AND CONSTRAINTS

Perhaps the two biggest challenges and constraints that affect this process are communication and information. Both, naturally, are tightly linked; the quality of one affects that of the other.

Communication becomes a challenge and constraint because effective communication is difficult to implement. Stakeholders have different styles and needs, and the larger the project, the more difficult it becomes to satisfy the latter. Some people prefer the personal touch when receiving communications while others want to communicate only through email. Some people prefer group sessions while others want a regularly scheduled one-on-one session. Some people want to communicate constantly while others only do so when an issue or problem needs attention.

Information is the other challenge and constraint. Too much information is just as problematic as too little. A balance is needed to ensure effective communications. People vary, too, on how information is presented and delivered. Some people want summary information while others want detail. Some people want it graphically while others desire it in narrative form. Some people want it in hard copy while others want it electronically.

Some common creative challenges and constraints confronting this process are shown in Table 12.1.

TABLE 12.1

Monitoring and Controlling Process and Challenges and Constraints

Challenge and Constraint	Example
Craving for predictability	Relentlessly pursuing facts and data when more than enough is already available
Dominance of brain thinking	Weaving detail analysis with an overall assessment of a project's performance
Faster, better, cheaper philosophy	Encouraging people to produce a deliverable replete with defects to meet a key milestone date
Fear	Being afraid of reprisals for coming up with a solution to a technical problem that will upset certain stakeholders
Focus on the past or future, not the present	Allowing a detected defect to pass through inspection in order to maintain schedule performance
Groupthink	Allowing team members to suppress individual suggestions for improving the performance of a project
Inability to adapt	Adhering to a communications plan that is ineffective
Lack of data and information	Not having access to information and data to come up with solutions to quality problems
Lack of sharing	Failure of team members to impart knowledge and experience to help resolve slides in the current schedule
Lack of tools	No software to conduct analysis to determine the cause of a problem
Leaping to judgment	Asking for additional funds from the management reserve before determining if other alternatives exist
Management's lack of responsiveness	Awaiting an important approval by key stakeholders to pull money from the management reserve
Methodism	Paying more attention to following a process described in a management plan than the resulting quality of the output
Mores, beliefs, values	Following traditional practices for raising issues to management, regardless of priority
Overemphasis on by-the-book philosophy	Adhering strictly to a process described in a management plan
Poor communications	Failing to inform stakeholders of a key decision that could affect the quality of deliverables
Poor coordination	Failing to include other key stakeholders in a change management meeting

(Continued)

TABLE 12.1 (*Continued*)

Monitoring and Controlling Process and Challenges and Constraints

Challenge and Constraint	Example
Silos	Not being able to bridge gaps among functional areas (e.g., Finance, Marketing, Engineering, etc.) on a project
Specialization	Not being able to translate the jargon from one discipline into that of another
Stretching resources too thin	Relying too much on a few resources assigned to activities on the critical path
Success	Taking a deserved but dangerous respite after a major delivery that is soon followed by another, thereby causing work to pile up

CREATIVE ABILITIES

Most of the creative abilities for this process involve compiling, analyzing, and interpreting data and information about a project. To do so, requires being objective and independent to avoid skewing interpretation and judgment. It also requires disciplined thinking so that the information generated allows making the best possible decisions. It also requires inspecting information to determine whether it is sufficient enough to make decisions and to allow the discovery of patterns hidden within the data and information.

Some relevant creative abilities required for this process are shown in Table 12.2.

GROUNDWORK FOR CREATIVE ENVIRONMENT

During the monitoring and controlling process, project managers need to eliminate barriers that impede data and information release and sharing. They need to provide stakeholders with easy-to-use tools and access to important data and information, facilitate communication and interaction to avoid groupthink, and eliminate any red tape and unnecessary meetings that fail to further the interests of a project.

Some actions that project managers can take to lay the groundwork for a creative environment are shown in Table 12.3.

TABLE 12.2

Monitoring and Controlling Process and Creative Abilities

Creative Ability	Example
Applying cross-domain thinking	Taking specific corrective action to improve schedule performance while determining the overall impact on the project
Being analytical	Reviewing a schedule to determine the cause of a slide on the critical path
Being observant	Watching the team to determine a more effective approach for executing a change management plan
Being precise	Determining the exact cause of a persistent technical problem
Being self-critical	Being willing to look at your own performance and how it impacts that of the overall project
Conceptualizing	Keeping the vision, goals, and objectives in mind when monitoring performance
Defining a problem	Knowing exactly what the problem is with the cost management process that produces inaccurate data
Embracing ambiguity	Recognizing that progressing on an activity or an entire project sometimes involves not having enough facts and data
Generalizing	Coming up with high-level conclusions about the quality of deliverables after reviewing performance data
Looking from the outside, in	Attempting not to lose your objectivity when trying to determine the cause of a cost performance problem
Nonlinear thinking	Taking a systemic view of a project's schedule performance
Reasoning	Attempting to come up with a rational answer for why team members are circumventing the change management process
Seeing multiple answers	Performing what-if analysis in a schedule tool to determine which revisions to the schedule will increase the likelihood of meeting a key milestone date
Shifting between convergent and divergent thinking	Reviewing an activity in the schedule and determining the impact of progress made on the overall schedule
Shifting from analysis to synthesis mode of thinking	Adding activities to the work breakdown structure and then assigning dependencies in the baseline schedule
Shifting from linear to nonlinear thinking	Reviewing the logic of the current schedule and ascertaining its impact on the cost performance baseline
Shifting perspectives	Taking a cost perspective and then a schedule perspective when reviewing performance data
Suspending judgment	Avoiding jumping to conclusions before all facts and data are available concerning a quality issue
Synthesis	Bringing cost and schedule data together to assess performance against their baselines

(Continued)

TABLE 12.2 (*Continued*)

Monitoring and Controlling Process and Creative Abilities

Creative Ability	Example
Uncovering patterns	Reviewing data and information about performance to ascertain the overall behavior of a project
Using linear thinking	Reviewing the schedule in logical sequence to determine what is causing key dates on the critical path to slide
Verbalizing	Preparing narrative descriptions of a project's cost and schedule performance
Visualizing	Preparing graphics about a project's cost and schedule

TABLE 12.3

Monitoring and Controlling Process and Groundwork for Creative Environment

Action	Example
Align individual with project goals and objectives	Making every feasible effort to align the interests of the individual to that of the project
Allow time for issue definition	Setting aside time for team members to define a technical problem
Build and maintain trust	Encouraging people to share knowledge and experience at team meetings
Counter groupthink	Bringing consultants on board temporarily to review cost and schedule performance and provide recommendations for improvement
Emphasize coordination	Providing opportunities for different functional areas or specializations to work together to address quality issues
Relax rules, procedures, etc.	Allowing for exceptions to processes when doing so will allow for corrective actions to be more effective
Stress communications	Providing meaningful, ongoing communications about progress to key stakeholders

GROUNDWORK FOR INDIVIDUAL CREATIVITY

From an individual perspective, project managers need to lay the basis for people to have the time and knowledge to provide data and to use tools related to cost, schedule, and quality performance of their projects. They also should emphasize the necessity for independent and objective analysis to avoid prejudicial judgments. Another challenge is avoiding the tendency to filter information in such a way that satisfies emotional needs.

TABLE 12.4

Monitoring and Controlling Process and Groundwork for Individual Creativity

Action	Example
Have a diverse background	Bringing team members on board who have a wide range of experience
Have self-discipline	Guiding people to exercise restraint in their prejudices when determining new estimates for remaining activities in a schedule
Have the ability to be self-critical	Encouraging people to question their own assumptions when conducting replanning
Realize that sooner or later, creativity must be implemented	Reminding team members that any idea for corrective action requires action to make progress
See outside the box	Extricating yourself, mentally or physically, from the current environment if replanning is necessary to preclude pride of authorship
Tolerate failure	Providing support for individuals who try but fail to succeed when trying something new on a project

Some actions that project managers can take to allow individuals to be creative are outlined in Table 12.4.

GROUNDWORK FOR TEAM CREATIVITY

Independence and objectivity can be quickly sacrificed in an environment where pressures like time, cost, and speedy delivery become extremely important. If the circumstances get out of control, decisions may be based, sometimes more often than not, on erroneous assumptions, data, and information. Certain stakeholders will face pressure to make quick decisions that are not well thought out, either through customer or other stakeholder pressure to meet within a specific cost or schedule target, thereby skewing analysis and behavior. Project managers especially find themselves in this pressure cooker. They are the only ones who usually have the opportunity to interact with all stakeholders, thus exposing them to the pressure most acutely. Project managers, therefore, must continually emphasize priorities, offset social pressure, adjust processes accordingly, and do whatever is necessary to ensure greater communication and collaboration.

Some actions that project managers can take to allow a team to be creative are outlined in Table 12.5.

TABLE 12.5

Monitoring and Controlling Process and Groundwork for Team Creativity

Action	Example
Act as if on a mission	Keeping the team focused on the vision, goals, and objectives of a project when replanning
Allow for open discussion and have a tolerance for ideas	Encouraging team members to identify the cause of a schedule slide, and not settle for a quick fix
Avoid noncontributory activities	Isolating a team from group meetings that offer no value to it
Be emotional and logical	Looking for opportunities to improve performance while simultaneously keeping everyone motivated to succeed
Have a diverse membership	Having people with different backgrounds share their knowledge and experience at team meetings
Have facilitative and supportive leadership	Keeping the team motivated to come up with creative ideas to improve cost performance
Know the priorities	Keeping the vision of the project constantly at the forefront of the team
Seek balance among creating, planning, and implementing	Reminding the team that a creative idea needs to become reality, sooner or later

---

RELEVANT TOOLS AND TECHNIQUES

The tools and techniques of the monitoring and controlling process center on maintaining an objective understanding about the status of a project. The emphasis is on collecting, compiling, and interpreting facts, data, and information to derive creative solutions enabling decisions and actions that truly address a problem or issue, not the symptoms.

Some common creativity tools and techniques that project managers can apply for this process are shown in Table 12.6.

TRADITIONAL CREATIVITY LIFE CYCLE MODEL

Within the monitoring and controlling process, project managers can apply the five phases of the creativity life cycle model. Each phase plays an instrumental role in clarifying and resolving an issue or problem.

TABLE 12.6

Monitoring and Controlling Process and Tools and Techniques

Tool and Technique	Example
Analogies, metaphors, and similes thinking	Comparing the logic of a schedule to something unrelated to the project (e.g., a chain link)
Benchmarking	Comparing the cost performance of a project with that of other projects within and outside the parent organization
Devil's advocate	Assigning someone on the project with responsibility for challenging assumptions, such as ones made when taking corrective action for poor schedule performance
Interviewing	Asking key stakeholders for any emergent risks and some ideas on how to mitigate them
Matrices	Compiling risk in a matrix form with associated deliverables, and then recording in each cell the appropriate mitigation action
Observation	Watching the performance of team members on other projects to get ideas on how to perform responsibilities more efficiently and effectively
Pareto chart	Developing a chart to determine which variable has the most impact in causing a technical problem with a deliverable
PDCA cycle	Using the cycle to continuously implement a corrective action to cost performance and to ascertain its effectiveness over several iterations
Problem solving	Making a concerted effort to determine a specific, measurable solution to a problem
Scatter gram	Collecting data on two variables and determining if there is a relationship between the variables (e.g., such as a certain defect and cost)
Trend chart	Plotting discrete points of data over time to determine if a trend exists, and if not, what could be contributing to the deviation

Preparation Phase

The purpose of the preparation phase is to learn as much information as possible about a topic and to compile any necessary information that will prove useful in coming up with creative ideas. This phase focuses largely on people, process, and performance.

For example, stakeholders differ on the approach for collecting status information on a project. Some stakeholders want what they refer to as "project management lite" status collection and reporting. Others want detail in reporting. Some stakeholders also disagree over how often status collection should occur (e.g., weekly, biweekly). The team prefers minimal data collection and reporting, preferably every two weeks. The sponsor and the customer want detailed collection and reporting.

The project manager assembles a subteam to conduct research on how past projects of a similar nature conducted status collection and reporting. The team also performs benchmarking to compare its project in scale and complexity with others in different organizations inside and outside the company.

Concentration Phase

The purpose of the concentration phase is to focus on exactly defining a problem or issue to address. The project manager needs to distinguish between what is and is not relevant, and just as importantly, what is and is not significant.

Continuing with the status collection example, the project manager assembles the members of the subteam. Disagreements quickly erupt among those stakeholders wanting minimal status collection and ones seeking a much more rigorous approach. Everyone agrees that status collection is needed but disagree over extent.

Incubation Phase

The purpose of the incubation phase is to allow the subconscious part of the mind to work by suspending judgment and avoiding concentration on a conscious level.

Continuing with the status collection example, the project manager has everyone take a break from the topic of status collection to focus on other concerns, such as another project. The project manager also suggests having everyone allow the subconscious to work, but also knows that it allows a cooling-off period during what seemed to be a tense impasse that occurred in the concentration phase.

Illumination Phase

The purpose of the illumination phase is to allow an idea to rise to the conscious level of its creator. This phase involves coming up with solutions to difficulties identified earlier.

Continuing with the status collection example, the project manager assembles the members of the subteam. All the stakeholders share their thoughts and any additional information. The project manager captures all the input in a matrix and then appoints a devil's advocate for each side of the issue. The members of the subteam list their proposed options on a white board. The project manager then applies the nominal group technique to determine the best one.

Verification and Production Phase

The purpose of the verification and production phase is to test and implement an idea.

Continuing with the status collection example, the project manager engages the members of the subteam to prepare a management plan to describe the approach for the monitoring and controlling process of the project. After receiving approval by key stakeholders for the management plan, the project manager then applies the Plan-Do-Check-Act cycle to implement the contents of the plan.

CONCLUSION

The monitoring and controlling process is highly reliant upon good communications and information. Unfortunately, despite the rise of modern technology, it seems that both are not present on many projects. If they exist, both are often inadequate. Creativity is necessary for this process in two ways. It enables building a cost-effective infrastructure that encourages good communications and information sharing. It also capitalizes on the availability of good communications and information if they exist.

Getting Started Checklist

Question	Yes	No
1. During this process, determine the challenges and constraints that could impact the creativity of your project team:		
Craving for predictability		
Dominance of brain thinking		
Faster, better, cheaper philosophy		
Fear		
Focus on the past or future, not the present		
Groupthink		

(Continued)

Getting Started Checklist

Question	Yes	No
Inability to adapt		
Lack of data and information		
Lack of sharing		
Lack of tools		
Leaping to judgment		
Management's lack of responsiveness		
Methodism		
Mores, beliefs, values		
Overemphasis on by-the-book philosophy		
Poor communications		
Poor coordination		
Silos		
Specialization		
Stretching resources too thin		
Success		
Other(s):		

2. Determine the creative abilities that are applicable to this process:

Applying cross-domain thinking

Being analytical

Being observant

Being precise

Being self-critical

Conceptualizing

Defining a problem

Embracing ambiguity

Generalizing

Looking from the outside, in

Nonlinear thinking

Reasoning

Seeing multiple answers

Shifting between convergent and divergent thinking

Shifting from analysis to synthesis mode of thinking

Shifting from linear to nonlinear thinking

Shifting perspectives

Suspending judgment

Synthesis

Uncovering patterns

Using linear thinking

Verbalizing

Visualizing

Other(s):

Getting Started Checklist

Question	Yes	No
3. Determine the actions that are necessary to lay the groundwork for a creative environment:		
Align individual with project goals and objectives		
Allow time for issue definition		
Build and maintain trust		
Counter groupthink		
Emphasize coordination		
Relax rules, procedures, and so on		
Stress communications		
Other(s):		
4. Determine the actions to take to improve individual creativity:		
Have a diverse background		
Have self-discipline		
Have the ability to be self-critical		
Realize that sooner or later creativity requires being implemented		
See outside the box		
Tolerate failure		
Other(s):		
5. Determine the actions to take to improve team creativity:		
Act as if on a mission		
Allow for open discussion and have a tolerance for ideas		
Avoid noncontributory activities		
Be emotional and logical		
Have a diverse membership		
Have facilitative and supportive leadership		
Know the priorities		
Seek balance among creating, planning, and implementing		
Other(s):		
6. Identify the creativity tools and techniques to use:		
Analogies, metaphors, and similes thinking		
Benchmarking		
Devil's advocate		
Interviewing		
Matrices		
Observation		
Pareto chart		
PDCA cycle		
Problem solving		
Scattergram		
Trend chart		
Other(s):		

13

Creativity and the Closing Process

INTRODUCTION

The closing process involves bringing a project to conclusion efficiently and effectively. It entails ensuring that all administrative, financial, and legal requirements have been addressed and closed. It also entails conducting reviews and capturing lessons from the project.

BENEFITS

There are many benefits attributed to the closing process. It ensures that the company or parent organization does not have any legal or financial issues outstanding, provides an efficient way to release resources and at the same time finish work, and offers an opportunity to capture any lessons experienced on the project that will be helpful to other future projects of a similar nature.

CONSEQUENCES OF FAILURE

Failure to perform this process has tremendous consequences, especially after the completion of a project. There can be legal and financial ramifications if contractual requirements are not addressed or payments related to accounts payable and receivable are not reconciled. A loss of vital information could be lost if no effort is made to capture the explicit and tribal knowledge acquired during the project.

Finally, as the project winds down, work could be incomplete as people move on to other projects and the morale of the remaining ones deteriorates.

DELIVERABLES

The closing process has several project management deliverables (see Figure 13.1), including:

- Contractual closure
- Financial closure
- Lessons learned
- Requirements verification and validation
- Reviews and audits
- Winding-down activities (e.g., release of resources)

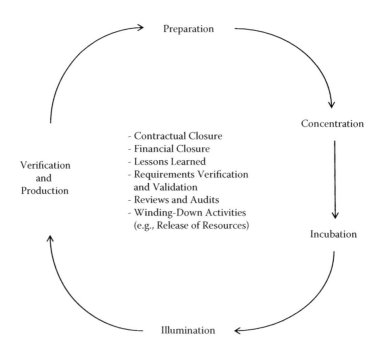

FIGURE 13.1
Closing process and deliverables.

IDEAL STATE

Ideally, project managers have a high-spirited team that wants to remain until all work is complete. It is especially useful that people who have finished their responsibilities volunteer to help others with remaining work. Resources are completely at the project managers' discretion on how long to keep and when to release them. In addition, all data and information are readily available to compile final statistics about performance. All financial and legal records are easily accessible, and project managers simply have to gather them from the repository and obtain the necessary signatures from applicable stakeholders. Any reviews and audits come at the right time and are unobtrusive with respect to the remaining activities of the project. Everyone feels they have been fairly recognized for their contributions. Finally, all stakeholders want to participate in a lessons-learned session in the best interests of the project.

Of course, reality is considerably different as the case is with the other processes. Several people begin leaving the project before they complete their remaining responsibilities. Some may be so eager to depart that they do a quick fix that ends up causing problems in the long run. Unless the project is managed perfectly (and few are), people are constantly pushed to complete their work. Differences frequently exist with contractors or suppliers over whether the work was done and, if so, according to expectations. Not everyone is thrilled about a lessons-learned session because it might get tempers up and accusations pouring out. If the project is large enough, someone will likely complain that they did not receive the degree of recognition that they thought they deserved. Finally, the customer expresses dissatisfaction because the project costs too much, took too long, and did not meet all expectations. Fortunately, a good many projects do not experience such a dismal state of affairs, but some do so to one degree or another.

CONTEXT

There are several contextual factors that project managers often face during the closing process. Here are just a few: Usually in the closing process, the project is something akin to a mopping-up operation.

Some remaining work occupies the attention of fewer people. Project managers apply a managerial style that is a mixture of being facilitative and directive. Relationships with key stakeholders are being addressed to ensure that no outstanding issues remain. They are also working with other stakeholders to assess how well everything went and trying to capture any useful information about the experience. Individual and team recognition occurs. The whole focus is one of getting the job done and moving on to a new project or returning to the home organization.

CHALLENGES AND CONSTRAINTS

The biggest challenges and constraints for the project are remaining committed to the project as it comes to a conclusion, having the availability of data and information to collect and compile to satisfy business and legal documentation requirements, capturing lessons learned, meeting the needs of performance reviews or audits, and maintaining objectivity and independence to determine if a project is complete.

Some challenges and constraints confronting this process are shown in Table 13.1.

CREATIVE ABILITIES

Of all the creative abilities for this process, perhaps the most important ones are related to data compilation and information generation. These abilities cover both automated (e.g., pulling data from different files) and manual means (e.g., interviewing people). By compiling data and generating information, decisions can be made regarding whether the project is complete according to the original or revised vision, goals, and objectives, and whether all technical, legal, and financial requirements have been addressed, both from a macro and from a micro perspective.

Some relevant creative abilities required for this process are shown in Table 13.2.

TABLE 13.1

Closing Process and Challenges and Constraints

Challenge and Constraint	Example
Dominance of brain thinking	Placing more emphasis on statistical collection than on keeping the team motivated to the very end of the project
Faster, better, cheaper philosophy	Pushing people to just complete remaining work as quickly as possible at the expense of quality
Fear	Failing to assure team members about their fate during the latter phases of a project, thereby inhibiting some people from contributing
Groupthink	Having people who all think alike at a lessons-learned session
Hierarchy	Allowing senior management to dictate the content of a lessons-learned document
Infighting	Allowing finger pointing to take over a lessons-learned session
Insecurity	Failing to address the fear that contributing to the completion of remaining work translates into loss of employment
Lack of data and information	Failing to have access to the source of data to generate cost information about the project
Lack of sharing	Failing to facilitate the sharing of knowledge and experience when conducting a lessons-learned session
Leaping to judgment	Concluding that the product or service delivered meets the customer's requirements and standards without verification and validation
Management's lack of responsiveness	Requesting statistical information and insights about the performance of the project and not receiving any response
Poor communications	Failing to communicate to key stakeholders the plan to release people as a project winds down
Poor coordination	Failing to coordinate with key stakeholders to approve key documents required for completing a project
Silos	Failing to bridge the differences among multiple functional areas when participating in a lessons-learned session
Specialization	Failing to bridge the differences among multiple specializations when participating in a lessons-learned session
Success	Lacking the motivation to perform many of the activities in the closing process after the successful delivery of a product or service
Team composition imbalance	Having too many left brain-dominant people remaining, thereby skewing the results of a lessons-learned session
Too many positive and negative incentives	Lacking the motivation to cooperate as well as to share knowledge, experiences, and data after not receiving an award

TABLE 13.2

Closing Process and Creative Abilities

Ability	Example
Applying cross-domain thinking	Balancing the need to collect statistical data while at the same time keeping the project team excited about completing the project
Being analytical	Collecting and compiling financial data and converting it into information
Being self-critical	Contributing to a lessons-learned session
Reasoning	Reviewing the logical sequence of the schedule to determine lessons learned
Shifting between convergent and divergent thinking	Reviewing the vision, goals, and objectives of the project and collecting specific data to validate their achievement
Shifting from analysis to synthesis mode of thinking	Collecting and compiling data and information, and generating conclusions from it
Shifting from linear to nonlinear thinking	Reviewing the logical sequence of the schedule and then determining all the contextual factors that impacted it during the project's life cycle
Suspending judgment	Collecting and compiling data and generating information before developing conclusions about the performance of the project
Using generalization	Reviewing data and information and coming up with some patterns of behavior
Using linear thinking	Reviewing the performance of the schedule to determine where opportunities for improvement exist for projects of a similar nature to leverage
Using nonlinear thinking	Identifying what contextual factors impacted the project and recording them in the lessons-learned document
Verbalizing	Producing a lessons-learned document in a narrative format
Visualizing	Generating graphics (e.g., histograms, trend charts, etc.) from cost and schedule data to show the overall performance of a project

---

GROUNDWORK FOR CREATIVE ENVIRONMENT

Initially, it is difficult for people to see the need for creativity during the closing process. Nothing could be further from the truth. Collecting data, converting it into information, and displaying it require creativity to some degree or another. Creativity is also required in motivating team members as a project concludes and, even more so, when capturing lessons learned.

TABLE 13.3

Closing Process and Groundwork for Creative Environment

Action	Example
Align individual and team goals and objectives with the parent organization	Articulating how the project satisfied the parent organization's strategic plan
Build and maintain trust	Following a plan for releasing resources as the project nears completion
Counter groupthink	Ensuring that a mixed group of disciplines and personalities attend a lessons-learned session
Emphasize coordination	Involving customers and other stakeholders to participate in verifying and validating requirements and standards as having been met prior to product delivery
Grant access to data to do the job	Granting access to cost and schedule performance data and information to key stakeholders who themselves need to generate reports
Grant access to necessary tools	Providing the necessary tools to assess and provide data and information for reviews
Reward risk taking	Recognizing people who, during the project, look on challenging responsibilities despite the potential for failure
Stress communications	Keeping key stakeholders informed about the progress of winding-down activities

Some actions that project managers can take to lay the groundwork for a creative environment are shown in Table 13.3.

GROUNDWORK FOR INDIVIDUAL CREATIVITY

Project managers will likely need the help of individuals to collect data and generate information. Data and information will probably reside in different locations, from electronic files to team members' minds. The key is to stress the importance of this effort because many people, especially people building a product or delivering a service, will feel that this work is red tape or bureaucratic. Project managers must stress the importance of the closing process and determine an equitable expectation of time and effort to devote to this process. They will also need to stress the necessity of being independent and objective.

Some actions that project managers can take to allow individuals to be creative are outlined in Table 13.4.

TABLE 13.4

Closing Process and Groundwork for Individual Creativity

Action	Example
Be destructive	Encouraging individuals to look for opportunities to perform their responsibilities more efficiently and effectively to reduce costs by eliminating non-value-added processes and activities
Be theoretical and experiential at the same time	Encouraging individuals to keep the vision of the project in mind when performing activities in a way that expedites the schedule but requires cutting corners
Have a diverse background	Encouraging individuals with diverse backgrounds to ensure quick fixes to meet the schedule without causing collateral damage after the product is delivered to the customer
Have the ability to be self-critical	Encouraging people to question their assumptions about the output of their work as the rush to completion accelerates

GROUNDWORK FOR TEAM CREATIVITY

Not only will individuals be involved in the closing process, but so will the entire team. The team's creative insights will likely be required to conduct lessons-learned sessions, respond to review or audit findings, and collect and compile information. As with individuals, project managers must determine the appropriate balance between completing work and providing the necessary data and information.

Some actions that project managers can take to allow a team to be creative are outlined in Table 13.5.

RELEVANT TOOLS AND TECHNIQUES

Many of the tools and techniques listed in Table 13.6 are used to compile and display data and information at detail and summary levels regarding cost, schedule, quality, and technical performance. This data and information can identify patterns and anomalies of behavior about performance, as well as counter the impact of groupthink to ensure greater independence and objectivity.

Some common creativity tools and techniques that project managers can apply for this process are shown in Table 13.6.

TABLE 13.5

Closing Process and Groundwork for Team Creativity

Action	Example
Adapt	Allowing teams to adjust to working together as people begin leaving the project
Allow for open discussion and have tolerance for ideas	Preventing the intensity and momentum of a project coming to an end to curtail different opinions and insights
Be curious	Encouraging the team to come up with better ways to perform work until the product or service is delivered
Have a diverse membership	Continuing to populate the team with individuals having a variety of backgrounds, knowledge, and experience
Have facilitative and supportive leadership	Helping the team by removing administrative obstacles as the project nears completion
Have no fear of the unknown	Keeping the team motivated even in the presence of everyone eventually departing
View failure as a learning experience	Trying to prevent the tendency of giving up if something goes wrong at the first attempt as the completion milestone approaches

TRADITIONAL CREATIVITY LIFE CYCLE MODEL

Within the closing process, project managers can apply the five phases of the creativity life cycle model. Each phase plays an instrumental role in clarifying and resolving an issue or problem.

Preparation Phase

The purpose of the preparation phase is to learn as much information as possible about a topic and to compile any necessary information that will prove useful in coming up with creative ideas. This phase focuses largely on process and performance.

For example, a project manager needs to figure out a painless way to collect data and information from different sources. The primary challenges are that most data and information reside within incompatible systems, while the remainder is in hard, rather than electronic, form. The project manager decides to interview other project managers and some subject matter experts as well as review lessons learned from similar projects.

TABLE 13.6

Closing Process and Tools and Techniques

Tool and Techniques	Example
Affinity diagramming	Collecting data about the cost and schedule performance and placing them in related categories
Benchmarking	Comparing the performance of the project with that of another to determine what went well and what areas need improvement as a basis for performing a lessons-learned session
Brainstorming	Assembling team members and other key stakeholders in a room and listing what went well and what needs improvement to create a lessons-learned document
Brainwriting	Having individual team members and other key stakeholders record on a piece of paper what went well and then passing it on to another colleague for review and revision
Checklists	Using a listing of ideas to expedite the closing of a project
Devil's advocate	Assigning someone during verification and validation meetings to counter prevailing thinking
Idea bulletin board	Setting up a white board to capture remaining ad hoc responsibilities to finish before the project can end
Interviewing	Meeting individually with key stakeholders to capture lessons learned
Nominal group technique	Assembling team members and other key stakeholders to compile lists of what went well and areas for improvement, and then voting for those considered to have the most impact
Offsite	Holding a lessons-learned session off premises to lessen pressure to hold one's thoughts, insights, etc.
Role playing	Taking the perspective of a key stakeholder to ascertain what statistical data and information they can provide related to the cost, schedule, and quality performance of the project
Scatter gram	Plotting the relationship between two variables over time to ascertain any important patterns or anomalies
Statistical process control	Plotting discrete data over time to identify any anomalies, such as defects, that could require postimplementation analysis
Trend chart	Plotting discrete data over time to ascertain improvement (e.g., a decline in defects)

Concentration Phase

The purpose of the concentration phase is to focus on exactly defining a problem or issue to address. The project manager will need to distinguish between what is and is not relevant and, just as importantly, what is and is not significant.

Continuing with the data and information example, the project manager briefly describes the problem he faces and then lists the possible options.

Despite drawing a strength, weakness, opportunity, and threat (SWOT) table, the project manager remains confused. Some time is available to make a decision, and he decides to let the problem rest for a while by proceeding to the incubation phase.

Incubation Phase

The purpose of the incubation phase is to allow the subconscious part of the mind to work by suspending judgment and avoiding concentration on a conscious level.

Continuing with the data and information example, the project manager focuses his mind on managing the project. This approach allows his subconscious to work on a possible solution rather than letting his conscious mind get fixated on the data and information incompatibility issue. During a brief walk around in the park adjacent to his office building, the project manager comes up with multiple solutions.

Illumination Phase

The purpose of the illumination phase is to allow an idea to rise to the conscious level of its creator. This phase involves coming up with solutions to difficulties identified earlier.

Continuing with the data and information example, the project manager revisits the problem statement and the SWOT table. It becomes clear to the project manager that he needs to select an approach that combines both automated and manual solutions. The project manager decides to interview a few more subject matter experts and then come to a conclusion. He soon does, deciding to pick someone on the team to help extract and combine data and information from compatible systems, but outsources the same work for incompatible systems due to the effort required.

Verification and Production Phase

The purpose of the verification and production phase is to test and implement an idea.

Continuing with the data and information example, the project manager, with the help of a team member, develops a high-level milestone schedule for extracting and compiling data and information from compatible systems. The project manager also adds milestones to perform the same work on incompatible systems.

CONCLUSION

The closing process is often the most overlooked process in project management. The reason is obvious. The project is winding down and people focus on seeking other opportunities with other projects. This situation complicates matters for the project managers. They, unlike other stakeholders, are responsible for ensuring project completion. To accomplish that, they must exercise the utmost creativity during the closing process to keep the team motivated and gain access to data and information about a project before closure occurs.

Getting Started Checklist

Question	Yes	No
1. During this process, determine the challenges and constraints that could impact the creativity of your project team:		
Dominance of brain thinking		
Faster, better, cheaper philosophy		
Fear		
Groupthink		
Hierarchy		
Infighting		
Insecurity		
Lack of data and information		
Lack of sharing		
Leaping to judgment		
Management's lack of responsiveness		
Poor communications		
Poor coordination		
Silos		
Specialization		
Success		
Team composition imbalance		
Too many positive and negative incentives		
Other(s):		
2. Determine the creative abilities that are applicable to this process:		
Applying cross-domain thinking		
Being analytical		
Being self-critical		
Reasoning		
Shifting between convergent and divergent thinking		
Shifting from analysis to synthesis mode of thinking		

Getting Started Checklist

Question	Yes	No
Shifting from linear to nonlinear thinking		
Suspending judgment		
Using generalization		
Using linear thinking		
Using nonlinear thinking		
Verbalizing		
Visualizing		
Other(s):		
3. Determine the actions that are necessary to lay the groundwork for a creative environment:		
Align individual and team goals and objectives with the parent organization		
Build and maintain trust		
Counter groupthink		
Emphasize coordination		
Grant team members access to data to do their job		
Grant access to necessary tools		
Reward risk taking		
Stress communications		
Other(s):		
4. Determine the actions to take to improve individual creativity:		
Be destructive		
Be theoretical and experiential at the same time		
Have a diverse background		
Have the ability to be self-critical		
Other(s):		
5. Determine the actions to take to improve team creativity:		
Adapt		
Allow for open discussion and have a tolerance for ideas		
Be curious		
Have a diverse membership		
Have a facilitative and supportive leadership		
Have no fear of the unknown		
View failure as a learning experience		
Other(s):		
6. Identify the creativity tools and techniques to use:		
Affinity diagramming		
Benchmarking		
Brainstorming		
Brainwriting		
Checklists		

(Continued)

Getting Started Checklist

Question	Yes	No
Devil's advocate		
Idea bulletin board		
Interviewing		
Nominal group technique		
Offsite		
Role playing		
Scattergram		
Statistical process control		
Trend chart		
Other(s):		

14

A Baker's Dozen of Takeaways

By its very nature, creativity does not lend itself to applying a paint-by-number approach on projects; too much is happening, quickly and stressfully. Project managers are not helpless, however. They can encourage creativity on their teams by following these takeaways.

TAKEAWAY NUMBER 1

The first takeaway, and one of the major points of this book, is that everyone on a project team has some degree of creativity. In other words, it is not reserved for a select few or people in a narrow field, such as art. As inventor James Jorasch notes, "Creativity has been put up on such a pedestal. ... People associate it with the arts and being for the anointed few struck by lightning. In reality, it's much less exciting. It's something everyone can do—and, like everything else, it takes practice."[1] Choreographer Twyla Tharp agrees, observing, "It is an absolute mismatch to think that art is not practical—or that business cannot be creative."[2]

Naturally, some people have a greater capacity than others to be creative, say 20 percent of the population, but everyone has some of it. Individuals and teams alike need to recognize this capacity and know how to activate and channel it into their work. That takes effort. As psychologist John Houtz notes, "I think if we want everyone to have a way to be more creative, we have to convey the message that they have to work at it; creativity isn't necessarily going to come naturally."[3]

TAKEAWAY NUMBER 2

The second takeaway is that project managers can help lay the ground-work to enable creativity to occur. They can play an instrumental role when certain factors are under their control; when they are not under their control, they can help ameliorate the impact of inhibiting creativity. "You can't methodically teach creativity," observes Mario Almondo of Ferrari, "but you can provide an environment that nurtures it."[4] Because many project managers often lack the necessary power to alter their environment, they sometimes feel helpless about what they can do to enhance creativity on their project teams. Fortunately, they can still enhance individual and group creativity by such actions as encouraging frequent breaks, furthering openness to allow sharing of ideas and information, involving people in decision making, and bringing in outside experts. The point is that project managers do not have to act helpless about encouraging creativity on a project; they can be proactive.

TAKEAWAY NUMBER 3

The third takeaway is that project managers should encourage as much defiance as compliance. Following the "rules of the game" is, of course, necessary. Taken to the extreme, however, all creativity goes to the wayside except, perhaps, for a few incremental changes.

The first part is having individuals and groups that are willing to ask questions related to the most important one of all; "Why?" For example: "Why are we doing this?" "Why don't we think of a better way to approach this problem on the project?" Asking such questions can peg people as iconoclasts or nihilists because they rebel against the status quo, both in terms of thought and action. They do not care, however; they enjoy it and it is their nature. Project managers should try to capitalize on their rebelliousness. These individuals would agree with innovator and entrepreneur Steve Jobs that "it's better to be a pirate than to join the Navy."[5] The other part is to develop truly creative solutions that entail thinking outside the box. That may require everyone adapting what has been attributed by some as "positive deviance," meaning certain people have evaded capture by their organization and have not succumbed to the modus operandi.[6] Complacency through compliance is the greatest threat to creativity and innovation projects. Project managers must keep that very thought in mind, keep alive the piratical spirit that Jobs mentioned, and direct it to produce unprecedented results. "Being a pirate means going beyond what people thought possible," further observes Jobs. "A small band of people doing some great work that will go down in history."[7]

TAKEAWAY NUMBER 4

The fourth takeaway is that creativity is fuzzy. That is, following a logical pattern, based upon a precise premise or set of assumptions, may impair creativity by restricting perspective, perception, and practicality. Project managers and their team members need to expose, explore, and experiment when generating creative ideas. Thinking can be logically correct, but can also come up with ineffective solutions to problems or issues. In other words, precision can hamstring creativity, due to a mental framework that filters and masks data, information, and thoughts. It also limits critical thinking so crucial for coming up with creative ideas and innovations. Critical thinking is instrumental to a project's success, according to a poll by AllPM.com, in which 42 percent of respondents considered it a core competency.[8] Coupled with critical thinking is imagination. With imagination, the constraints of a mindset can be circumvented or altered, leading to creative ideas. That is because it is easier to see connections among seemingly unrelated ideas (e.g., unconnected insights and contradictions) by asking questions like, "Why", and as Albert Einstein did, performing mind experiments.[9]

TAKEAWAY NUMBER 5

The fifth takeaway is that creativity requires working closely with the customer. This relationship should be more than at arm's length. It should be a close one, to encourage sharing needs and wants without fear of anything negative, such as either party taking advantage of the other. Trust and confidence are critical to this relationship. The team should know the customer well enough to provide value. The customer should know the team well enough to communicate requirements. To quote musician Yo-Yo Ma, "If I know what music you love and what music I love, we start out having a better conversation."[10] Communication is critical for this takeaway. How the customer and team share their knowledge, insights, expertise, and desires leads to greater satisfaction. Often, this communication means adapting the Japanese concept of Genchi Genbutsu, also known as Gemba, meaning the team literally visits the place where the work actually occurs. Regardless of approach, however, the key to creating and innovating is to communicate. As architect Maya Lin says, "I'm asking for a one-on-one relationship between the viewer and the work. ... In the end, it breaks down to an intimate, psychological experience."[11]

TAKEAWAY NUMBER 6

The sixth takeaway is that creativity is as much about failure as it is about success. In fact, just about every successful creator and innovator will emphasize that they learned as much, if not more, about themselves and their product or service, when facing failure. In the world of project management, plenty of projects have, and will, offer learning experiences. The key is how a project's leadership (e.g., project manager) and team members perceive failure.

Failure should be seen as a springboard for eventual success if they subscribe to what Julia Cameroon, author of the celebrated *The Artist's Way*, refers to as "optimism in the face of creative despair.[12] Project managers need to continually serve as cheerleaders, for themselves as well as others, in the midst of failure, reminding all stakeholders that, as Kevin Kelly says, "the most creative environments allow for repeated failure."[13] Or, as psychologist Robert Epstein says, "You have to learn not to fear failure and rejoice in it."[14] In the end, it all comes down to a project team's resiliency in the face of failure. Although in reference to individuals, John Houtz's insight also applies to teams: "The creative individual thinks of failure as a new opportunity. 'Okay, why did I fail?' Let me try to do something else. Let me go forward with it."[15]

Perhaps the best attitude expressed about failure is viewing it as a "return on experience," rather than return on investment.[16] Such a perspective makes it easier for team and individual alike to experience a resurgence by identifying new interconnections among ideas.[17]

TAKEAWAY NUMBER 7

The seventh takeaway is that creativity still requires focus and discipline. Creativity is not an excuse to perform haphazardly and operate without order. A degree of aim and organization are necessary to apply creativity and innovation successfully. Just about all great artists, engineers, architects, and writers build a model or prototype and then follow a strategic, structured approach. Individuals, like Jobs, knew the importance of vision while at the same time following an unorthodox strategic path to achieve results.[18] Author Brent Schlender quotes Steve Jobs on the importance of a vision when founding Pixar: "Pixar has been a marathon, not a sprint. There are times you run a marathon and you wonder why I am doing this? But you take a drink of water, wind back, remember the finish line, and keep going."[19] Vision and discipline are instrumental, therefore, in creating a product or service of value. The degree of discipline, too, is as important as the vision itself. This discipline should be rigorous enough to further the vision yet provide enough latitude for creativity and innovation to flourish. A clean mission, strategic direction, accountability, and performance indicators all give stakeholders reasonable assurance that the goals and objectives of a project will be met.[20]

TAKEAWAY NUMBER 8

The eighth takeaway is that creativity requires as much emotion as it does logic or reason. Individuals and teams need engagement in their work. Otherwise, people perform perfunctorily, that is, with little or no energy. Mixing emotion with reason serves as a powerful catalyst to perform beyond expectations. With emotion comes initiative, ownership, fervor, and pride in workmanship. Eventually, it draws a line between ordinary and exceptional performance, especially with regard to creativity; Carlos Castaneda observes, "The basic difference between an ordinary man and a warrior is that a warrior takes everything as a challenge while an ordinary man takes everything, either as a blessing or curse." In other words, it is a matter of perspective.

Emotion gives work meaning. Instead of just occupying one's time, projects give individuals and groups alike a purpose for existence beyond that of earning a paycheck. As General George S. Patton said, "Challenges are what makes life interesting; overcoming them is what makes life meaningful." Again, the fuel for doing that is emotion.

TAKEAWAY NUMBER 9

The ninth takeaway is that creativity must overcome resistance from others, and perhaps just as importantly, from oneself. Everyone is a product of their knowledge, training, and experience. A person's background may be an asset or a liability, with the latter locking the mind into a framework that prevents new ideas, previous experiences, and knowledge from coming to the surface. For individuals, the liability takes the form of a mental block or something similar to it; for a team, groupthink. Either way, it hurts creativity and innovation. For example, one of the most creative of individuals, Thomas Edison, allowed his mental model to restrict his thinking. Despite inventing the movie camera, he saw it simply for peep shows rather than for the large screen.[21] He also believed that his invention of the phonograph was more for office use, not entertainment.[22]

The key is to free the mind, whether for an individual or a group. Cracking the metal casing enveloping the mind is not easy, but it can be done, simply by first acknowledging its existence and then opening the mind or minds to varied experiences, knowledge, and backgrounds. Inventor James Jorasch makes a special effort to do just that, recommending to "push yourself to do things you've never done before, reach out to people you've never talked to before, and ask a lot of questions."[23] The result? Perspective changes, opening one's mind to new ideas, as author Gordon Parks observes: "My perspective keeps changing. I see the same events differently than I did 40 or 50 years ago."[24]

TAKEAWAY NUMBER 10

The tenth takeaway is that creativity requires the individual and team alike to work together to provide value to themselves and others.

No doubt, history is replete with examples of a solitary genius contributing to mankind. However, such contributions are rare. More often than not, creativity and its companion, innovation, arise from individuals and teams working hand in hand to produce and deliver a product or service of value. Observes Kevin Kelly, "Innovation is about more than just having the idea yourself; you also have to bring everyone else to where your idea is. And that becomes difficult if you're too many steps ahead."[25] Gianframo Zaccar, president of Continuum, agrees: "Real design is seldom done by one person, but rather it is best done by a group of people, with different skills and sensibilities, working together."[26]

Perhaps the best way to view the individual and team coexisting is to view a project like a hand. Each finger is different in shape and purpose, but work together harmoniously to execute a common task, such as picking up a cup of coffee or writing with a pen. Each finger contributes and cooperates with the others to transform a complex task into a simple one; if the fingers were all the same and did not work together, an ordinarily simple task becomes a complex one.

TAKEAWAY NUMBER 11

The eleventh takeaway is that creativity requires all kinds of people. Diversity is the spice of life on a project. Different personality types with varying backgrounds, knowledge, and experiences contribute a variety of perspectives and ideas that enhance rather than impede creativity. Project managers find this variety challenging, but they will also discover the richness of insights. They can then capitalize on the strengths of others while simultaneously compensating for their weaknesses.

The difficulty, of course, is that reaching consensus, let alone agreement, can be extremely challenging, if not impossible. Some people may be mavericks, whose unconventional insights and uncompromising attitude might pose a challenge if not managed and led well. Others, such as procrastinators and indecisive people, may add to delays without the right incentives, thereby killing the creativity of others on a team. Such people, fortunately, are the exception rather than the rule.

Perhaps the best rationale for having a diverse team of people is the one offered by Steve Jobs in his description of the Beatles. "My model of management is the Beatles. The reason I say that is because each of the key people in the Beatles kept the others from going off in the directions of their tendencies. They sort of kept each other in check. And when they split up, they never did anything as good."[27] In an article in *Fortune*, John Byrnes wrote about who he considered to be the twelve greatest entrepreneurs of all time, which all seemed to come from recent memory. Nonetheless, the article was striking in that all these creative individuals—from Jeff Bezos of Amazon, who was described as a dreamer and patient, to Narayana Murthy of Infosys, who could create a business out of limited resources—brought different personalities and capabilities to the environment and created something of value.[28]

TAKEAWAY NUMBER 12

The twelfth takeaway is that creativity on projects requires taking a holistic perspective, meaning the importance of using both sides of the brain to create and deliver a product or service. The right brain is often associated with integration and the left is associated with burrowing into the details. The combination of the two provides a powerful opportunity to generate creative and innovative results. The perspective of using both sides of the brain becomes useful when determining the levels and types of creativity.

From a thinking perspective, the parts of the brain need each other to do divergent and convergent thinking, the former generating many unique ideas and the latter combining them. The right brain is used to produce several creative ideas and the left brain to combine them in some organized manner to produce something of value.

From a creativity perspective, Wendell Williams of Scientific Selection. com takes a different perspective, suggesting that there are two types of creativity—breadth and depth, the former drawing connections among ideas and the latter doing so in a narrow field, again reflecting the important relationship between left- and right-brain thinking.[29] Still another perspective on creativity is taking an incremental rather than radical approach toward creativity. An incremental approach involves improving on what currently exists, while the radical approach involves seeking a breakthrough that entails creating something dramatically new.[30] Regardless of perspective on thinking and creativity, the bottom line is that the entire brain is needed to create and innovate. The left side provides the necessary depth, while the right side offers the required breadth. Combining the two bridges the gap between imagination and practicality.

TAKEAWAY NUMBER 13

The final takeaway is that creativity requires action as well as thought. To a large extent, that explains the difference between creativity and innovation; the former results in something unique, and the latter converts the creation into something of value for the customer. Thought and action transform imagination into the reality that both sides of the brain created.

From a creativity and innovation context, two parts make up the mixture of thought and action. The first part is that the knowledge of the day along with contemporary technology and the laws of physics enable the development of a creative idea, and then the technology and the laws of physics turn it into something real.

The other part, and just as important and perhaps even more so on projects, a creative idea requires the support of an organization's infrastructure, as Thomas Davenport, Laurence Prusak, and H. James Wilson in the *Harvard Business Review* observe: "No business idea takes root within an organization purely on its own merits. Instead it has to be sold—to senior executives, to the rank and file, to middle managers."[31] Rolf Smith, whose company offers thinking expeditions, summed up the relationships among creativity, thinking, and action very well:. "Being creative is when you think about your thinking," he says. "Being innovative is when you act on your actions."[32] Projects that are nothing more than glorified thought experiments have their place, of course; so do projects that seek solely to implement ideas. Combining the two provides a synergistic effect of harnessing the combinatorial qualities of people, processes, systems, and data to deliver a product or service of value.

CONCLUSION

Throughout this entire book, emphasis has been on tapping everyone's creative potential and the role of project managers doing so. Whether by design or accident, project managers often fall into the role of "good cop, bad cop," with the emphasis on the latter. Unfortunately, such a perspective is too negative and, quite frankly, counterproductive from a creativity and innovation perspective. Think about it: How creative and innovative would you be if a cop was continually looking over your shoulder and correcting your every thought and action? Chances are that you would probably consider it countercreative and counterinnovative, which translates into being counterproductive.

What project managers should and need to do is stress the positive side of people's potentialities by laying the groundwork for creativity and innovation and then leveraging such contributions to increase personal satisfaction, add value to customers, and contribute to the overall success of the parent organization—a win-win for all stakeholders.

ENDNOTES

1. Marina Krakovsky, "Father of Invention," *Psychology Today*, November/December 2010, pp. 31–32.
2. "Creativity Step-by-Step," *Harvard Business Review*, April 2008, pp. 48–49.
3. Mariette DiCristina, "Let Your Creativity Soar," *Scientific American Mind*, June/July 2008, p. 26.
4. Gardiner Morse, "Sparking Creativity at Ferrari," *Harvard Business Review*, April 2006, p. 23.
5. Steven Levy, "Ringside at the Revolution," *Wired*, December 2011, p. 234.
6. Craig Mindrum, "Harvesting Innovation," *Talent Management*, May 2010, pp. 20–21.
7. Levy, "Ringside at the Revolution," p. 234.
8. "Think Really Hard," *PM Network*, November 2007, p. 17.
9. Jeffrey H. Deyer, Hal B. Gregersen, and Clayton M. Christensen, "The Innovator's DNA," *Harvard Business Review*, December 2009, p. 34.
10. Joshua Kosman, "Yo-Yo Ma," *Smithsonian*, November 2005, p. 87.
11. Michael Parfit, "Maya Lin," *Smithsonian*, November 2005, p. 101.
12. DiChristina, "Let Your Creativity Soar," p. 24.
13. Kevin Kelly and Steven Johnson, "Where Ideas Come From," *Wired*, October 2010, p. 124.
14. DiChristina, "Let Your Creativity Soar," p. 28.
15. DiChristina, "Let Your Creativity Soar," p. 29.
16. Stacy Collet,. "Ready, Set, Compete," *Computerworld*, January 14, 2013, p. 20.
17. DiChristina, "Let Your Creativity Soar," p. 29.
18. Nancy F. Cohen, "His Legacy," *Fortune*, November 23, 2009, p. 110.
19. Brent Schlender, "I Just Knew in My Bones That This Was Going to be Very Important," *FastCompany*, May 2012, p. 82.
20. Woulter Alan and Adi Alan, "Promote Innovation as a Business Discipline," *Talent Management*, May 2010, p. 22.
21. Richard Corliss, "Lights. Camera…Edison!" *Time*, July 5, 2010, p. 51.
22. Randall Stross, "The Incredible Talking Machine," *Time*, July 5, 2010, p. 49.
23. Krakovsky, "Father of Invention," p. 9.
24. Roy Rowan, "Gordon Parks," *Smithsonian*, November 2005, p. 68.
25. Kelly and Johnson, "Where Ideas Come From," p. 122.
26. Steve Hamm, "Fifty Years at the Drawing Board," *Businessweek*, January 21, 2008, p. 39.

27. Schlender, "I Just Knew in My Bones That This Was Going to be Very Important, p. 76.
28. John Byrne, "The Twelve Greatest Entrepreneurs of All Time," *Fortune*, April 9, 2012, pp. 68–86.
29. "How to Hire for Creativity," *Inc.*, October 1, 2010, p. 2.
30. "How to Hire for Creativity," *Inc.*, p. 2.
31. Thomas H. Davenport, Laurence Prusak, and H. James Wilson, "Who's Bringing Your Hot Ideas and How Are You Responding?" *Harvard Business Review*, February 2003, p. 60.
32. Anna Muoio, "Idea Summit," *Fast Company*, January/February 2000, p. 160.

Glossary

affinity diagramming: A technique used to logically group a wide number of items having similar characteristics.

Alchemist: Developed by Annette Moser-Wellman, one of the five thinking skills that generates ideas from multiple sources via the manipulation of components and relationships among them.

Amiables: One of the four social styles identified by Robert Bolton; tends to focus on people over facts and data.

analogy: The comparison of dissimilar ideas, problems, things, etc., that share a common feature or characteristic.

analysis: The breaking of the object of study into components.

Analyticals: One of the four social styles identified by Robert Bolton; tends to focus on the task to get done and less on people.

Artist: One of the four key roles identified by Roger von Oech; uses information from the Explorer to generate a new idea.

Bar Coding: Identified by Dave Allan et al., it is the jumping from one responsibility or task to another before completion, and then resuming work on it.

benchmarking: A technique used to compare the performance of a process to another one in another organization to determine its efficiency and effectiveness.

Birkman Model: Developed by Roger Birkman; a model of human behavior predicated on the interests, needs, style, and stress, represented by four colors red, green, blue, and yellow.

Black Hat Thinking: One of the six thinking hat styles identified by Edward de Bono to symbolize addressing a problem or issue using skeptical, even pessimistic thinking to shoot holes through an idea.

Blue Hat Thinking: One of six thinking hats identified by Edward de Bono to symbolize addressing a problem or issue by developing and implementing good managerial practices.

brainstorming: A facilitated group discussion session that encourages free generation of creative ideas to solve a problem or provide alternate solutions.

brainwriting: A technique that requires each person to record their ideas on a sheet of paper and then pass it to the next person for additional input.

Bravery: One of the six behaviors identified by Dave Allan et al.; involves implementing a creative idea in the midst of challenges like resistance to change.

checklists: A technique used to help remember or account for key concepts, data, etc., which in turn lead to creative ideas.

closing process: One of the six project management processes; involves bringing a project to conclusion, efficiently and effectively.

Color Code: Developed by Taylor Hartman, a psychological model that assumes everyone has a core personality to direct their personality based upon motive, needs, and wants, and is represented by four colors: Red, Blue, White, and Yellow.

compare and contrast: A technique used to choose and evaluate ideas to determine the pluses (pros) and minuses (cons) of an idea to address a problem or issue.

concentration phase: One of the five phases in the traditional view of the creativity life cycle requiring focus on defining exactly a problem or issue to be addressed.

conceptualizing: A chain of abstract thinking that results in one or more ideas.

convergent thinking: Solving a specific problem or issue focusing on some scoping criteria.

Crawford slip technique: A variant of brainstorming that, with the aid of a facilitator, defines a problem or issue and then records thoughts on slips of paper, which are compiled, grouped, and summarized.

Creative Behavior Model: Developed by Dave Allan et al.; a half dozen set of behaviors that flow sequentially to create and deploy ideas; these behaviors are Freshness, Greenhousing, Realness, Momentum, Signaling, and Bravery.

creative collaboration: Individuals and groups work in concert to achieve a common goal.

creative problem solving: Eight essential processes for creatively solving problems or issues; these processes are understand the environment, increasing awareness, gather information, generate assumptions, determine alternatives, choose an option, implement the option, and take corrective action, if necessary.

creativity: Developing a new or improved product or service that adds value to the customer upon its implementation, consisting of the formula: novelty + value + implementation.

crippling conservatism: A concept developed by Dietrich Dorner that a comfort level engenders compliancy with the existing way of doing business or hiding behind the rules.

cross-domain thinking: The ability to transcend restrictions of one field by applying its tools, concepts, and techniques to derive something creative in the new field.

defining process: One of the six project management processes; requires determining, at a high level, the goals, scope, deliverables, major tasks, responsibilities, schedule milestones, risks, and other pertinent issues.

deliberate practice: Developed by Keith Sawyer; a team learns from failure as a way to avoid repeating the same mistake and experiencing the same mishap in the future.

deliverable: The tangible or intangible result of a project management process and technical phase used to manage a project.

Delphi technique: A technique used to achieve the consensus of independent experts by submitting a questionnaire multiple times.

devil's advocate: A technique of having someone take the opposite stance on an idea with the specific purpose of identifying flaws.

divergent thinking: Solving a specific problem or issue by suspending judgment during the collection of data and generation of ideas.

Drivers: One of the four social styles identified by Robert Bolton; tends to focus on results and being highly active.

Enneagram: A psychological model that identified nine personality types that are grouped into triads (Feeling, Doing, and Relation) that affect how people deal with the world.

executing process: One of the six project management processes; involves the actual application of the plan to achieve the goals and objectives of the project.

Explorer: One of the four key roles identified by Roger von Oech; the Explorer goes on a journey of discovery when addressing or defining an issue.

Expressive: One of four social styles identified by Robert Bolton; tends to operate on emotion and on generalities.

field trip: Traveling to different places to observe and collect facts and data that can be used to broaden perspective and come up with ideas to address the current problem or issue.

fishbone diagram: Also known as the Ishikawa diagram, this tool is used to determine the sources of a problem.

flow: A state that people experience whereby they are consumed in what they do while simultaneously finding themselves rooted in reality.

Fool: Developed by Annette Moser-Wellman, one of the five thinking skills; has a perspective that nobody else thinks about, paying particular attention to imperfections and discrepancies to generate ideas.

force field analysis: A technique that assumes that for every action, one or more counter-actions (constraining and restraining forces) exist.

freshness: One of the six behaviors identified by Dave Allan et al.; involves holding back on accepting assumptions and challenging existing rules.

Green Hat Thinking: One of the six thinking styles identified by Edward de Bono to symbolize addressing a problem or issue by coming up with alternatives for making an idea a reality.

greenhousing: One of six behaviors identified by Dave Allan et al.; involves suspending judgment and nurturing an idea.

groupthink: Peer pressure that is so intense that it alters individuals' judgment even in the midst of contrary facts and data.

Group Flow: Developed by Keith Sawyer; a phenomenon involving a team performing at the top of its ability, similar to the flow experienced by individuals.

Group ID: Developed by Robert Sternberg; a concept that reflects a team functioning greater than the sum of its parts.

hemispheric thinking: Using one or both sides of the brain to generate and evaluate ideas.

hypothetical analyzer: One of the four strategic styles, identified in Organizational Engineering, that prefers conceptual ideas after careful analysis and takes a structured approach toward completing work.

hypothetical scenario: A technique that encourages individuals and teams in thinking about how to deal with a problem or issue potentially occurring in the future.

iconoclastic: Radical thinking that challenges and seeks to destroy widely held symbols of a paradigm.

Idea Bulletin Board: A technique to capture ideas as they arise by having people record them on some medium placed in a common area.

illumination: Allowing a creative idea to arise from the subconscious, accompanied by an "Aha!" feeling.

illumination phase: One of the five phases in the traditional creativity life cycle that allows an idea to rise to the conscious level of its creator.

imagineering: Also known as visualization, a technique using one's imagination to describe an ideal state for an idea.

incubation: Allowing the subconscious part of the mind to work by suspending judgment.

incubation phase: One of five phases in the traditional creativity life cycle that allows the subconscious part of the mind to work.

innovation: New creative output that adds value to the customer.

interviewing: A technique that involves, through question and answer, obtaining data, information, or ideas that can help address a problem or issue.

intuition: An unconscious sense or gut feeling telling someone to try or do something different.

Judge: One of the four key roles identified by Roger von Oech that uses critical judgment by asking penetrating questions; also known as shooting holes through an idea.

lateral thinking: Developed by Edward de Bono, this approach involves looking at an idea differently by combining and recombining components and promoting an idea better than the current one.

left-brain thinking: Thinking with the side of the brain that seeks tangible, concrete results associated with analysis.

linear thinking: Viewing the world as sequential in action (e.g., do step 1, then step 2, and so on).

literature reviews: A technique that involves researching primary (e.g., interview) and secondary (e.g., read articles) to provide additional information and guidance.

Logical Processor: One of the four strategic styles identified in Organizational Engineering; prefers to take a methodical approach and prefers concrete action.

looking from the outside, in: View the object of study from an independent, objective perspective.

matrices: A technique using a table to capture the relationships between two or more variables under varying circumstances.

Moser-Wellman's Mental Skills of Creativity: A model of five thinking skills developed by Annette Moser-Wellman for developing a creative idea: Seer, Observer, Alchemist, Fool, and Sage.

metaphor: Combining description with an idea, problem, thing, etc. that seems unrelated.

methodism: An overemphasis on compliance with a process, procedure, technique, etc. at the expense of experimenting with something new.

mind mapping: Advocated by Tony Buzan; a technique used to identify and expand upon concepts and their relationships to one another in a graphic format.

modeling: A technique used to capture how an idea or object works using symbols to reflect components, their relationships, states, signals, and roles.

Momentum: One of six behaviors identified by Dave Allan et al.; involves giving an idea a sense of urgency and direction.

monitoring and controlling process: One of the six project management processes; involves collecting and assessing information about the performance of a project and taking the necessary corrective actions to improve that performance.

Multiple Intelligences: Developed by Howard Garner, this model identifies individual intellectual proclivities that represent one's frame of mind.

Myers-Briggs: Based upon the work of Carl Jung, this psychological model offers an assessment for identifying sixteen patterns of behavior regarding individual personalities.

nihilism: Viewpoint involving radical thinking that seeks to destroy widely accepted premises of a paradigm.

nominal group technique (NGT): A variant of brainstorming that takes a structured and methodical approach using criteria to select one or more ideas.

nonlinear thinking: Looking at the world as a series of complex relationships that occur simultaneously and proportionally.

normal science: Puzzle solving that does whatever it can to suppress novel ideas by requiring the use of accepted and known rules and procedures.

observation: A technique used to open perspective by visiting and watching an individual or organization execute its activities to learn or enhance creative ideas.

Observer: Developed by Annette Moser-Wellman, one of the five thinking skills that compiles data and information to generate one or more ideas.

offsite: A technique that involves taking a group, such as a project team, away from the work environment to address burning problems and issues.

Organizational Engineering: A model predicated on the behavior styles of how people process and respond to information, known as strategic style, which consists of a method and mode; the four styles are Reactive Stimulator, Relational Innovator, Hypothetical Analyzer, and Logical Processor.

organizing process: One of the six project management processes; involves identifying and putting in place the infrastructure for effectively and efficiently managing a project.

Pareto chart: A chart used to identify the causes of problems predicated on the theory that a small quantity of issues, problems, etc. will cause 80 percent of the effects.

People Styles: Best described by Robert Bolton, this behavioral model emphasizes people's behavior patterns and habits, and their effect on relationships through two variables: assertiveness and responsiveness.

Plan-Do-Check-Act (PDCA) cycle: Also known as the Deming Wheel, a technique that focuses on continuous incremental improvement using a repetitive cyclic approach involving planning, executing, measuring, and analyzing.

planning process: One of the six project management processes; requires determining the roadmap for achieving the goals and objectives of the project.

preparation phase: One of the five phases of the traditional creativity life cycle requiring learning as much as possible about a certain topic.

problem solving: The process of coming up with a targeted, unambiguous solution to a problem or solution.

product life cycle: The phase used to manage the technical output of a project.

project: A temporary endeavor to achieve a specific result, such as developing a product or delivering a service for the first time.

project life cycle: The processes used to manage the work effort of a project.

project management process: One of the six processes applied during the entire product life cycle or a specific phase for managing the work.

psychosclerosis: A term developed by Daniel Goleman for describing rigid thinking.

reactive stimulation: One of the four strategic styles identified in Organizational Engineering that takes information only to the extent needed after selecting an option.

realness: One of the six behaviors identified by Dave Allan et al.; involves expressing an idea in different ways.

Red Hat Thinking: One of six thinking styles identified by Edward de Bono to symbolize addressing a problem or issue through the use of feelings to select facts and data.

reductive hypothesis: A concept developed by Dietrich Dorner that a danger exists in reducing the operations of a system, from a conceptual perspective, resulting in incomplete assessments.

reengineering: An overall radical approach that seeks to identify a more efficient and effective process than the one that currently exists.

Relational Innovator: One of the four strategic styles identified in Organizational Engineering that likes to investigate problems and explore ideas to create something innovative.

relearning: Viewing the world under a different paradigm that means adhering to a different set of assumptions and beliefs.

reverse thinking: Taking a perspective that is opposite of the prevailing thoughts.

right-brain thinking: Using the side of the brain that accepts ambiguity, intuition, and emotion; associated with synthesis.

role playing: A technique that entails putting a person in another individual's position to understand the thoughts, emotions, values, beliefs, etc., and then using that information to attain greater insight.

Sage: Developed by Annette Moser-Wellman, one of the five thinking skills that develops a vision and uses it to align everything else to it; anything irrelevant goes to the wayside.

Seer: Developed by Annette Moser-Wellman, one of the five thinking skills that visualizes an idea or multiple ones through imagination.

Semi-structures: Developed by Keith Sawyer, a blend of structure and order that enables innovation without falling into a chaotic state.

shifting perspectives: The ability to see a problem or issue from multiple vantage points to help step beyond the restrictions of a prevailing viewpoint.

signaling: One of the six behaviors identified by Dave Allan et al.; involves merging a creative idea with logic by performing preparatory work before its implementation.

simile: Comparing dissimilar ideas, problems, things, etc., but including the use of *like* or *as*.

Six Thinking Hats: Developed by Edward de Bono, this creativity approach involves pretending to wear one of several colored hats to assume one of these thinking styles: White, Red, Black, Yellow, Green, and Blue.

stage gate: A checkpoint at the end of each phase in the creative life cycle to evaluate ideas.

stakeholder: An individual or organization that has an interest in the outcome of a project.

statistical process control (SPC): A technique that plots discrete data points over time to reveal any anomalies exceeding specific ranges.

storyboarding: A variant of brainstorming that is used to capture, link, and evaluate ideas by applying creative and critical thinking.

synectics: A technique that requires suspending judgment and using analogies to develop ideas to address a problem or issue.

synthesis: Putting together all the components of an object of study after analysis is complete.

traditional creativity life cycle: A five-phase approach toward developing, analyzing, and implementing a new idea; the five phases are preparation, concentration, incubation, illumination, and verification and production.

transactional leadership: Performing routine managerial tasks that keep the group functioning.

transformational leadership: From a creativity standpoint, taking risks that challenge the status quo.

tree diagram: A quality tool to display data and information at various levels of abstraction, from general to specific detail.

trend chart: Also known as a run chart, this tool enables plotting data over time to reveal a pattern of behavior.

unlearning: Removing the constraints that inhibit thinking to ensure that false assumptions and beliefs do not inhibit thinking.

verification and production phase: One of the five phases in the traditional creativity life cycle where an idea is tested and implemented.

Von Oech's four creative types: A model, developed by Roger von Oech, consisting of four roles for developing, evaluating, and implementing a creative idea; these roles are Explorer, Artist, Judge, and Warrior.

Warrior: One of four key roles identified by Roger von Oech; takes an idea and puts it into the real world.

White Hat Thinking: One of six thinking styles identified by Edward de Bono to symbolize addressing a problem or issue with facts and data.

workflow analysis: Capturing or revising a process to determine key elements of information and primary controls regulating their behavior to identify opportunities for creative solutions.

Yellow Hat Thinking: One of six thinking styles identified by Edward de Bono to symbolize addressing a problem or issue using a positive perspective on an idea, such as looking at its benefits and future possibilities.

References

ARTICLES

"100 Most Creative People in Business 2009". *Fast Company*, June 2009.

"100 Most Creative People in Business 2011." *Fast Company*, June 2011.

"100 Most Creative People in 2012." *Fast Company*, June 2012.

"101 Gadgets That Changed the World." *Popular Mechanics*, July 2012.

Alon, Adi, and Woulter Alon. "Promote Innovation as a Business Discipline." *Talent Management*, May 2010.

Anders, George. "The University of Disruption." *Forbes*, June 25, 2012.

Arndt, Rachel Z. "Take a Nap, Be More Creative." *Fast Company*, March 2012.

Austen, Ben. "Steve Jobs?" *Wired*, August 2012.

Austin, Robert D,. and Richard L. Dolan. "Bridging the Gap between Stewards and Creators." *MIT Sloan Management Review*, winter 2007.

Baker, Bud. "Creativity Counts." *PM Network*, September 2004.

Bagley, Katherine. "Invent Your Own Anything." *Popular Science*, June 2012.

Baldwin, Howard. "Time Off to Innovate." *Computerworld*, November 5, 2012.

Begley, Sharon. "Buff Your Brain." *Newsweek*, January 9 and 16, 2012.

Bronson, Po, and Merryman, Ashley. "The Creativity Crisis." *Newsweek*, July 19, 2010.

Bryne, John A. "The 12 Greatest Entrepreneurs of Our Time." *Fortune*, April 9, 2012.

Buchanan, Leigh. "How the Creative Stay Creative." *Inc.*, June 2008.

Buchanan, Leigh. "How to Stay Creative." *Inc.*, June 2008.

Caudron, Ahari. "Strategies for Managing Creative Workers." *Personnel Journal*, December 1994.

Christensen, Clayton. "The Rules of Innovation." *Technology Review*, June 2002.

"CIO 100 by the Numbers." *CIO Magazine*, August 15, 2007.

Cole, K. C. "Sally Ride." *Smithsonian*, November 2005.

Collett, Stacy. "Ready, Set, Compete." *Computerworld*, January 14, 2013.

Conlin, Michelle. "Champions of Innovation." *Businessweek*, June 2006.

Corliss, Richard. "Lights, Camera … Edison." *Time*, July 5, 2010.

"Creativity Counts." *PM Network*, September 2004.

"Creativity Step by Step." *Harvard Business Review*, April 2008.

Davenport, Thomas H., Laurence Prusak, and James H. Wilson. "Who's Bringing You Hot Ideas and How Are You Responding?" *Harvard Business Review*, February 2003.

DeSalvo, Tina. "Unleash the Creativity in Your Organization." *HR Magazine*, June 1999.

DiChristina, Mariette. "Let Your Creativity Soar." *Scientific American*, June/July 2008.

Dyer, Jeffrey H., Hal B. Gregersen, and Clayton M. Christensen. "The Innovator's DNA." *Harvard Business Review*, December 2009.

Ehin, Charles. "Are You Promoting Innovation?" *Baseline Magazine*, April 2007.

Elkins, Aaron. "Douglas Owsley." *Smithsonian*, November 2005.

Finn, Bridget. "Brainstorming for Better Brainstorming." *Business 2.0*, April 2005.

"Flying Aces." *PM Network,* November 2012.

Goetz, Thomas. "How to Spot the Future." *Wired*, May 2012.

Goodell, Jeff. "The Steve Jobs Nobody Knew." *Rolling Stone*, October 27, 2011.

Grayling, A. C. "7 Reasons Why People Hate Reason." *New Scientist*, July 26, 2008.

Grove, Andy. "All about Steve." *Fortune*, November 23, 2009.

Guglielmo, Connie. "Untold Stories about Steve." *Forbes*, October 22, 2012.

Haeckel, Stephan H. "How to Create and Lead an Adaptic Organization." *CIO Insight Whiteboard*, date unknown.

Hamel, Gary. "The Why, What, and How of Management Innovation." *Harvard Business Review*, February 2006.

Hamm, Steve. "Fifty Years at the Drawing Board." *Businessweek*, January 21, 2008.

Hammer, Michael. "Making Operational Innovation Work." *Supply Chain Strategy*, October 2005.

Heintz, Nadine. "Managing Employee Creativity Unleashed." *Inc.*, June 2009.

Helft, Miguel. "Steve Jobs' Real Legacy: Apple Inc." *Fortune*, September 26, 2011.

Herbert Wray. "Got an Original Idea? Not Likely." *Scientific American Mind*, June/July 2008.

Hildebrand, Carol. "Creative Genius." *PM Network*, January 2007.

"How to: Hire for Creativity." *Inc.,* October 1, 2010.

Isaacson, Walter. "The World Needs More Rebels Like Einstein." *Wired*, April 2007.

Isaacson, Walter. "Steve Jobs: The Biography." *Fortune*. November 7, 2011.

Isaacson, Walter. "Keep It Simple." *Smithsonian*, September 2012.

Jones, Malcolm. "Our Mysterious Stranger." *Newsweek*, August 9, 2010.

Joni, Saj-nicole A., and Damon Beyer. "How to Pick a Good Fight." *Harvard Business Review*, December 2009.

Katz, Jamie. "Unleash Your Inner Genius." *AARP Magazine*, date unknown.

Kelley, David. "The Mouse First." *Wired*, December 2011.

Kelley, Kevin, and Steve Johnson. "Where Ideas Come From." *Wired*, October 2010.

Koehn, Nancy F. "His Legacy." *Fortune,* November 23, 2009.

Kosman, Joshua. "Yo-Yo Ma." *Smithsonian*, November 2005.

Krakovsky, Marina. "Father of Invention." *Psychology Today*, November/December 2010.

Lafley, A. G,. and Ram Charan. "Making Inspiration Routine." *Inc.*, June 2008.

Lanting, Frans. "David Attenborough." *Smithsonian*, November 2005.

Lashinsky, Adam. "The Decade of Steve." *Fortune*, November 23, 2009.

"Leadership Track." *PM Network*, October 2010.

Lehrer, Jonah. "Cultivating Genius." *Wired*, March 2012.

Lev-Ram, Michael. "The Big Idea." *Business 2.0*, May 2007.

Levy, Steven. "Ringside at the Revolution." *Wired*, December 2011.

Levy, Steven. "The Revolution According to Steve Jobs." *Wired*, December 2011.

Long, Richard. "Maya Angelou." *Smithsonian*, November 2005.

Mangalindan, J. P. "Apple's Other Operations Whiz." *Fortune*. September 26, 2011.

Martin, Jean, and Conrad Schmidt. "How to Keep Your Top Talent." *Harvard Business Review*, May 2010.

McHie, Stewart. "Unite the Processes of Innovation." *Intelligent Enterprise*, November 2006.

McKie, Stewart." Let Innovation Thrive." *Intelligent Enterprise*, January 1, 2004.

Meyer, Liz. "Risk, Survive, Repeat." *Fast Company*. November 2011.

Mindrum, Craig. "Harvesting Innovation." *Talent Management Magazine*, May 2010.

Mone, Gregory. "The Idea Factory." *The Atlantic*, October 2011.

Morse, Gardiner. "Sparking Creativity at Ferrari." *Harvard Business Review*, April 2006.

Muoio, Anna. "Idea Summit." *Fast Company*, January–February 2000.

Murphy, Chris. "Innovation Atrophy." *Informationweek*, May 30, 2011.

Newman, Jolie. "The Innovative Imperative." *Global Services*, November 2008.

Ohlson, Kristin. "Get Creative." *Entrepreneur*, July 2008.

"On the Record." *PM Network*, November 2007.

Parfit, Michael. "Maya Lin." *Smithsonian*, November 2005.

Pink, Daniel H. "What Kind of Genius Are You?" *Wired*, July 2006.

Prahalad, C. K., and R. A. Mashelkar. "Innovator's Holy Grail." *Harvard Business Review*, July–August 2010.

Pratt, Mary K. "Managing Mavericks." *Computerworld*, February 13, 2006.

Project Management Institute. "Think Really Hard." *PM Network*, November 2007.

Project Management Institute. "The Leadership Pack." *PM Network*, October 2010.

Project Management Institute. "Flying Aces." *PM Network*, November 2012.

"Risk, Survive, and Repeat!" *Fast Company*, November 2011.

Rizova, Polly. "Are You Networked for Successful Innovation?" *MIT Sloan Management Review*, spring 2006.

Rowan, Roy. "Gordon Parks." *Smithsonian*, November 2005.

Sawhney, Mohanbir, R. C. Wolcott, and Inigo Arroniz. "The 12 Different Ways for Companies to Innovate." *MIT Sloan Management Review*, spring 2006.

Schlender, Brent. "Steve and Me." *Fortune*, November 7, 2011.

Schlender, Brent. "I Just Knew in My Bones That This Was Going to be Very Important." *Fast Company*, May 2012.

"Secrets of the Most Productive People." *Inc.*, June 2012.

Sinar, Evan, and Richard S. Wellins. "Who's Leading Innovation." *Chief Learning Officer*, October 2012.

"Six Teams that Made Business History." *Fortune*, June 12, 2006.

Smolowe, Jill. "Steve Jobs." *People*, October 24, 2011.

Spolsky, Joel. "How Hard Could It Be?" *Inc.*, February 2008.

"State of the CIO." *CIO Magazine*, January 1, 2009.

Stross, Randall. "The Incredible Talking Machine." *Time*, July 5, 2010.

Sutton, Robert. "Weird Ideas That Spark Innovation." *MIT Sloan Management Review*, winter 2002.

Sutton, Robert. "Eight Rules to Brilliant Brainstorming." *Inside*, September 2006.

Tatum, C. B. "Fostering Innovation on the Project Team." Project Management Institute, Newton Square, PA. Project Management Symposium, September 17–21, 1988.

Tharp, Twyla. "Creativity Step by Step." *Harvard Business Review*, April 2008.

"Think Really Hard." *PM Network*, November 2007.

"Unhappy Execs." *Computerworld*, August 11, 2008.

Walsh, Brian. "The Electrifying Edison." *Time*, July 5, 2010.

Wellner, Allison Stein. "Creative Control." *Inc.*, July 2007.

"When Are You Most Creative?" *Entrepreneur*, April 2009.

"Workplace Ticker." *Computerworld*, December 17, 2007.

Wright, Robert. "Edward O. Wilson." *Smithsonian*, November 2005.

BOOKS

Ackoff, Russell L. *The Art of Problem Solving*. New York: John Wiley & Sons, 1978.

Adams, James L. *Conceptual Blockbusting*, 2nd ed. New York: W. W. Norton & Company, 1979.

Allan, Dave, et al. *What If?* Oxford: Capstone Publishing Limited, 1999.

Armstrong, Thomas. *7 Kinds of Smarts.* New York: Plume, 1993.

Barron, Frank, Alfonso Montuori, and Anethea Barron, Eds. *Creators on Creating.* New York: Penguin, 1997.

Bennis, Warren, and Patricia W, Biederman. *Organizing Genius.* Reading, MA: Addison-Wesley, 1997.

Birkman, Roger. *True Colors.* Ontario: Thomas Nelson, Inc., 1997.

Birren, Faber. *Color & Human Response.* New York: Van Nostrand Reinhold Co., 1978.

Bohn, David, and David Peat. *Science, Order, and Creativity.* Toronto: Bantam Books, 1987.

Bolton, Robert. *People Skills.* New York: Touchstone, 1979.

Bolton, Robert, and Dorothy G. Bolton. *People Styles at Work.* New York: AMACOM, 1996.

Bragdon, Allen D., and David Gamon. *Building Left-Brain Power.* Bass River, MA: Brainwares Books, 1999.

Brassard, Michael. *The Memory Jogger Plus+.* Methuen, MA: Goal/QPC, 1989.

Brown, Kenneth A. *Inventors at Work.* Redmond, WA: Tempus Books, 1988.

Buckingham, Marcus. *Go Put Your Strengths to Work.* New York: The Free Press, 2007.

Buckingham, Marcus, and Donald O. Clifton. *Now, Discover Your Strengths.* New York: The Free Press, 2001.

Buckingham, Marcus, and Curt Coffman. *First, Break All the Rules.* New York: Simon & Schuster, 1999.

Butler, Gillian, and Freda McManus. *Psychology.* Oxford: Oxford University Press, 1998.

Buzman, Tony. *Use Both Sides of Your Brain.* New York: E. P. Dutton, 1983.

Cameron, Julia. *The Artist's Way.* New York: Perigee Books, 1992.

Campbell, David. *Take the Road to Creativity and Get Off Your Dead End.* Niles, IL: Argus Communications, 1977.

Campbell, Linda, Bruce Campbell, and Dee Dickinson, Dee. *Teaching and Learning through Multiple Intelligences.* Needham Heights, MA: Allyn & Bacon, 1996.

Castleden, Rodney. *Inventions That Changed the World.* Edison, NJ: Chartwell Books, Inc., 2007.

Csikszentmihalyi, Mihaly. *Flow.* New York: HarperPerennial, 1990.

Csikszentmihalyi, Mihaly. *Creativity.* New York: HarperCollins, 1996.

Day, Laura. *Practical Intuition for Success.* New York: HarperPerennial, 1997.

de Bono, Edward. *The Mechanism of Mind.* New York: Simon and Schuster, 1969.

de Bono, Edward. *Lateral Thinking.* New York: Harper and Row, 1970.

de Bono, Edward. *Practical Thinking.* New York: Penguin Books, 1971.

de Bono, Edward. *Atlas of Management Thinking.* Middlesex, England: Penguin Books, 1983.

de Bono, Edward. *Six Thinking Hats.* Boston: Little, Brown, and Company, 1985.

de Bono, Edward. *The Use of Lateral Thinking.* New York: Penguin Books, 1990.

de Bono, Edward. *Serious Creativity.* New York: HarperBusiness, 1992.Dodgson, Mark, and David Gann. *Innovation.* Oxford: Oxford University Press, 2010.

Dorner, Dietrich. *The Logic of Failure.* Cambridge, MA: Perseus Books, 1996.

Epstein, Robert. *Creativity Games for Trainers.* New York: McGraw-Hill, 1996.

Foster, Jack. *How to Get Ideas,* 2nd ed. San Francisco: Berrett-Koehler Publishers, Inc., 2007.

Fox, William M. *Effective Group Problem Solving.* San Francisco: Jossey-Bass Publishers, 1990.

Freud, Sigmund. *Civilization and Its Discontents.* New York: W. W. Norton and Company, Inc., 1961.

Gardner, Howard. *Creating Minds.* New York: Basic Books, 1993.

Gardner, Howard. *Frames of Mind.* New York: Basic Books, 1983.

Gardner, Howard. *Multiple Intelligences.* New York: Basic Books, 1993.

Gelb, Michael J. *How to Think Like Leonard da Vinci*. New York: Delacorte Press, 1998.

Gelb, Michael J. *Discover Your Genius*. New York: HarperCollins, 2002.

Goleman, Daniel, Paul Kaufman, and Michael Ray. *The Creative Spirit*. New York: Dutton, 1992.

Gregory, Richard L., ed., *The Oxford Companion of the Mind*. Oxford: Oxford University Press, 1987.

Gwain, Shakti. *Creative Visualization*. Novato, CA: Nataraj Publishing, 1995.

Hartman, Taylor. *The Color Code*. New York: Fireside, 1998.

Hayes, Nicky. *Psychology*. London: Hodder & Stoughton, 1994.

Hesselbein, Francis, Marshall Goldsmith, and Iain Somerville. *Leading beyond the Walls*. San Francisco: Jossey-Bass Publishers, 1999.

Higgins, James M. *101 Creative Problem Solving Techniques*. New York: The New Management, 1994.

Higgins, James M. *Innovate or Evaporate*. Winter Park, FL: The New Management Publishing Co., 1995.

Hirsh, Sandra, and Jean Kummerow. *Life Types*. New York: Warner Books, 1989.

Janis, Irving. *Victims of Groupthink*. Boston: Houghton Mifflin Co., 1972.

Johnson, Steven. *The Innovator's Cookbook*. New York: Riverhead Books, 2011.

Kao, John. *Jamming*. New York: HarperCollins, 1997.

Keirsey, David. *Please Understand Me II*. Del Mar, CA: Prometheus Nemesis Book Company, 1998.

Keirsey, David, and Marilyn Bates. *Please Understand Me*. Del Mar, CA: Prometheus Nemesis Book Company, 1984.

Klauser, Henriette A. *Writing on Both Sides of the Brain*. San Francisco: Perennial Library, 1977.

Kliem, Ralph L. *The Project Manager's Emergency Kit*. Boca Raton, FL: St. Lucie Press, 2003.

Kliem, Ralph L., and Harris Anderson. *The Organizational Engineering Approach to Project Management*. Boca Raton, FL: St. Lucie Press, 2003.

Kliem, Ralph L., and Irwin S. Ludin. *Tools and Tips for Today's Project Manager*. Newtown Square, PA: Project Management Institute, 1999.

Kosko, Bart. *Fuzzy Thinking*. New York: Hyperion, 1993.

Kuhn, Thomas S. *The Structure of Scientific Revolutions*, 2nd ed. Chicago: University of Chicago, 1970.

Langoon Books. *Brain-Boosting Lateral Thinking Puzzles*. Boston: Langoon Books, 2000.

Leavitt, Harold J. *Corporate Pathfinders*. New York: Penguin Books, 1987.

Levi, Daniel. *Group Dynamics for Teams*. Thousand Oaks, CA: Sage Publications, 2001.

Maesel, Eric, and Susan Raeburn. *Creative Recovery*. Boston: Shambhala, 2008.

Maslow, Abraham H. *Toward a Psychology of Being*. Princeton, NJ: D. Van Nostrand Company, Inc., 1968.

May, Rollo. *Man's Search for Himself*. New York: Signet, 1967.

May, Rollo. *The Courage to Create*. New York: Bantam Books, 1980.

Merrill, David W., and Roger H. Reid. *Personal Styles & Effective Performance*. Radnor, PA: Chilton Book Company, 1981.

Mersino, Anthony. *Emotional Intelligence for Project Managers*. New York: AMACOM, 2005.

Michalko, Michael. *Cracking Creativity*. Berkeley, CA: Ten Speed Press, 2001.

Miller, Arthur I. *Insights of Genius*. New York: Copernicus, 1996.

Miller, William C. *The Creative Edge*. Reading, MA: Addison-Wesley Publishing Company, Inc., 1987.

Moore, Geoffrey A. *Dealing with Darwin.* New York: Portfolio, 2005.

Moser-Wellman, Annette. *The Five Faces of Genius.* New York: Penguin, 2002.

Myers, David. *Exploring Psychology*, 7th ed., New York: Worth Publishers, 2007.

Nierenberg, Gerard I. *The Art of Creative Thinking.* New York: Cornerstone Library, 1982.

Nirenberg, Jesse S. *Getting through to People.* Englewood Cliffs, NJ: Prentice Hall, 1963.

Oldham, John M., and Lois B. Morris. *Personality Self-Portrait.* New York: Bantam, 1991.

Ornstein, Robert. *The Right Mind.* New York: Harcourt Brace & Company, 1997.

Osborn, Alex. *Your Creative Power.* Schaumburg, IL: Motorola University Press, 1991.

Paul, Richard. *Critical Thinking.* Santa Rosa, CA: Foundation for Critical Thinking, 1995.

Peters, Tom. *Re-imagine!* London, DK, 2003.

Petroski, Henry. *To Engineer Is Human.* New York: Vintage Books, 1992.

Pike, Robert W. *Creative Training Techniques Handbook.* Minneapolis, MN: Lakewood Books, 1989.

Pink, Daniel H. *A Whole New Mind.* New York: Riverhead Books, 2006.

Pretzer, Williams S. *Working at Inventing.* Baltimore: John Hopkins University Press, 2002.

Raudsepp, Eugene. *How Creative Are You?* New York: Perigee Books, 1981.

Rees, Fran. *How to Lead Work Teams.* Amsterdam: Pfeiffer & Company, 1991.

Rich, Ben R., and Leo Janos. *Skunk Works.* Boston: Little, Brown and Company, 1994.

Riso, Don R. *Personality Types.* Boston: Houghton Mifflin, 1990.

Rogers, Everett M. *Diffusion of Innovations*, 4th ed., New York: The Free Press, 1995.

Rohr, Richard, and Andreas Ebert. *Discovering the Enneagram.* New York: Crossroad Publishing Company, 1997.

Rylatt, Alastair, and Kevin Lohan. *Creating Training Miracles.* San Francisco: Pfeiffer, 1997.

Sawyer, Keith. *Group Genius.* New York: Basic Books, 2007.

Schrage, Michael. *No More Teams!* New York: Currency Doubleday, 1995.

Scott, Ian. *The Luscher Color Test.* New York: Washington Square Press, 1969.

Senge, Peter, et al. *The Dance of Change.* New York: Currency, 1999.

Senge, Peter M. *The Fifth Discipline.* New York: Currency Doubleday, 1994.

Shiraev, Eric, and David Levy. *Cross-Cultural Psychology*, 2nd ed., Boston: Pearson, 2004.

Sloane, Paul, and Des MacHale. *Brain-Busting Lateral Thinking Puzzles.* New York: Sterling Publishing Co., Inc. 2004.

Sonnenschein, William. *The Diversity Toolkit.* Lincoln Wood, IL: Contemporary Books, 1999.

Springer, Sally P., and Georg Deutsch. *Left Brain, Right Brain.* San Francisco: W. H. Freeman and Company, 1981.

Stoltz, Paul G. *Adversity Quotient @ Work.* New York: William Morrow, 2000.

Taylor, Jill B. *My Stroke of Insight.* New York: Plume, 2009.

Thorpe, Scott. *How to Think Like Einstein.* New York: Barnes and Noble, 2000.

Tieger, Paul D., and Barbara Barron-Tieger. *Do What You Are.* Boston: Little, Brown, and Company, 2001.

Tubbs, Stewart L. *A Systems Approach to Small Group Interaction*, 6th ed. Boston: McGraw Hill, 1998.

Vance, Mike, and Dianne Deacon. *Think Out of the Box.* Franklin Lakes, NJ: Career Press, 1997.

VanGundy, Arthur B. *Creative Problem Solving.* Westport, CT: Greenwood Press, Inc., 1987.

von Oech, Roger. *A Kick in the Seat of the Pants.* New York: Harper and Row, 1986.

von Oech, Roger. *A Whack on the Side of the Head.* New York: Warner Books, Inc. 1990.

Wanless, James. *Intuition @ Work.* Boston: Red Wheel, 2002.

Weisberg, Robert W. *Creativity*. New York: W. H. Freeman and Company, 1986.

Whyte, David. *The Heart Aroused*. New York: Doubleday, 1994.

Williams, Linda V. *Teaching for the Two-Sided Mind*. New York: Touchstone, 1983.

Wonder, Jacquelyn, and Priscilla Donovan. *Whole Brain Thinking*. New York: Ballantine Books, 1984.

Index